Moving Objects

Moving Objects

A Cultural History of Emotive Design

Damon Taylor

BLOOMSBURY VISUAL ARTS
LONDON · NEW YORK · OXFORD · NEW DELHI · SYDNEY

BLOOMSBURY VISUAL ARTS
Bloomsbury Publishing Plc
50 Bedford Square, London, WC1B 3DP, UK
1385 Broadway, New York, NY 10018, USA
29 Earlsfort Terrace, Dublin 2, Ireland

BLOOMSBURY, BLOOMSBURY VISUAL ARTS and the Diana logo
are trademarks of Bloomsbury Publishing Plc

First published in Great Britain 2020
Paperback edition published 2023

Cover design by Louise Dugdale

A catalogue record for this book is available from the British Library.

Library of Congress Cataloging-in-Publication Data
Names: Taylor, Damon, author.
Title: Moving objects: a cultural history of emotive design / Damon Taylor.
Description: London; New York: Bloomsbury Visual Arts, 2020. |
Includes bibliographical references and index. |
Identifiers: LCCN 2020011447 (print) |
LCCN 2020011448 (ebook) | ISBN 9781350088610 (hardback) |
ISBN 9781350088627 (epub) | ISBN 9781350088634 (pdf)
Subjects: LCSH: Design–Psychological aspects.
Classification: LCC NK1520.T39 2020 (print) | LCC NK1520 (ebook) | DDC 745.4–dc23
LC record available at https://lccn.loc.gov/2020011447
LC ebook record available at https://lccn.loc.gov/2020011448

ISBN: HB: 978-1-3500-8861-0
PB: 978-1-3503-6000-6
ePDF: 978-1-3500-8863-4
ePub: 978-1-3500-8862-7

Typeset by Newgen KnowledgeWorks Pvt. Ltd., Chennai, India

To find out more about our authors and books visit
www.bloomsbury.com and sign up for our newsletters.

Contents

Figures

Acknowledgements

As with all creative works, there are many who stand behind the person named as the author who should be recognized for their contribution in bringing the thing into being. First and foremost, I would like to thank Deborah Sugg Ryan for helping to set this process in motion and her invaluable contribution throughout this project. Thank you to Giovanni Marmont for insisting that I publish this work (long before he was included in it). Thank you to all the designers who have talked to me over the years, and given their kind permission to publish images. Thanks go to the galleries who have also allowed me to use their photographs. I would also like to thank the anonymous reviewers, whose thorough responses made this a much better book than it might have been. Thanks also go to everybody at Bloomsbury. I would also like to thank the School of Architecture and Design at the University of Brighton for their support in the completion of this book. Financial support for the early research was provided by Falmouth University and the European Social Fund. Sections of Chapters 1 and 4 have appeared in a different form as the journal article, 'After a Broken Leg: Jurgen Bey's Do Add Chair and the Everyday Life of Performative Things', *Design and Culture* 5, no. 3 (2013): 357–74, DOI:10.2752/175470813X13705953612246'. The definitive version of this article can be found at: https://www.tandfonline. com/doi/abs/10.2752/175470813X13705953612246.

I am grateful to Taylor & Francis for permission to republish this material here.

I would like to thank my parents, John and Carol Taylor, whose unstinting support has always kept me going when I may otherwise have flagged. Finally, I would like to thank Helena and Hope, whose love and belief in me make it all worth doing.

Introduction

Some time in the early hours of Wednesday, 13 June 2012, burglars broke into the Los Angeles home of rapper Kanye West. As the intruders were searching for valuables, having entered the living room and swung their torches around, would they have been surprised by the six-foot-high action figure that caught the light? Or the large neo-pop prints on the walls? Perhaps for a moment, in their fear and heightened state of arousal, they would have glimpsed a chair made from soft toys, an overflowing of furry heads and bodies, hard eyes glinting in the light, and thought, 'What the hell's that?' That would have been an *All Animals Banquette* chair by the Brazilian designers Humberto and Fernando Campana (Figure 1). This was made, according to the designers, not because such a thing would solve a problem, but to make people smile.[1] Whether this was the burglars' reaction is not recorded.

Around the turn of the millennium, something changed in the design world. Designers started to behave like artists. There have been star designers before. In the 1950s, Charles and Ray Eames were lauded as American pioneers of modern design. In Italy, in the 1960s, Joe Colombo acted like a design playboy and in the 1980s Ettore Sottsass and the Memphis group courted publicity like the pop stars they were. In the 1990s, design proliferated to service the burgeoning lifestyle industry and Philippe Starck and his postmodernism-lite seemed to be everywhere. Yet, they still remained designers, servicers of industry and mass production. Those who had been working at the fringes, attempting to establish an avant-garde design practice were marginal figures, outliers known of only by a few who worked directly in the field. At the turn of the new century, furniture designers started to act and work specifically as though they were contemporary artists, authors of their work who demanded recognition, and achieved some degree of fame for what they produced, as galleries started to represent them and museums showed their work. As the presence of the Campana brothers' chair attests, collectors such as West were buying their work and putting it in their homes.

Figure 1 Humberto and Fernando Campana, *All Animals Banquette Chair*, 2007. © DACS 2019

The pieces produced are not generally created to commission or to fulfil the requirements of a particular client. Instead, the people who make these things have been setting their own briefs, creating exploratory projects that operate to examine the designer's concerns rather than fulfil a pre-existing need or solve a problem. Just as with prints or various casts of a sculpture, the work is generally produced as limited editions or sometimes as one-off prototypes meant primarily to stimulate thought and discussion. Some of the work is shown in museums. Many of the pieces have been exhibited and sold through galleries such as the Carpenters Workshop Gallery in London, Paris, New York and San Francisco, Vivid in Rotterdam, the Moss Gallery in New York and Contrasts in Shanghai. They are shown and traded at fairs such as Design Miami/Basel and the fringes of the Salone del Mobile in Milan; just as with contemporary art, it is then through the auction houses of Sotheby's, Christies and Philips de Pury that the secondary market operates to further cater for collectors of this type of design. Unlike contemporary art, however, when such things appear in the living rooms of the wealthy people who make up much of their market it is not simply as objects of contemplation or conversation pieces (though they certainly do fulfill such roles), but also as functional elements of their everyday lives.

In many cases, to really regard the objects under discussion as useful everyday things might feel like something of a stretch. Often these are works of design that operate at the top end of the market, that are so expensive that only the rich can afford them, or they exist as singular propositions or speculative prototypes to be viewed in a museum setting. Yet, the people who make these things describe themselves as designers, and the things they make are actually chairs and tables, sofas and sideboards, useable household devices, even if at the moment they are of a type that is often materially available only to a select few. Though these are sometimes highly crafted objects, it does not seem correct to call them 'craft', as such. Though a lot of handwork can go into their construction, these are pieces that can and do exist outside of the traditional field of craft based on genre or the nature of the materials used, and it is what they do rather than how they are made that defines them, both practically and in terms of the economies in which they operate.

When the actor Brad Pitt bought a limited-edition marble *Cinderella Table* from the Verhoeven twins at Design Basel in Switzerland in 2008 (Figure 2), he caused quite a stir by paying over $200,000 for it. Though the example Pitt bought was in marble, the first examples of the *Cinderella* were in plywood and the designer used Computer Aided Design (CAD) and Computer Numerically Controlled (CNC) routing to create an object that morphs from the outline of an eighteenth-century commode into that of a console table of the same period.

Figure 2 The Verhoeven Twins, *Cinderella Table*, 2005. Courtesy of Carpenters Workshop Gallery

Of course, Pitt will have had a number of reasons for buying the piece, including his aesthetic and connoiesseurial interests as a collector, perhaps investment considerations would have come into it (though like contemporary art this would have been something of a risk), and he may have also been telegraphing his knowledge and status. However, within this mix, it seems a little hasty to dismiss the fact that this is still a table.

He bought the expensive marble version; the plywood model would have been cheaper yet perhaps would not have had the presence that Pitt was looking for. Nevertheless, the alteration in material demonstrates how quickly something can transition from one state to another, how a piece of furniture created as a technical experiment in modest materials can, as its context shifts, become a luxury status symbol. Because it is design, it is all about reproducibility and seriality. Different versions can be made. The design can be applied in varying ways, creating a series of physical actualizations of the original principle. Given the technical possibilities of reproducibility offered by the likes of CAD and CNC milling, transpositions of form and material have become viable routes for exploring the possibilities of certain designs and approaches in a way that only a generation ago would have seemed unthinkable. This is, therefore, not mass production, but it is certainly technological reproduction, and this takes place in a wider economy of reproducibility. In such a situation, an object that has an aura of authenticity and exclusivity can be made in multiples, allowing it to be both unique and reproducible at the same time. This then happens in conditions in which the image of the design can be reproduced almost infinitely, allowing it to flow through the channels of the media and information exchange, thus making it possible for the object to gain prestige as its visibility grows, even as it retains its status as a unique design.

Emotive design

The emotive in design is a quality of the work that is arousing, but which does not operate to add to its functionality. It is recognizable in the sense that it is something the object is *doing* in the emotional register that is not concerned directly with what it is *for*. All use-objects are to one degree or another emotive, in that we have feelings about what we engage with. The work referred to here as emotive design amplifies this quality and plays upon it. In his *Smoke* series of 2002, the Dutch designer Maarten Baas took a blowtorch to pieces of furniture: a Rococo armchair, a chandelier, cheap IKEA chairs and tables. He burnt them

Figure 3 Maarten Baas, *Smoke Chair*, 2002. Photo credits: Frank Tielemans. Courtesy of the designer

until they resembled things rescued from a house fire (see Figure 3). The surface was stabilized using epoxy resin and the objects finished with new upholstery and fittings. To look at, the elegance of the chair's frame has been transformed into something that is both beautiful and disturbing. By being burnt, the object has taken on an emotive quality. It appears to be some form of relic, suggesting that it has come through a cataclysm, yet the pristine nature of the upholstery jars with this as it speaks of craftsmanship and elegance. It is clearly a high-status object, but the way it has been altered provokes a sensation, and the feelings that it stirs are ambiguous.

To those with a knowledge of design history, the act of burning a chair may almost inevitably bring to mind an iconic image of Italian radical design, a 1975 cover of *Casabella* magazine, edited by the designer and critic Alessandro Mendini, which showed his *Lassù* chair in flames. This was a deliberately poetic act and an intellectual provocation, whereby the burning chair was meant to represent a challenge to modernism's concentration on the object as functional device.[2] Yet, Mendini's intervention was a deliberately symbolic posture intended to provoke a response. Baas is quite adamant he was not trying to make a point. Later, in 2004, he went on to burn a number of design 'classics' by the likes of Gerrit Rietveld and Ettore Sottsass. Yet, this was done at the request of the Moss Gallery. Baas has been at pains to point out that the *Smoke* project was about the aesthetics of charring, not making a symbolic statement.[3] Thus, the reason that

Baas has needed to be so adamant about this is because what he has produced
has such powerful latency. Whether he meant it to or not, what he has made
creates an impression, and this is not simply an intellectual association (though
this may be part of it), it is powerfully affecting: it goes to the gut as much as to
the head.

When we encounter burnt pieces of furniture, we cannot help but have a
strong reaction. Baas may not have meant for this to be symbolic of anything,
indeed it is interesting that this was actively not what he was trying to do, but no
matter what the intention of the person who creates such a piece, the inclusion
of qualities such as charred wood, particularly in contrast to pristine upholstery
and fittings, cannot help but set up a situation where the work will provoke a
response. It seems that emotion is coming out of and through such furniture,
almost in spite of what the maker intended, rather than as a direct consequence.
He has created an emotive object, one that arouses intense feelings, whether he
set out to or not.

In pieces such as the Campana's banquette chairs, a similar struggle can be
seen. On one level, each example appears to be quite a fun piece of furniture, as
the exuberant mass of soft toys tumble out to form a chair in a way that certainly
may make those who encounter it smile. Yet, the blank stares of the animals'
faces seem to belie this. The profusion can be seen as disturbing, unsettling.
What could be the innocent jumble of a child's bed crammed with toys, with a
slight turn of the head, becomes a more upsetting vision of the excrescence of
mass production and the uncanny gaze of the doll. This is not to say that the
Campanas deliberately set out to create such an effect, but that in the relations set
up lie the work's potency, as the dynamics and contradictions of the conditions
in which it was created can be seen in its configuration.

When, at the end of the 1990s, this kind of work first started to become visible,
particularly the furnishings and products disseminated under the banner of
Droog Design from the Netherlands, for example, these strange and exuberant
designs appeared difficult to account for. They were certainly not playing by the
rules of modernism, but nor did they have the flavour of the postmodern. Too
playful to be 'serious' functional design yet too sincere to be ironic, they seemed
to be doing something that was if anything unmodern. At first, certainly, there
was an improvisational quality to much of what was created. The designers used
already existent objects and re-appropriated them to different ends. The use of
archaic forms and materials seemed to be less of a reaction to modernism than a
sigh of relief that this fiction was over, that the frills and curls of more vernacular
styles could be taken out from the storage spaces where they had been kept as we

all pretended to live in minimalist showrooms. The mixing together of styles and periods, the montaging together of elements, and the use of novel materials spoke not of postmodern intellectual games, but rather a deeper search for effects that depended upon more than wry reflection on the nature of our material lives.

What has been discernable in such work is not any form of overt ideology, or even a conscious set of concerns, but more an underlying tendency. Through the use of these methods and approaches, designers have been making things that seem to be involved with arousing feelings in those who encounter and use them. This coincided with a turn in design towards a recognition of the importance of emotion. With the development of User-Centred approaches to design in the 1990s, there was an increasing appreciation that the things we use can as much be about feeling as practical function, even if in the User-Centred paradigm, the examination of the former has tended to be directed to the maximization of the latter. In the past twenty years, emotion has increasingly moved to centre stage in the discourse of design. The establishment of the Design and Emotion Society in 1999 marked the beginning of a surge of interest in emotion in the field of design research, whilst the idea that design engages us on an emotional level was popularized in the early 2000s by the professor of computer science and advocate of 'Human Centred Design', Donald Norman.[4] Coming very much from a cognitivist position that emphasized 'product experience' and 'engagement' in relation to concepts such as usability, this approach sought to render emotion quantifiable and measurable, with the goal of improving consumer products. What is remarkable about such work is that, for research on emotion, it all seems rather affectless and a little clinical. In this sense, such an approach seems actually to be an attempt to rationalize emotion, to render it better available to analysis intended primarily to serve market forces, rather than examine emotion on its own terms.

As part of the affective turn in design those taking a more material culture approach began to examine the nature of human relationships with objects. In her 2007 work *Evocative Objects: Things We Think With*, the social theorist of technology Sherry Turkle collected together accounts by designers, artists, scientists, and professionals from the humanities in which they reflected upon the way that they used meaningful things to work through issues and ideas.[5] In *Love Objects: Emotion, Design and Material Culture* edited by Anna Moran and Sorcha O'Brien, published in 2014, a range of theorists and practitioners examine what objects can and do mean in everyday life from a broadly anthropological position. Such explorations of how we cherish things are useful counterpoints to the loose scientism of more cognitivist approaches to emotion in design, but the very nature of the work means that it concentrates on personal meanings and individual experience more than offering any systematic political account of the issues.

In his book *Emotionally Durable Design: Objects, Experiences and Empathy*, first published in 2005, the designer and critic Jonathan Chapman suggested that this concentration on the emotional qualities of design was a possible route to a sustainable practice of manufacture and use. His thesis was that if products could be designed to alter and age well then it would be possible for people to have stronger emotional bonds with them, and then less would be thrown away and wasted.[6] This is an attractive idea, but it is clear that there is really very little evidence that this is the case. Loving things does not mean that we will necessarily have less of them, or that the objects that we will have will be better by dint of being more lovable. Though the later edition of the book published in 2015 goes some way to accounting for the fact that consumerism is the political context in which the design and use of objects currently takes place, an idea that is rather neglected in the first version, he still begins from an assumption that then structures the rest of his investigation. Having noted that consumer culture encourages certain forms of emotional identification with the things we use, he posits that the role of design should be to create 'deeper' bonds between people and the commodities they consume.[7] He then suggests that such 'empathy' can be fostered by creating objects that have similar capacities for change as people do. Yet, this does still seem to be missing the point of how human beings are changing, and why. It appears to take our identification with the commodities we consume as a given, as an almost natural quality of such a relationship when, as will be demonstrated, this can be understood as a politically and historically determined set of circumstances.

One factor that unites the more nakedly consumer-oriented work of Norman and others who adopt similar approaches, and the more idealistic work of the likes of Chapman, is the assumption that the fundamental structure of how we make and use things can and will remain the same. The suggestion being that we can find new materials or production processes and what we are doing can be sustained, that the broader system can continue with little alteration. Another factor that such positions share is the assumption that emotion is innate, and therefore transcultural; a 'fact' of being human that derives from our biology in a straightforward manner.

Such work on design and emotion has tended to regard design as an essentially instrumental process in which these issues are only really of interest to the extent that they contribute to a product's 'usability' or improve its sustainability.

What here is described as emotive design eschews such consequentialism, as it operates in the realm of emotion for its own ends, because feeling is valuable in itself. Thus, this book is an exploration of what design can be if it is not simply a rationalist attempt to make better consumer goods. It also suggests that in the strange and often unsettling world of emotive objects, the ultimate instability of the consumer capitalist project can be glimpsed, just as the first glimmer of the possibility of an alternative may be discernable. In examining the social relations that are floridly manifest in such work, and which can be demonstrated to be historically determined, the intention is to show how this larger infrastructure of action and interaction is serving to define how we live.

In some cases, the designers discussed in this book have a stated agenda to arouse an emotional reaction for certain ends. In Chapter 5, where the discussion takes in the field of practice that is characterized as Critical or Speculative Design, the suggestion is that this is work that is essentially different to much of the rest of the design discussed in the book, in that it has a certain programme or stated set of aims, so part of the reason for examining it is to show that, in terms of how it deals with emotion, it is perhaps not quite doing what some of its main proponents declare.

Where designers are producing things that are more recognizably made to be use-objects, those making them are generally more interested in the internal relations of the objects, how the elements interact, than they are with overt meaning or message. There are, though, interesting exceptions to this. Julia Lohmann is a German-born designer who has worked mainly in the UK during the period covered by this book. Her practice is concerned with the human relationship to the natural world, and she consciously makes works that are meant to stir people who use the object, or see it in an exhibition or online, to think about their own place in relation to the making and using of things. She argues that in a world that is 'increasingly mediated through objects' and which revolves around consumption, 'it is the responsibility of the designer to embed in objects an added emotional and ethical functionality'. This is because, she believes, 'design should stop us from becoming numb to the world and instead prompt us to rethink how we lead our lives'.[8] Yet, in this regard, Lohmann is something of an exception. As with Baas, most of the designers discussed in *Moving Objects* profess to be more interested in the aesthetic or material qualities of the objects they create than any overt political or critical agenda. They often allude to diffuse narrative elements within what they produce, but there is little explicit political drive or programme in their personal accounts as authors.

The intention here is thus not to concentrate on the intentionality of the authors as the defining quality of the work, though such motivations will of course be discussed. Rather the point is to see these works as the conflicted products of an age in which the politics of emotion is being played out, where the intimate objects of everyday life, their qualities turned up to often absurd proportions, have become a site of expression and contestation where the desires and anxieties of the age have become visible.

Emotive design is recognizable as a tendency where the piece has clearly been made to effect an emotional reaction, but this is not treated as an instrumental quality of the work. It is not then accidental that it is often domestic furniture and furnishings, the everyday devices we use to live our lives, that are the location of such activity. These things, by being so intimate, are the site of our daily dramas. They are the landscape we inhabit; they are the characters we relate to and use in the formation of who we are. It is, therefore, not so surprising that designers should begin to manipulate them in an exploration of our emotional relationship to the physical matter of life.

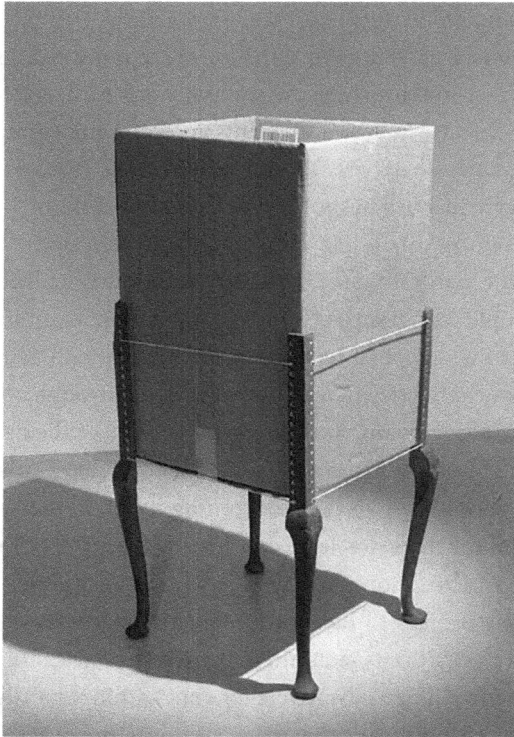

Figure 4 Peter Marigold, *Box Legs*, 2010. Courtesy of the designer

This book is an examination of the means and methods employed in emotive design that act to destabilize an ideological status quo that exists in material culture, which is so deeply embedded that we struggle to see it. The minor rebellion of emotive design need not reside in expensive or technically elaborate work. Arguably, it is often the very twisted ordinariness of much of it that makes it powerful. Peter Marigold's *Box Legs* (Figure 4) consists of four cabriole legs with pierced angled struts connected to the top of each one. These can then be attached to any cardboard box using a string tourniquet, thus turning the box into a piece of furniture. The mechanism is delightfully simple and the effect is to convulse the humble cardboard box into an object of utility and status. Yet, a moment of disjuncture is experienced upon encountering an object such as this, as the formality and historical resonance of the shape of the leg meets the low-status quality of the box. There is also a level of slightly disturbing animation taking place, as the addition of the legs seems to bring the object to life, suggesting that it may scuttle away at any moment. What could have been seen as amusing or witty begins to reveal a certain darkness underlying our relationship to objects, which when pried open has the potential to make legible a certain instability at the heart of the consumerist cosmology of things.

Domestic art

When it first began to appear as a recognizable form of practice, this kind of work was often referred to as Design Art, with the coining of the term popularly attributed to Alexander Payne of the auction house Philips de Pury.[9] As its derivation suggests, such a name operated primarily to identify what was a newly sellable category of designed goods. It also, however, pointed to a central tension in such work. Since these are objects that were made not only to be shown and thought about, but also used, this seemed to suggest that a new type of practice was developing that existed between art and design. As the critic and historian Christopher Reed notes, one of the guarantees that modernist art was serious and genuinely avant-garde was its disavowal of the domestic sphere.[10]

In modernity, the home is a space that has generally been characterized as feminine.[11] It has not, therefore, traditionally been seen as a legitimate territory for artistic practice. In the work discussed in this book, these experiments with everyday use-objects, through a concern with domesticity, seems to be leading 'gallery design' directly into the domestic interior. This then is an underexplored realm, the affective space of the domestic as a site of expression

Figure 5 Wieke Somers, *Bath Boat*, 2005. Photographed by Elian Somers. Courtesy of Studio Wieke Somers

and experimentation, not just on the level of applied art, of the prettifying of domestic goods for use, but as a space where issues can be worked through and explored in depth.

Bath Boat, for example, made in 2005 by the Dutch designer Wieki Somers (Figure 5), is a working bathtub, which takes the form of a boat. The designer did not create a bath-shaped sculpture, rather she made a fully functional object with a form that evokes certain feelings; it is a useful thing which makes allusion and suggests narratives, meanings and relations beyond its basic utilitarian functioning. Certainly, designers have made work that has referential or narrative qualities before, indeed this was a feature of Arts and Crafts practice a century earlier,[12] but what is striking about work such as that of Somers is the extent to which it materially exists in economies of meaning and exchange that straddle the artistic and the domestic, that relate to sensation and use.

The question that an artefact such as the *Bath Boat* suggests is not 'can design be exhibited and sold like art?' (the existence of the market for such goods proves this is the case) but 'what if the things we used everyday operated as art?' That is to say, what would everyday life be like if it worked to imperatives dependent upon expression and exploration, not the sterile choices and false notions of efficiency promulgated in consumer capitalism? Though one way in which this piece has come to be well known is through the engaging photographs of it that move through the channels of the media, what makes it interesting is the potential for affective domestic design which is not instrumentally aligned. This is then less about the creation of spectacular objects that work entirely as a form of display, and more about the possibilities of some of the tactics and techniques of art being co-opted by makers of useful things that can actually take their place in daily life.

In its penetration into the home, this form of artful design seems to suggest not only the possibility of commenting on the domestic through the creation of functioning furniture and products, but the material alteration of what it means to inhabit such a space. *Bath Boat* is not only rhetorical, it does not just make a point, nor is it simply narrative, in that it tells a story about bathing. Rather through the way the piece has been materially rendered it makes a certain kind of experience possible. And experience always has an emotional dimension.

So, what would it be like to live with such an object? What would it mean for this to be a part of everyday life? It is one thing to discuss it as though it were sculpture, to examine its aesthetic effect, the meanings and connotations engendered by its form. It is quite another to think of being with it day-in-day-out. After a while would you still notice it? Would it not recede into the fabric of habit and routine, as the things we live with most intimately tend to do in this age of mass-produced excess? Or would its form and the way in which it functions keep on having an effect, even if you did not notice it? Perhaps exactly because it was no longer fully present to consciousness, it would sneak under the radar and affect you all the more.

This is one of the most delicious things about thinking of pieces like the *All Animals Banquette* chair in the living room of Kanye West: imagining the surrealist possibilities that such a scenario would allow for. This is to smuggle subversion into the lives of the rich. Emotion, real feeling, not its artificially produced consumerist stand-in, is volatile and difficult to contain. It has effects that are unexpected and unpredictable. It is this possibility of domestic sedition that forms the main subject of this book. The things we live with are a material part of life. In our relationship to domestic furniture and household products, there is a closeness that means that they become part of who we are. The design in question here is made, for a range of reasons, in a way that disrupts the frictionless nature of so much of what we consume, or at the very least makes it less comfortable and available to straightforward assimilation. Thus, the intention is to examine the techniques employed by designers in the creation of emotive objects and to place this against the background of these pieces' circulation through the channels of culture in an attempt to map such effects and render visible the dynamics in play.

The practitioners discussed do not form any sort of coherent group. It is not a movement or even a clearly identifiable approach that is being examined. Rather what is noticeable in the work of the designers discussed here is a shared attentiveness to certain effects, and a similarity of method and means that centre around the emotional life of people and things. Some are clearly commercial product designers, keen to sell on a world stage. Others are more experimental and involved in the investigation. Some are using emotional intervention and expression as a way to ask questions. Others are just playing, because it's fun. Yet with all of them there is a sincerity to the way these designer-authors are exploring sensibility that gives the things they create a presence and complexity in a manner that has become rare in the objects that we use.

The politics of stuff

Until the end of the twentieth century, if you were interested in design it was necessary to seek out information in specialist magazines or locate a particular book or article in physical space. Now, like everything else, it is a click away. The approach to design examined in the following chapters has developed during roughly a thirty-year period that has seen the most rapid alteration in the conditions of existence in human history. This has involved the continued expansion and refinement of the mass production of physical things in an increasingly globalized world, which has made consumer goods more available than ever. This is an extension of a process that has been a feature throughout modernity, whereby commodities are produced in ever-increasing amounts to maximize economic growth. At the same time, the proliferation of digital technologies of reproduction has reached the point whereby daily life in the developed West has become saturated with information, and space and time feel as though they have folded in on themselves as all have become available to us at once.

Objects created by designers can now be picked up and circulated online as sign value almost instantaneously, and we can consume them on this level without ever leaving the chair pulled up before the screen, yet the chair is still there. Objects have become radically mobile, in that they can be experienced as images across the globe in a way that was unimaginable thirty years ago, they can transition between platforms and be shared in ways that have allowed them to become superfluid as data. Objects now exist as much in their representation as they do in their materiality; they can appear to be unique and exclusive whilst also being available for mass consumption in their virtual form, and this is the age in which branding and PR operate to give the products we use identity, to give character and presence to the commodities we consume. Yet, this has not rendered the things we live with less physically present, it does not appear to have diminished their materiality, it has had led to them gaining a certain intensity as their existence in the world becomes multivalent and fluid.

In such circumstances, work that stimulates us emotionally can be seen to exist on a spectrum. At one end is its spectacular manifestation, its celebrity form. Here such design fulfils a role similar to those who are familiar to us through their images. Just as the soap star or internet influencer allows those consuming their messages to feel an ersatz form of friendship, a sense of intimacy that is fostered through that very modern value of being 'relatable', so experiencing highly wrought furniture through the channels of communication allows us to feel a sense of ownership and connection, it makes it possible for us to be moved by such work whilst not being physically in contact with it.

Pieces such as the *All Animals Banquette* chair or Baas's *Smoke* series do open up a space where we can be excited by objects, to feel sensations of joy, intrigue and novelty, and this can be experienced simply by looking at it on a screen and knowing that they exist. At the other end of the spectrum is the reality of use. Particularly with the early work of Droog Design discussed here, much of what was created was intended to be mass-produced for general consumption. The plan was very much that these would be actual use-objects. With more recent works made as limited edition or exhibition pieces, the objective can be seen to more akin to haute couture fashion, whereby these are real things that have use value, but which imply their use and demand that the viewer imagine a world where such things could exist as part of daily life. In either manifestation, such pieces perhaps become their most interesting when thought of as actual use-objects. In their present form, many of them have to be taken as foreshadowings, prefigurations of a world in its becoming, as the first intimations of ways of being that are taking form, but it would be reductive to say that simply because they *also* exist as spectacle, their qualities as real, functioning devices are entirely absented.

At this point in history, we face unprecedented challenges precipitated by the way we live: impending ecological disaster, economic turmoil, social upheaval created by the emergence of a networked and increasingly virtual way of living, and the myriad pressures caused by the processes of globalization. It may, therefore, seem strange to study the political and moral problems of making and using things through the analysis of odd furniture and domestic design: limited-edition furniture and speculative products, which are available to few, used by fewer and of interest to only a minority. As has been argued, there is certainly a subversive potential in such work, but given that there are so many clear problems with the conditions of mass consumption and the structures of mass production upon which they depend, why take the time to examine a few highly wrought and often absurd domestic items that are generally so expensive they will only be bought by a particular elite, or are not even for sale at all, when it might seem more sensible to be using our energy to find realistic solutions to the practical problems we face?

One part of the answer lies in the very fact that these things have been made and exist in the world at the point of crisis. In the past thirty years, what it means to live daily life has changed enormously. Throughout this period, designers have been making things that express their concerns. In this way, the designs discussed here are as much a response to the pressures of our era as the technical attempts to answer our needs in more rational ways. Understanding how our relationship to objects forms who we are is to begin to comprehend what it means to be an embodied self in such an era. A critical study of new forms of material culture gives insight into the processes that act upon and through us. We cannot help but have an emotional relationship to the objects we use to make our lives, and our relationship to materiality is changing. With so much material abundance, the things we live with, the objects that make up so much of everyday life, have lost some of their sheen, at just the same time that through the effects of marketing and the dominance of consumerist materialism they are coming to mean more to us than ever before. It is in the space of this paradox that emotive design happens.

In an article titled 'Towards Relational Design', the curator and critic Andrew Blauvelt has proposed a history of modern design whereby an initial phase developed in the early part of the twentieth century based on a search for a language of form, a period essentially coterminous with the development of modernism. He then suggests that a second wave in the 1960s was centred around meaning-making in design 'its symbolic value, its semantic dimension and narrative potential', which roughly coincides with postmodernism. Finally, he argues that a third wave has swept in, that began in the 1990s and which 'explores design's performative dimension: its effects on users, its pragmatic and programmatic constraints, its rhetorical impact, and its ability to facilitate social interactions'.[13] It is this 'performative dimension' of design and its relation to context that is explored in *Moving Objects*, how this is intimately tied up with the rhetorical possibilities of design, the way that anything made or used by human beings will always be interpreted and become entangled in our emotional lives.

A cultural history of emotive design

The following is a work of design theory. It is a study in design history informed by a theoretical understanding of material culture as a means to examine the social life of things and subject–object relations as political features of a changing world. Although the design discussed in the book can broadly be described as that which has been called Design Art, Conceptual Design, or Critical Design, the scope of the book is broader than being a simple review of such work from the 1990s onwards. Instead, the intention is to provide a new approach in design history and theory that is premised on an attention to the embodied, emotive qualities of design, at the same time as placing this against a background whereby any understanding of material culture must be a study in the nature of mobility.

It is not a comprehensive history of the field. It is certainly not a sequential narrative, the story of emotive design. Rather it is a connecting together of moments, the piecing together of fragments, and the unearthing of clues as to the nature of the emotive tendency in design, the techniques employed in its creation, and the political consequences of its existence. The events and practices considered are examined because of their thematic resonance; the examples are chosen quite partially because they offer particular insights and allow for certain ways of looking at the problem. Much is missed out or glossed over in pursuit of the underlying significance of the evidence that is addressed. This book is useful not because it gives a detailed account of the phenomenon, but because it builds a theoretical groundwork upon which to begin to construct an analysis of the issues involved. The intention is to lay out some coordinates that may then be of use in further study of our changing physical and emotional topography. In this way, it is meant to be a new way of looking at design that takes account of the political nature of its emotive dimension.

Chapter 1 begins with Droog. As is made clear, this should not be seen as an historical zero-point. Droog had antecedents, of course, and a particular place in history, but as the first organization to systematically promote work that relied upon emotive techniques, this seems like a good place to start. As the design and craft critic Glenn Adamson observes, the early output of Droog in the 1990s can be seen as relatively unified project based upon allusions to craft processes and an inventive use of materials. By the end of the first decade of the twenty-first century, arguably, its range of products had descended, in Adamson's words, into a collection of 'disparate one-liners'[14] that were being offered to the market through a store on the Las Vegas Strip. It is, therefore, necessary to sketch out the story of Droog, but in the process the intention is to show how far from being simply an exercise in 'dry' humour, the Dutch project was one which depended upon a darker and altogether more unsettling effect beneath its playful surface. Chapter 2 then seeks to tease out some of the theoretical concerns that need to be addressed in understanding such work. In order to do this, the intention is to examine a number of different dynamics, what could be called dialectical tensions in the work: the relationship between reason and emotion; the way that functionalism and expression coexist; the role of the author and the way this works in relation to the power of discourse; how such overblown pieces of design bear upon the concept of everyday life. These currents are explored to allow for an understanding of how designers are drawing from the techniques of art, but in the process, through not being quite subsumed into the discourse or economies of this field of practice, they have opened up a new space of the expressive use-object, or emotive design. Of these techniques, the idea of 'estrangement' is given some prominence as it is asked to what extent designers are trying to shock those who encounter their work in some form of consciousness, or whether something more complex is going on.

The next chapter looks at how anything that is described as emotional must deal with the embodied nature of existence. Through the examination of a series of works that deal with bodily concerns, the intention is to explore how designers have been relating to the body, at the same time that the emotive can be understood to be both physical and societal at the same time. By confronting troubling emotions that consumerist design generally avoids, such as disgust, the analysis examines how designers are working with the power of emotion in a way that is very different to the problem-solving paradigm. Similarly, through a discussion of comfort as a concept, the limited nature of scientific or ergonomic attitudes to use-objects is explored, just as it is posited that what such approaches hide becomes clearly visible in emotive design.

Chapter 4 looks at how we value design. It charts the rise of the market in this kind of work, and examines how it can function as 'high design'.[15] It also seeks to explain how material things made by real people can become radically mobile and take on a virtual dimension in their informational volatility. The rest of the chapter is an examination of how forms of value other than monetary operate through these strange and sometimes disturbing things and their relationship to daily life. In Chapter 5, the early development of Critical Design is placed in its historical context to show why this practice developed as it did, how this work operates rhetorically, and in what ways this relates to the way we react emotionally to things. This then makes it possible to examine other speculative approaches that are more concerned with creating things that people can actually use, and seeing what implications this has for the development of the poetic and playful in daily life. Finally, Chapter 6 looks at how the affective shift in design can be seen as a form of relational practice, whilst it is asked how the alteration in human sensibility that is being wrought by the technological revolution is being materialized in design, and what this may mean for our emotional lives in a digital future.

Moving Objects, therefore, sets out a new approach to design, one that does not emphasize the ability of designers to solve all our problems, yet nor does it simply celebrate the expressive qualities of the designed objects under review. The book is meant to be a history of the phenomenon, but it is not just a retelling of the events, rather it is an attempt to show the relations between the parts, to reveal the dynamics at play in designed objects that have come about in a situation where the implicit tensions serve to generate the work's effects. The analysis centres upon design that is presently highly exclusive, but the purpose of this is to show how it relates to the everyday. In the end, the point of this work is to show, through the adoption of a certain destabilized perspective and a dialectical approach, how subversive potential can be discerned in emotive design. To do this then, it seems necessary to begin with the problem that is Droog.

1

Droog: The dry and the moist

Just before Christmas of 2010, Droog Design opened a new retail space in *The Cosmopolitan*, a $3.9 billion hotel and gambling complex in Las Vegas. The interior, designed by Marcel Schmalgemeijer, was modelled on the final sequences of the film *2001: A Space Odyssey* and the underfloor lighting gave the strange and outlandish furniture presented an other-worldly glow. A few days before the opening of the store, John Unwin, CEO of *The Cosmopolitan*, gave a journalist from the publication *Travel and Leisure* a tour of the hotel site. Having pointed out the 'casino cabanas' and the lobby columns patterned with high-definition video screens, they reached the building's eastern edge, where it opens onto the sidewalk of the Las Vegas Strip. Here, Unwin remarked, 'We're going to put a Droog in this corner.' 'A what?' the journalist asked, bemused. 'You know: Droog, the Dutch design store,' replied his host, explaining, 'slots [slot machines] would make more money, but I think Droog is cooler.'[1] It is clear then what the hotel gained from this: prestige and the glamour of appearing cutting-edge. But what was Droog getting from the deal?

Nearly two decades before, in April 1993, in an old villa in the centre of Milan, Droog Design showed their first collection at the prestigious Salone del Mobile. Droog is a commercial collective established by the historian and critic Renny Ramakers and the designer and educator Gijs Bakker, which was formed to act as a vehicle for a new wave of Dutch design. At this point, Ramakers was one of the most important and well-known design commentators in the Netherlands. Bakker and his partner Emmy van Leersum had been central to the Dutch and German studio jewellery movement of the 1970s, and in the 1980s, his activities had broadened out to include furniture and product design, making him a leading figure in the Dutch design world at the time, allowing him to lend creative and academic weight to the project.[2] At the Salone show, Droog presented a range of furniture and utilitarian domestic objects, which included 'a bundle of second-hand drawers, a chair made of rags, piled up lamp shades, a coffee maker in which bicycle lamps were mounted, a bookcase made of paper'.[3] Reviewing the show, the French newspaper *Libération* suggested that the 'unknowns' responsible for Droog should be 'given a medal for spiritual savoir vivre', saying that 'they tell the most improbable of stories. Fairytales without fairies. Fleeting. They are brilliant in that they arouse the desire to revivify the quotidian in life. Design for them is not a question of taste but an ongoing issue. That makes you feel better. The way a stroll through the flea market does.'[4]

In the past, much has been made of the Dutch origins of this type of design. Gareth Williams, one of the main commentators on this kind of work and the former curator of contemporary furniture at the Victoria and Albert Museum, has observed that there are 'common themes and shared concerns' that are observable in this kind of design 'which has led to what we might describe as a Dutch inflection in international design today'.[5] Ramakers was certainly keen to promote the idea that there is something basically Dutch in such an approach, particularly in the idea that there is an essentially humorous quality to it. She states that 'the Dutch tradition of simplicity and clarity links arms with the nose-thumbing element' which is typified by a '"dry" (droog) humour'.[6] Similarly, Paola Antonelli, the curator of design at the Museum of Modern Art in New York, has observed that Droog designs 'did not necessarily have much in common but shared a similar sensitivity' which was identified as 'typically Dutch and thus exquisitely dry'.[7] However, as the following history of this kind of work will show, though the origins of the Droog approach (and that of work that followed it) can certainly be attributed to a way of working developed in the Netherlands, not least at the Design Academy Eindhoven, there were broader influences at work. In many ways more than being typical of a particular national approach, what was special about Droog when it launched was the way it seemed to capture a certain attitude that was in the air at the time, one that was iconoclastic whilst also being sensitive to the growing importance of feeling in design.

Seventeen years later, they were a cool loss leader for a hotel and casino. Ramakers, her co-founder Bakker having departed by this point, stated that 'Droog has always pioneered new directions for design, we see our role as a design company in creating new content and also in setting new boundaries in how and where our work is encountered. Las Vegas is a new context for us and we are excited about the opportunities it will bring.'[8] Yet, this seemed a strange trajectory. How did an organization that began life challenging the design profession by presenting work that appeared to revitalize the everyday come to be selling its wares in the gaudy environs of the Las Vegas Strip?

It might be observed that it was a change in the way in which design was marketed that had primarily led to the development of this type of work. As Williams suggested some time later, it could be seen that 'the mechanisms of the art world, specifically the art market' had at this time 'increasingly leeched into the practices of designers'.[9] Though he acknowledges that the situation was much more complicated than this initial statement might suggest, such an assertion illustrates the way in which commentators have stressed the importance of the market in the appearance of emotionally laden, content-heavy design.[10] Whilst it should be acknowledged that the commercial development of the market was crucial in shaping how we ascribe value to such objects (and this is discussed in detail in Chapter 4), the intention here is to place the artefacts into a context whereby they are understood *as* design, rather than being valued as a form of pseudo-art. This will then involve taking into account the way in which commercial concerns shaped them, but at the same time keeping in view the way that particular formal and functional considerations, associated with the discourse of design rather than art, have served to determine their nature.

Droog was established by Ramakers and Bakker as a way of showcasing the work of young designers from the Netherlands, both to raise the status of Dutch design and to market it on the international stage. Influenced by work such as Jasper Morrison's *Some New Items for the Home Part 1*, shown at Milan in 1988, Ramakers detected what she described as a 'back-to-basics' approach that was more playful than the neo-modernist design that dominated at the time.[11] Morrison's show has the feel of an installation. A spartan room is populated by a few pieces of simple furniture. The bookcase is drawn onto the wall and three green bottles stand on the table. Here, therefore, something interesting is happening, in that the viewer is directed to examine the table and chairs, but a broader narrative is implied. The stage-set-like appearance of the show seems to suggest a domestic life interrupted. That is, the set-up seems to say something about *use*. This approach, if not co-opted by Ramakers, then at least was used as a form of compass as she selected works that were to exemplify the new Dutch tendency she wished to sell.

The following chapter is not a narrative history of Droog, but it does follow the path of the organization from the early works appropriated into the organization by Ramakers and Bakker through to its move to Las Vegas to discover how the form of highly expressive design they promote came to move from the margins of the design world to occupy a place at the top end of the market for designed goods. In the process, the intention is to ask what tools need be applied if we are to understand what happened to allow for these circumstances to pertain. To do this it will be necessary to consider what qualities this form of design possesses, what techniques have been applied in their creation and how our relationship to such objects has changed in the intervening years. Throughout, Droog products are examined, not to form a chronological account of the organization's history or to catalogue their output but to allow a window onto practices that reveal how these marvellous things actually represent a darker and more interesting undercurrent in design than their reputation as quirky status symbols may suggest.

The presence of things

What makes Droog's early output exciting is that the strange things they produced really were meant to be manufactured, sold and used. The central feature that makes design design, rather than art or something simply to be mused upon is *use*. Designed objects, no matter how absurd they are, by being presented as design, suggest that they will actually be employed by someone to do something. Yet, use is about much more than simply the application of the object as a tool. Tejo Remy's *Rag Chair* of 1991, for example, which was a feature of Droog's first show, has been made by wadding together rags which are held in the shape of a chair by being bound in metal tapes (Figure 6). As is discussed below, in a piece such as this, we have a strong sense of the creator of the object, its author. Its improvised feel gives the impression that another person has spent time putting this thing together. Crucially, however, upon encountering an object such as this, there is also a sense that this is a thing that has been made for somebody to use; its adoption of the formal chair archetype and its titling as a chair, all place it in the field of domestic use objects, even if it is a florid example.

Remy's chair is made from the appropriated detritus of modern life. In this way, it seems to be a far cry from functionalist furniture. It has been put together from elements that have initially been created for a different purpose, suggesting some form of recycling or reuse. This might then appear to imply that Remy was in some way 'upcycling' the materials (though this word would not have been used at the time, of course), to effect a more ecologically sound form of design. Indeed, Ramakers was keen to promote this reading of the work.[12] Yet, this was not the designer's intention,[13] and the effect of the piece is certainly not limited to a conscious recognition of such an agenda. Rags speak of change, of one thing turning into another. Consequently, Remy's chair invokes a sense of the transience of manufactured goods and the way that modernity is as much

Figure 6 Tejo Remy, *Rag Chair* for Droog, 1991. Photographer: Robaard/Theuwkens (Styling by Marjo Kranenborg, CMK)

about waste and decay as it is about the construction of a shiny new future. As the critic Walter Benjamin notes, Charles Baudelaire, the lyrical poet of high capitalism in the nineteenth century, was much concerned with the ragpicker as a feature of modernity. He observed:

> Here we have a man who has to gather the day's refuse of the capital city. Everything that the big city threw away, everything it lost, everything it despised, everything crushed under foot, he catalogues and collects. He collects the annals of intemperance, the *capharnaüm* (stockpile) of waste. He sorts things out and makes a wise choice; he collects like a miser guarding a treasure, the refuse which will assume the shape of useful or gratifying objects between the jaws of the goddess of Industry.[14]

In just this way, Remy's chair appears to be the work of a designer who has sorted through the detritus of modern production to create a useful or gratifying object. In the process, we are offered a chair, one that can be sat on and used in the standard way, but it is also a thing that stimulates a certain reaction, one that is outside of the bounds of the normal functions of furniture.

Things such as Remy's chair can certainly be regarded as functional pieces of design, in that they do what they were intended to in a practical sense. That they are also expressive objects, which demonstrate a poetic approach to how they operate, does not then disqualify them as functional, rather it exemplifies the way that, as the design historian John Heskett has argued, a more fully inclusive definition of function is needed.[15] When the designer and theorist of Critical Design, Matt Malpass, notes that the function of an object 'depends on the practices that situate it in a system of use', he does so to extend the idea of what something does beyond what its author intended.[16] Yet, it is perhaps necessary to go even further than this to observe that objects have always have qualities that are not concerned with their function, but which are a significant part of use.

Certainly, to attempt to separate an object's material function from its sociocultural role is a false division.[17] As the social psychologists Mihaly Csikszentmihalyi and Eugene Rochberg-Halton observe, 'Even the use of things for utilitarian purposes operates within the symbolic province of culture.'[18] Yet, what should be noted here is the fact that what we may call the realm of the symbolic is as much about emotion as it is about meaning. So, as will be examined in more detail in the next chapter, despite modernism's fetishization of functionalism, engineering function cannot be separated from the emotional utility of an object, which is necessarily cultural in nature. However, to reduce the emotive qualities of the things we live with simply to utility, to see them as functional at all (never mind to what ends), is to impoverish the depth of our affective experience of the world.

In design that depends for its effect upon the amplification and exploration of the emotive qualities of things the complexity of such relationships can be seen. For example, Pablo Reinoso is a Brazillian product designer who has lived and worked in Paris since the late 1970s. Well established as a commercial maker of furniture, lighting and jewellery, he began to make more fanciful and expressive furniture in the late 1990s that sell as unique or limited-edition pieces through galleries and at auction. Therefore, it would be easy to suggest that a piece such as his *Spaghetti Bench* of 2006 (Figure 7) was created to service the growing market in such design, but there is clearly more going on than this. Hand-carved from Portuguese chestnut with each example existing as a single unique piece, this is not object as archetype or everyday piece of furniture. The familiar form of the garden bench has convulsed beyond its boundaries as it writhes and grows voraciously up the wall. It appears as though something escaped from a dream

Figure 7 Pablo Reinoso, *Spaghetti Bench*, 2006. Courtesy of Pablo Reinoso Studio

or a nightmare. It seems to exist in an interzone where the mundane has become the marvellous. It is involving. It is clearly a thing of consequence, and as a highly crafted object we would expect it to be worth a lot of money. So, on one level it can be accounted for as a product of market forces, in that mechanisms of such cultural processes (its unique status, the manner in which it is traded) have been utilized to allow the object to exist. Yet this does not seem to account for the content of the piece. It does nothing to tell us why it should take on this affecting and dream-like form.

On one level, Reinoso is effectively stimulating the affective qualities of the piece in the same manner as Droog designers such as Remy did in the 1990s. Similarities can also be seen to techniques adopted by Art Nouveau designers a century before. The art critic, Hal Foster, suggests that Art Nouveau was created as a response to the increasing industrialization of the manufacture of domestic-use objects at this time. He argues that the organic form of these products stemmed from the struggle by the designer 'to impress his subjectivity on all sorts of objects through the idiom of the vitalist line – as if to inhabit the thing in this crafted way was to resist the advance of industrial reification somehow'.[19] This seems important. Foster is arguing that in an age when the nature of human subjectivity was being called into question by technological development, and human agency was seemingly being usurped by machines as people became more thing-like in the process, so a highly affecting design style developed that appeared to be trying to humanize the form of what was developing. Foster goes on to suggest that in Art Nouveau this then gave rise to a certain sterility in an approach to design that demanded a totalizing effect. Paradoxically, he observes, the attempt to re-inject life into designed objects threatened by the homogenizing effect of a commodity culture based on mass production and standardization, arguably created an interior which was so unified and complete that, in the words of the early twentieth-century critic and designer Adolf Loos, it precluded any 'future living and striving, developing and desiring'.[20]

Walter Benjamin, however, suggested that this style based in organicism and the vitalist line developed because, unlike the Arts and Crafts adherents who came before them, designers had ceased to treat new technologies, materials and production practices as a threat. Instead, it seemed that they intended to smother new materials and techniques with a honeyed mass of vegetal form to ornamentally sterilize them. Yet, this then meant that 'the confrontation with technology that lies hidden within it was all the more aggressive'.[21] In this way, Reinoso's bench can be understood as a functional object that asserts its presence through both its singular nature and its vitalist form, whereby an object that is now generally mass-produced has been convulsed into a unique thing. Many Droog products adopted similar tactics as they humanized manufactured goods. Joris Laarman's *Heatwave* radiator of 2003, for example, has a rampantly Rococo form, in contrast to the supposedly functional austerity of such devices. Far from standing mute at the edge of the room, it climbs up the wall like concrete ivy, solidified steam. The fact that Laarman used this shape, because it is actually more efficient (giving a greater surface area for the conduction of heat[22]), demonstrates how function and narrative allusion, actual heat and emotional warmth, are not diametric opposites, but can be part of the process by which things become useful to us.

Spirit of the nineties?

In 1998, Ramakers and Bakker published the book *Droog Design: Spirit of the Nineties*. As the Dutch design critic Timo de Rijk observes: 'The book was a pamphlet, an advertising brochure, a primary source, and a canonizing historiography all rolled into one.'[23] It is therefore worth considering how Ramakers's essay 'Spirit of the Nineties', contained in the larger work, served to act as a self-generated historiography, or origin myth for Droog. In it the work promoted by the organization is identified as a form of 'New Design', in that it is established as representative of a novel tendency in the making of use-objects, one, however, that had identifiably grown out of the Italian New Design of the 1980s. As she states: 'The developments in the New Design of the nineties as manifest in Droog design are inseparably linked with the design revolution of a decade earlier.'[24] Droog is, therefore, characterized as having developed concerns that had previously exercised the Italian pioneers.

The Memphis group, founded in Italy in 1981, which Ramakers suggests prefigured Droog, can itself be seen to have developed out of the radical design movement and countercultural tendencies of the 1960s and early 1970s.[25] At this time, groups such as Archizoom and Superstudio explored the power of architecture and design to create new worlds. Explicitly inspired by Marxist philosophy, and supported by academics such as Gillo Dorfles and Umberto Eco, who wished to explore the semiotic possibilities of such work, the designers created functional objects that challenged traditional notions of what furniture and domestic products could be.[26] By the late 1970s, much of the impetus had dissipated from the movement and Memphis was effectively formed as a secessionist group from Alchymia, which was organized around the editor of *Domus*, Alessandro Mendini. The new grouping's central figure, the industrial designer Ettore Sottsass, along with Michele De Lucchi, Aldo Cibic, Matteo Thun, Barbara Radice and others, wanted to develop an approach to design that moved away from what they saw as Mendini's nihlistic principle that 'design can do nothing but redesign'.[27] Instead, the direction that Memphis was intended to follow was concerned with confronting the functionalism of the modern movement and a concentration on 'product language', what Sottsass described as the attempt to create things with 'stronger stimuli, more concentrated, more rapid, more complex'.[28]

Ramakers suggests that this was done not to confront the developing consumer culture, as might perhaps be expected from radical design, but as an attempt to connect to it in a new way. Here she quotes Sottsass, when he states, 'If society plans obsolescence, the only possible enduring design is one that deals with that obsolescence, a design that comes to terms with it, maybe accelerating it, maybe confronting it, maybe ironizing it, maybe getting along with it... And then I don't understand why enduring design is better than disappearing design.'[29] That's a lot of 'maybes' and it is more than a little vague as a call to action. This statement, therefore, demonstrates the rather loose heritage that Ramakers claims for Droog in Memphis. She seems to be arguing for an approach to design that is related to consumer culture rather than being any programmatic response to it, but the nature of this connection is not resolved. It is to characterize consumerism as a motive force, certainly, but it is actually difficult to get a sense of what Ramakers believes design should actually *do* in such a situation, what is should be *for*. Instead we learn that in Memphis, and consequently in Droog, 'the psychological, symbolic and poetic values of the product now came to the fore', yet why this should be the case is left unclear. She notes that such an approach was based in an interest in semiotics, and referring to the work of the French post-structuralist philosopher Jean Baudrillard she observes that 'products are increasingly construed as signs, as a code distinguishable from other codes', but no tools for reading such codes are proffered, as such. We are told that Sottsass and company were concerned with the 'meaning of objects in today's everydays (sic) surroundings, and with manipulating that meaning',[30] but as to what these meanings may be we are left a little hazy.

With Memphis this very indeterminacy was a deliberate tactic adopted to allow an apparently critical stance to be assumed, just as they actually remained very much within the discourse of commercial furniture design and production. In a piece such as the well-known *Casablanca Cabinet* (Figure 8), it

Figure 8 Ettore Sottsass, *Casablanca Cabinet* for Memphis, 1981. Photograph by Pariano Angelantonio. Courtesy of Memphis S.r.l.

can be seen how Sottsass has given the object an expressive energetic form, but any references it may be making are opaque, even blank. This was, therefore, an exercise in creating use-objects that were meant to be outside of the arena of bourgeois good taste because they did not connect to what had come before in any way. As Michele De Lucchi argued, 'you don't relate them yet to anything or anybody and you can project new possibilities onto them right away.'[31] Declared to be the New International Style by the group themselves, this was therefore intended to be an antidote to what Sottsass and the other members of Memphis considered to be the sterility of tasteful good design. Using brightly coloured patterned plastic laminates and bold and exuberant forms created a recognizable aesthetic, which meant that, as the design historian Catharine Rossi notes, these objects quickly became 'postmodernist pin-ups'.[32] Such a tactic was therefore a useful way of allowing Memphis to both be a radical response to commercial orthodoxies, at the same time that it was a rather safe challenge to good taste which could then refresh consumerist design rather than negate it.

What is in evidence, looking retrospectively at Memphis, is not the extent to which it shocked the design establishment, which it certainly did in its initial appearance on the scene, but the speed at which this challenge was assimilated into popular culture and the canon of design. If Memphis represents a rupture in a narrative of good taste as related to modernist design, what it really can then be characterized as is a point at which the content of the aura of elite high design changed, rather than a withering away of this trope. In this way, Memphis, in its media-friendly photogenic form, actually momentarily opened up a space in which it became permissible for furniture to be ornamental, expressive and emotionally engaging.

In discussing the way that Memphis was received in the Netherlands, Ramakers quotes the Dutch art historian, Hein van Haaren, who spoke out against the work of Memphis, criticizing what he saw as 'indolent Milanese design ... a dangerous fashion that shirks critical analysis', condemning as he did so the elitist nature of the objects not simply because they had pretensions to being art but because they were incomprehensible to 'the masses'.[33] Here, for Ramakers, this is illustrative of a particular Dutch approach to design 'where symbols of power and status mean little',[34] and design should be for the many; yet, she still claims Memphis as a precursor and this goes to underline the inconsistent manner in which she constructs this sense of Dutchness. That Droog can be understood as developing in a very specific national context has already been noted, but it is worth mentioning here because Ramakers makes a claim for Droog as being a form of paradox: both representative of a Dutch mentality and in contradiction to it. So we see that she suggests Droog was based in the New Design of the 1980s, and this is characterized as communicative but without specific content. So, in Ramakers's book *Spirit of the Nineties* what is presented as an explanatory analysis of the Droog's origins actually layers mystification upon myth; in this way, it was an exercise in constituting Droog as much as explaining its emergence.

Expensive rubbish

In *Spirit of the Nineties*, Ramakers notes that in the first half of that decade the accent in Droog design 'lay on the assembling of existing components',[35] and as Williams observes, appropriation became a major tactic employed by a range of designers at this time.[36] He then goes on to discuss how this was far from being a new approach, suggesting that this tendency can be traced back from Marcel Duchamp's readymades through to Achille and Pier Giacomo Castiglioni's *Mezzadro* stool of 1957, made of a tractor seat, declaring that 'appropriation is a practice that has brought artists and designers close together'.[37] This is, however, problematic in that there is a clear difference in strategy between Duchamp's unassisted readymades used for artistic ends and the assemblage that can be seen in the work of the Castiglionis, and evidenced in Droog and more recent emotionally driven design work.[38]

Achille and Pier Giacomo Castiglioni's approach to design was avowedly based in the everyday, in that it was to be drawn from the components delivered by mass production and observation of how people actually interacted with these artefacts. With the *Sella* stool, also created in 1957, for example, the seat from that icon of functionalism, the bicycle, is attached to an upright that has been sunk into a curved base – allowing the stool great freedom of movement. Achille explained that 'when I use a payphone, I like to move around, but I would also like to sit – but not completely'.[39] These are therefore assemblages of the functional found. In a piece such as *Sella*, they are not attempting to distance the viewer, or defamiliarize the design in any way, in fact the appropriation of the saddle acts in the opposite way: to indicate how it may be used. Such works are also fundamentally not Duchamp's 'unassisted' readymades, as despite their apparent similarities the act of appropriating an object is fundamentally different in the discourse of design as it is to that of art.

If the Castiglionis' *Mezzadro* stool is compared to one of Duchamp's original unassisted readymades, it can be seen how such things share certain tactics but serve different strategies. That is to say the methods are similar, but the actual techniques are different. The first of Duchamp's readymades to be referred to as such was the snow shovel of 1916, which was given the title *In Advance of a Broken Arm*. Here Duchamp has taken a mass-produced industrial product and, without altering its form, transmuted it into an art object by an act of designation: by giving it a title and declaring it to be art. It is this case of ontological violence that defines the readymade in Duchamp's hands.

As an unassisted readymade, the snow shovel was created as an exercise in revealing how meaning cleaves to the object in terms of artistic production and presentation. As the art critic John Roberts has suggested, in art the readymade can be understood as a commodity that has been relocated from one productive sphere, that of the shop or the workplace, into another, the studio or the gallery. In such a specific act of transposition, he argues that *In Advance of a Broken Arm* constituted 'the production of an object in which productive labour and artistic labour are conjoined in a state of critical tension and suspension'.[40] This for Roberts then creates a form of 'delay'. In the readymade this is not the delay of aesthetic contemplation (Duchamp was quite clear that he was not attempting to make the viewer appreciate the aesthetics of these objects),[41] instead 'the spectator's attention is not held by the internal relations or surface of the object but by the object's conceptual identity'.[42] That is, the physicality of the object has not been altered, rather its place in the taxonomies of culture has been changed. It has been reframed, and this affects how it will be understood, how it can operate, how it functions.

An intervention such as the snow shovel, therefore, highlighted the way in which art works in a very particular arena or frame, and the fulcrum upon which the operation of the piece rests is that of the choice of the artist, as he moved the object from one category (common functional object) into another (a singular art piece). Given the lack of Duchamp's physical intervention into the object and its aesthetic opacity, the delay leads back to a reflection upon the act of the artist; the issue becomes what the intentional act of the creator has done to the object in the act of transposition. Here the art then lies in the relation between the artefact, the reception of the viewer and the delay caused by the artist's act. It is a work of authorship concerned with meaning, with the chain of signification heading back towards the intention of the artist.

Though both the Castiglionis' and Duchamp's acts of appropriation have the effect of taking common objects and making them singular, the techniques employed are actually quite different. The *Mezzadro* stool is manifestly not an unassisted readymade. In connecting the seat of the tractor to the steering handle, the designers have intervened and changed the materiality of the object. Duchamp transposed the snow shovel from one ontological category (the functional everyday) to another (art). The Castiglionis' piece is an act of appropriation that has not changed the ontological category the object inhabits: the components remain functional objects, but they have had their capacity to function altered by the way in which they are being used. This is then an act of authorship that depends upon use, upon the possibilities of action, whereby the chain of signification gestures onwards, towards the ongoing existence of the object.

With *In Advance of a Broken Arm*, the delay or point of reflection engendered by the piece depends upon the tension created between its form as a functional object and its presentation, in a very specific location, as a work of art. This means that the spectator's reflection depends upon the nature of this transmutation. It is the act of shifting categories from not-art to art that produces the object's conceptual identity; therefore, any contemplation of the object is directed back to this point, even as the viewer considers what the piece may mean to them. It can be observed, of course, that it was just this process that Duchamp was critiquing,[43] however, this actually then serves to emphasize the contrasting nature of appropriation in design to that of art.

In the *Mezzadro* stool, the Castiglionis have actually altered both the form and the internal relations of the object. The delay is therefore putatively ongoing, not temporally fixed to the moment of artistic creation or related back to authorship but focused on the chronic functioning of the object, its emergence into the world through its usefulness. When presented with a work of art we have been schooled to know that we ask, 'What is the artist trying to say? What does it mean to me?' When faced with a piece of design, that is to say a use-object presented as such, the question is less one of intrinsic meaning than of use, either actual or potential (or indeed, as shall be seen in Chapter 5, rhetorical). With the art object the spectator looks, experiences the delay and reflects upon what the artist was trying to say and what it says to them; with design, the delay can be said to occur in the moment of projected use, in that the user comes to the object and says: 'What is this? What is it for? How am I meant to use it?' There is then actual use, whereby the possibilities are collapsed through the interrelationship. With a use-object the user will attempt to reconcile the physicality of the piece, what it seems to be suggesting it can do, with its broader social narrative in the context of their needs.[44] This is because design as a form can be said to be predicated on the concept of use,[45] that is to say an iterative relationship whereby the thing is not encountered only once and contemplated or reflected upon subsequently, but rather the object is returned to again and again as a part of life as it is lived, allowing for a relationship to emerge, to come into being, in the use of the object.

In functional appropriation, the elements do not simply stand for themselves, they are not even metonymic signifiers, they are functioning components. They are very present as tools at the same time as they are not shorn of their meaning through relocation, as was the snow shovel. Instead, the significance and value to be found in everyday objects is pressed into service in these assemblages. Yes, the objects are to some degree made strange by their use in an unfamiliar setting, but this is not arbitrary in the Castiglionis' work, nor is this the case with early Droog products, in that the use of the found element does not shift the object from one ontological category to another. Instead, if the components employed are in any way alienated, this has been done because what is appropriated is, frankly, appropriate in its use-values.

A piece such as Peter van der Jagt's *Bottoms Up* doorbell of 1994 (Figure 9) illustrates the marriage of functional, symbolic and ultimately emotional appropriation adopted in many of the early Droog pieces. Rather than appealing to historicism to place the object in its story, the design takes a piece of social

Figure 9 Peter van der Jagt, *Bottoms Up* doorbell for Droog, 1994. Photograph by Mo Schalkx. © Droog.com

life as its symbolic drive. The use of found wine glasses does nothing to suggest recycling for ecological purposes, as such. Instead, they are employed for their physical qualities to represent an archetype of sociability and an emotional reaction to a functional device.

As one of the central conduits allowing those on the outside of a house to communicate to those within their desire to enter, the doorbell can be a source of anxiety. The standard 'ding-dong', or worse a buzzer, operates in the same way as a traditional telephone ring: it is an invitation and a command; it is a hailing of the subject. Van der Jagt's doorbell takes the potentially disturbing appeal of the doorbell and transmutes it into a social experience. Through striking the wine glasses, the immediacy of the doorbell becomes the clink of glasses, a sound that is firmly rooted in day-to-day experience as one of sociability and emotional warmth. This is, therefore, a humanization of the design object through the use of archetypal elements, not their alienation through displacement.

In *Spirit of the Nineties*, Ramakers comments on the way in which many connected this trope of reuse to environmental issues, but she suggests that whilst this held true for some designers 'it was more a way of thinking than keeping strictly to the letter: in no way did it mean applying the rules of environment-friendly design'.[46] In this context, it should also be noted that with the exception of perhaps Marcel Wanders, the designers shown by Droog in the early days were either graduating students or very early in their careers. Consequently, rather than being an environmental strategy of recycling, for practitioners with no real access to mass production techniques or expensive industrial processes, the use of found components represented a cheap and available way to construct new products. It is curious in this regard that Ramakers does not in *Spirit of the Nineties* refer to the influence of designers working in Britain in the early 1980s, such as Tom Dixon and Ron Arad, who had most recently made use of this version of product design created with found elements. For example, Ron Arad's *One Off* gallery was established in Neal Street in 1983, and it was just such a method that was employed here. Objects created by the likes of Arad, such as the 1981 *Rover Chair* made from an old car seat, demonstrated a concern for reuse which was not so much a comment on overproduction as a result of it: the availability of readymade elements. This was then combined with an approach to means and methods which was that of the outsider, who uses what they can to enter the game.

Similarly, along with Mark Brazier-Jones and Nick Jones, Tom Dixon formed the company *Creative Salvage* in Britain in 1984. They claimed that 'the key to Creative Salvage's success is not in the expensive research and development costs of modern-day products, but in the recycling of scrap to form stylish and functional artefacts for the home and office.'[47] As Williams notes, this DIY approach to the making of things was the furniture equivalent of punk and this approach based in appropriation and improvization could be seen to be mirrored in the graphic design of Jamie Reid and the sampling culture that was developing in music at this time.[48]

This could only happen at a certain point in history because of the availability of objects created through industrial production. In such a situation, the designer can become an arranger of elements, and as such is visible themselves as a labourer – one adding value to the matter manipulated. Rody Graumans's *85 Lamps* chandelier (Figure 10) takes a disposable everyday thing, the incandescent light bulb, and turns what was the faceless and inhuman multiple into a singular thing of consequence. In Marcel Wanders's *Set Up Shades* lamp, made from shades stacked upon each other, the problem is approached from the other direction to similar effect. By combining many replications of the same industrial product, he is using the archetype of the lampshade in an attempt to create an instant connection between the design and the user through the familiarity of the object deployed.

In this way, the early Droog pieces can be said to have owed more to the techniques of montage than they did to Duchamp's unassisted readymades. In

Figure 10 Rody Graumans, *85 Lamps* chandelier for Droog, 1993. Photographer: Stefanie Grätz (Styling by Marjo Kranenborg, CMK). © Droog.com

the interwar period, the Berlin Dadaists used photomontage because it provided them with an easily accessible method for taking parts of the industrial world, the newspaper, the magazine, which could then be reconstructed to make work that was manifestly not traditional art. As the leader of the Berlin Dada, Raoul Hausmann, declared: 'We call this process photomontage because it embodied our refusal to play the role of the artist. We regarded ourselves as engineers, and our work as construction: we assembled [in French: monteur] our work, like a fitter.'[49] The early Droog designers can be regarded as monteurs, crafting new constructions from what is to hand, not to create artistic statements as such, but making use of the design vocabulary available to them in the construction of objects that cannot help but emphasize the disjunctive nature of material reality. Montage as a form contains its juxtapositions *within* the work, it does not solely rely upon reference to the absent author for its operation.

Jurgen Bey was one of the original Dutch Droog designers and continues to be amongst the most interesting practitioners working in the field. Bey considers himself to be an 'industrial designer',[50] but he is clearly operating in an area that displays a conceptual sensitivity to the way in which objects become meaningful to us. His *Light Shade Shade* of 1998 (Figure 11), for example, is a traditional and somewhat kitsch chandelier with a foil shade wrapped around it. When switched off, it appears to be a sleek modern light fitting. When the room darkens and the light is switched on, the chandelier is illuminated and it hangs ghost-like within the now transparent outer layer. The elements of the object are at once

Figure 11 Jurgen Bey, *Light Shade Shade*, 1998. Courtesy of Studio Makkink & Bey

harmonious but in tension, the old meets the new, illumination reveals the archaic within the modern. Many of the most interesting of the objects discussed in this book are like this; the obsolescent is reclaimed to be incorporated within the new, the abject is pressed into the service of luxury, the discarded and outmoded becomes the novel and the coveted. The forgotten past returns as it is reclaimed in the present, as if in an act of human memory.

These objects are best understood not as readymades, they have been worked upon too much for this. Rather they should be seen as material montages, whereby the creators can often be seen to be employing emotive techniques in which the elements play upon each other, and the disjunctions, incongruities and contradictions created by putting available functional parts together to make assemblages that deny the reifying homogenization of mass production whilst still being functional and functioning design.

The dry and the moist

Accounts of Droog tend to stress how the designers created apparently humorous objects. Antonelli, for example, observes in her introduction to the 1998 Droog publication that non-indigenous texts always explain that 'Droog' means 'dry' in Dutch.[51] De Rijk also notes that Ramakers constantly stresses the idea that 'Droog possessed a liberal sprinkling of humor'.[52] Therefore, the name 'Droog' was intended to suggest that what was presented was somehow possessed of a dry or ironic wit.

This concept of ironic humour depends upon a certain relationship to the codes of communication concerned. The theorizing of irony usually proceeds from a semantic definition that it is involved with saying one thing and meaning another, yet as the literary theorist Linda Hutcheon observes, irony is actually characterized by having an 'edge', in that it is about attacking something within certain conditions.[53] For some form of figuration to be considered ironic in this sense, it is therefore not enough to simply say one thing whilst implying something else; this must have some form of intended effect. In her study of gender and humour, Nancy Walker has argued that 'irony engages the intellect rather than the emotions',[54] yet as Hutcheon argues, irony always has a 'target' and a 'victim', that is to say it is always actually emotionally charged and directed.[55] Irony, therefore, is about a relationship to power. For all the emotional content of work, such as the *Rag Chair* or the *Light Shade Shade* for example, in attempting to understand Droog's output as humorous it is difficult to get a sense of what exactly is being subverted or highlighted, what the target is supposed to be. It seems more likely, therefore, that this reading of Droog as somehow ironic is actually a more diffuse product of the time in which it was produced, the 1990s, when a clear programme of formal and ethical approaches to design was difficult to discern and 'postmodern' irony was a more general stance. This then ignores the emergent properties of Droog work, which was actually much more about the opening out of meaning, not the targeted and pointed action of the ironic.

Irony must perforce have a specific context, as Hutcheon continues, 'irony happens as part of a communicative process; it is not a static rhetorical tool to be deployed, but itself comes into being in the relations between meanings … between intentions and interpretations'.[56] That is to say irony always takes place within a discourse. There must be an expectation of something making sense a 'general expectation of sincerity and coherence',[57] before this can be subverted through the ironic stance. Thus, the Droog designs of the 1990s may have been deliberately departing from the neo-modernist orthodoxies of the day, but in the play of signifiers of the time they could perhaps be better described as ludic rather than ironic. Design writer Aaron Betsky has argued in relation to Droog that 'irony and wit … show that one is "in the know" and thus part of a tribe'.[58] Indeed, irony is always both exclusionary and inclusionary, in that it implies an assumption of superiority and sophistication on the part of both the ironist and the intended, comprehending, interpreter.[59] Yet, as is noted above, irony is not a static device, it is something that happens in the dynamic interplay of communication and discourse. This means that no fixed constituencies can be identified, particularly as these things transition through the course of the life histories. This is because irony is relational, in that it comes into being between the said and the unsaid, between intention and interpretation within specific contexts.[60]

These designs could be seen to be playing with codes of status and taste; yet, there does not seem to be enough actual direction to them to call what they are doing irony in any meaningful sense of the word. Rather what is presented in this early work of Droog is more dialectical than ironic; they mean what they say, but what is being said is contradictory. This then is different to irony. Droog may have been self-consciously presented as humorous or ironic in a dry manner, with the suggestion is that we will all get the joke because of our informed sophistication, but this does not mean that this was actually the case. Yes, much of what they were doing was dependent upon a disjuncture between elements or codes, but this did not necessarily signify irony or wry detachment at the time of their manufacture and mediation, and it certainly does not mean that they must be read or understood in this way now.

As de Rijk notes, these designers had received hardly any theoretical training.[61] They were not schooled in postmodern theory. Rather they had been exposed to the broader dominance of neo-modernism in Dutch design practice and discourse, and reacted against this. Therefore, almost inevitably, the vocabulary they adopted was essentially non-rational and self-consciously anti-functionalist. They did this, as all good students should, to get up the noses of their teachers and what was perceived as the design establishment, and it is arguable that this resulted in the work of early Droog having a clear surrealist bent. As the philosopher Jacques Rancière observes, such practices constitute 'a pure encounter of heterogeneities, testifying wholesale to the incompatibility of two worlds'. Therefore, for him, this can be seen as representing a material expression of the famous surrealist encounter of the umbrella and the sewing machine, which demonstrates 'the absolute power of dreams and desire against the reality of the everyday world, but using its objects'.[62] So, rather than constituting a dry irony, these early Droog assemblages actually reveal themselves as a more visceral surrealist practice.

Dick van Hoff's sewn together washbasin made from felt and then impregnated with polyester resin (1996), which was for the designer 'a criticism of the clogged-up attitude of the sanitary industry' as 'a washbasin to me is a receptacle for catching water, no more and no less'.[63] Yet this is much more than simply a receptacle for catching water. Through transposing the usually solid form of a washbasin into what appears to be flexible textile, the irony might be that what we expect to be hard, the basin, is made from a soft material, but the material has been made rigid by impregnation with resin. Yet in such examples it is in actuality difficult to see the joke, and if the humour is apparent it could be suggested that it is not as dry as has been implied. A piece such as Jurgen Bey's *Garden Bench* (1999) could be said to exemplify the conceptual dry humour claimed for much of the organization's output: it is essentially a machine which takes organic waste and extrudes a bench which will then slowly decompose, fertilizing the surrounding area. Yes, Bey's bench seems to be making a playful statement 'hey, why not just extrude the bench from the mulch we have?' But even if it is accepted that this is funny, is this not actually an object that to some degree refers to both the futility of production and the inevitability of decay? This is, therefore, not to deny that there is humour to be found in these pieces, it is to suggest that rather than being dry, distant and ironic, instead, as with surrealist practice, something darker and altogether more disturbing lurks beneath.

In van Hoff's washbasin, for example, can be seen a clear echo of the technique employed by Meret Oppenheim in her 1936 surrealist object

Breakfast in Fur, in which the usually hard porcelain of a tea cup has morphed into the sensuousness of fur. In just the same way, with the washbasin, it is not difficult to see how Freudian resonances of desire can be read into a piece which speaks of softness and hardness and the plunging of hands into hot wetness. Far from being 'dry', such connotations seem very clearly to have returned as moist. Similarly, in Jan Konings's and Bey's *Kokon* furniture, created in 1997 in conjunction with Technical University Delft, Faculty of Space and Aviation Technology (Figure 12), the products have been wrapped in a synthetic elastic fibre. These can be seen as marvellous and strangely threatening objects. Ramakers informs us that with these pieces 'the "skeleton" is a well-known chair, with the elastic skin adding an entirely new appearance. By cross-breeding and grafting, products and functions of a different nature can merge and develop into new products'.[64] Here, Ramakers speaks of the objects as though they were living things: 'cross-breeding' and 'grafting'. As with Reinoso's bench, so the objects seem to be convulsing beyond their normal boundaries, though here the physicality is repressed, contained within the new skin.

If in the early twentieth-century functionalist modernists dreamed of the transparent house filled with tools for living, then the surrealists looked in the other direction, as they delved into the fantastic nature of the modern interior.

Figure 12 Jan Konings and Jurgen Bey, *Kokon Furniture* for Droog, 1997. © Droog.com

The theorist Roger Caillois observes that 'it's clear that the utilitarian role of an object never completely justifies its form, that is to say the object always overflows the instrument. So it is possible to discover in every object an irrational residue determined among other things by the unconscious agency of the inventor or technician.'[65] This then is the unnameable, that part of experience that is not, and never can be, fully available to consciousness, which identifies a key element of the everyday things we encounter that is explored in the next chapter.

The surrealists certainly saw how the power of the influence of the unconscious of the creator could imbue the object with presence in an increasingly mass-produced material culture. Yet, this is not to argue that such work then entirely depends upon reference back to the intentions of the author. Rather it seems to point to a position whereby human actors cannot help but embody some of what they feel into what they make. We leave an imprint on what we create that is perceptible to those who encounter it. The emotive is encoded into the work. Its emergence is not then the release of what was intended, but the articulation of that which was unknown. In this way, more than Droog work representing a humorous or ironic stance on the part of its creators, rather such experiments can be seen as reservoirs of affect that speak to the anxieties and contradictions of the age in which they were brought into being.

The unheimlich

Droog examples such as those discussed above can therefore be seen as disturbing because they appear to draw upon a body of emotivity and association beneath the surface of the apprehended object. That is to say, they play on the emotional qualities of things. This then is a tactic that has been adopted by many designers working more recently. The *Cow Bench*, created by Julia Lohmann, in 2004, for example, is an uncanny object (Figure 13). It has been made by taking a cowhide and stretching it over a wood and hard-foam superstructure to exactly mimic the form of the animal, minus the head. It takes up the space that a cow would and, according to Lohmann, people who encounter it tend to react to it as though it were a living thing.[66] This is the 'uncanny' in operation. In surrealist thought, this concept is derived from Freud's concept of the *unheimlich*, literally the 'unhomely', which exists in contrast to the *heimlich*, the 'homelike', the familiar, the known. The word also has a double meaning, however, in that heimlich also refers to that which is hidden, or so known that it is no longer seen.[67] The unheimlich, or uncanny, therefore, is not simply what we are not at home with,

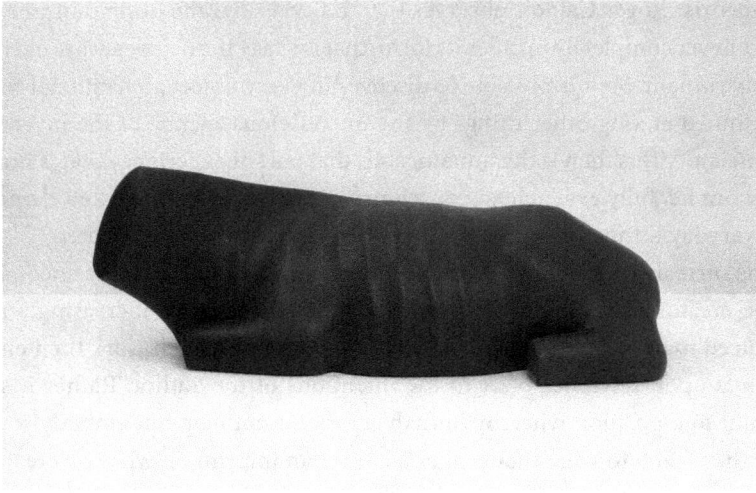

Figure 13 Julia Lohmann, *Cow Bench*, 2004. Photograph by Sylvie Chan-Liat. Courtesy of the Kreo Gallery

but rather it is the return of the familiar made strange by repression. It is the moment of recognition and alienation experienced when that which we come into contact with is both commonplace and strange at the same time. As the curator and critic Jane Alison observes, Freud noted that in some languages 'the uncanny can only be translated as "the haunted house" that gives rise to ghosts'.[68] So the surrealist uncanny is the recognition of the haunted nature of reality, haunted that is by our unconscious knowledge and desires, by the ultimate unassimilability of our emotional lives, the unnamable part of our selves. For the surrealists, this was certainly about beauty and eroticism, but for them these ideas were suffused with a darkness that was expressed in terms of the irrational residues of experience.

One of the ur-objects of surrealism was the mannequin or doll, which disturbs us because it appears to exist as both animate and inanimate; it is uncanny because it appears to be familiar as a human form yet monstrous because it is lifeless. What then is also disturbing is the object that transgresses from the other direction, whereby the artefact appears to be coming to life. For Foster this is the definition of the marvellous, a relation to objects whereby the distinction between the animate and the inanimate is ambiguous. This was then at the root of the surrealist project: 'the re-enchantment of the disenchanted world, of a capitalist society made ruthlessly rational',[69] and it is a methodology that is apparent in early Droog work and more recent emotive furniture and products.

Figure 14 Meret Oppenheim, *Table with Bird's Legs*, 1938–9. © Victoria and Albert Museum, London

Meret Oppenheim's *Table with Bird's Legs* of 1938–9 (Figure 14), for example, represents an object that demonstrates the surrealist preoccupation with the occult resonances of manufactured goods. As with Lohmann's creation, it is something that seems to have escaped from a dream, whereby the inanimate has somehow metamorphosized into the living. Inspired by Max Ernst's series of detourned engravings *Une Semaine de Bonté*, where the normality of the bourgeois interior is ruptured by marvellous manifestation, Oppenheim's piece is both humorous and horrifying. It has power because it appears to blur from one category (the inert, the object) into another (the animate, the living thing), consequently it can no longer recede into the background; it asserts its presence as it alludes to the suspicion that the things around us may be more animate than we wish to believe. In this way, the surrealists sought to disrupt the apparent seamlessness of the interior as 'etui' or comforting case filled with the bourgeois consumer's carefully accumulated objects, as Benjamin characterized it, not by its blank rejection but by its intensification.[70] There is no little humour in such an approach, but it is of a form that acknowledges the underlying uneasiness of everyday life, in just the manner that Lohmann's piece can be seen to operate.

From good design to 'design design'

Droog matured throughout the 1990s and the early 2000s in a context defined by the rise of design, both as an aspirational trope and as a feature of everyday life. If the twentieth century had begun with an intense esoteric debate as to the form designed goods should ideally take then by the end of the century to some the practices of industrial production appeared to have answered these questions.[71] As Ramakers observed, by the late 1990s, the word 'design' had become epithetic and 'Design design' had seeped everywhere.[72] That is, the discussion about what constituted design as a way of giving form to the objects we use had essentially been resolved by the rise of consumer design: the forming of objects to serve a particular market or economy of desire. The emphasis had shifted from a debate about how production could be modelled to create good design for all to one concerned with how manufactured goods could be formed to make them desirable and meaningful for consumers. The role of the designer had essentially become, in the minds of the public at any rate, that of stylist who rendered what was produced amenable to the market.

Through the 1990s in the UK supplements such as the *Guardian Space* magazine and *Elle Deco* told people where to source the latest trends and provided useful illustrations of how their purchases might look when artfully arranged. Into the new-century television programmes such as *Changing Rooms* presented consumers with templates that could be adapted in their construction of their particular look. The availability of cheap furniture meant that people had more of a chance than ever before to express themselves through their furnishings. The anthropologist Daniel Miller discusses the way in which such domestic choices can express a range of different social issues, such as class and generational differences,[73] and the development of the interior as a site of display and fantasy meant that this tendency became amplified. People had begun to use their homes as a canvas for painting 'who they really are' in a way that their parents would often have thought unimaginable.

The concept of design has begun to fulfil a very particular function in the culture of the West. It is a way of intervening in the world, the apparent application and guarantee of discernment. So a knowledge of design has become a form of cultural capital available to consumers.[74] As people started to understand design more as a collection of artefacts (as a noun to describe a certain form of thing), so they also began to see themselves as designers of their own lives, sculptors of the emotional landscape in which to live. However, what is obscured in such a process are the hegemonic structures in the raw materials available to the consuming public. Just as the development of the home computer allowed everybody to become a graphic designer – but within certain very defined limits and with literally preset parameters – so the availability of domestic objects meant that everybody could now become an interior designer, but with similar limits. Then as is always the case with the operation of ideology, what was not apparent was the extent to which the boundaries of possibility were set.

The rise of style and lifestyle publications and TV programmes meant that an agenda was being established. Through choice a certain form of subjectivity was being demanded. This was therefore not control through repression, but control through stimulation.[75] Increasingly, then, we are sold pre-packaged lifestyles. As consumer culture has developed, it has become increasingly possible for individuals to shop for a personality by buying the goods necessary to both present themselves to others as a certain sort of person, at the same time allowing them to believe that this is who they really are. Indeed the philosopher Anthony Giddens has gone as far as to state that this is now a requirement of consumerism: that it is necessary to identify oneself through the adoption of a lifestyle.[76] This can then be supplied by the furnishing of life with the correct objects. A central stimulus to the development of design, both as a body of goods and as a practice, has been this drive towards the acquisition of things predicated upon the need to be the right sort of consumer displaying the correct taste.

It was in such an atmosphere that the first Droog shop was opened. One problem that Droog faced was that despite the international interest shown in their work at exhibitions such as the Salone del Mobile, they found it hard to begin to really monetize their practices. In an attempt to bring Droog products, amongst others, into production, Marcel Wanders created the company Moooi in 2000 in conjunction with the Italian furniture manufacturer B&B Italia SpA. In May 2002, Droog established their first retail outlet, Droog & Co. in Amsterdam. Up until this time, the organization had operated out of a small office and from the number of visitors who seemed to expect to be able to buy what they had seen in the media, Ramakers and Bakker have argued that they believed that some form of shop was going to be necessary if customers were to be able to buy into the Droog brand.[77] It could be observed, however, that the organizers of the Droog project had also noted the rise of stores selling high-end design at top prices and wished to capitalize on this. A small outlet was also established in Tokyo in 2008 and a large two-floor showroom opened in New York in 2009.

Yet, by the end of the first decade of the twenty-first century, design had become a much more dynamic market, thanks to the opening up of the channels of communication and a growing awareness of the power of design, the growth of cheap manufacturing and the expansion of global trade. What really appeared to have changed for Droog, however, was that a trend of which they had originally been pioneers, for expressive and communicative design, had overtaken them. In many ways the turn of the millennium can be characterized as the point at which the world really became digital, when mass internet use made the world radically more available. As is discussed in Chapter 4, it is in such circumstances that spectacular, emotionally charged design thrives, as it can pass through the circuits of culture as representation in a way not dreamed of only a decade before. Droog seemed to be somewhat wrong-footed by this. Such mechanisms definitely favoured the emotive objects they had been championing but it is not clear that they had realized that such a shift in the informational economics of culture meant that the whole ethos of what it means to design and be a designer (or design promoter) had changed.

The descent of Droog

Things do not go away on the internet. If they are deliberately removed or somebody does not pay the hosting fee they will disappear, but if they exist somewhere maintained or they are forgotten about and simply not taken down, things can persist indefinitely. In this way, in the information age, the past has started to become a material part of the present. It is a little melancholy, then, to see the press from the opening of the New York Droog shop now, as it breezily announces their arrival in the city in 2009, as less than two years after the opening it closed almost overnight in November 2010. Ramakers claimed that this was because the stock was needed for the opening of the Las Vegas store, thus leaving the New York venue empty.[78] Yet, given the unannounced closure of the premises and the almost immediate relocation to Las Vegas, Ramakers's explanation does not seem convincing.

Throughout the 1990s, Droog were pioneers of an expressive form of design, the legacy of which can be seen in the emotionally complex design produced more recently. Approaches such as the use of found elements and disjunctive combinations of materials served to emphasize the presence of simple use-objects to the point where not only were the alienating effects of mass production mitigated, but they became objects of desire in a new political economy of design founded on the protocols of consumer culture. Far from representing a smooth passage of inevitable evolution, the history of furniture and domestic products over the past hundred years or so has been characterized by a dialectical tension between the development of mass culture predicated on mass production and its concomitant standardization and homogenization, and the attempt by designers to periodically assert the emotive qualities of objects as products of human labour and will. Yet, in a capitalist culture, as William Morris found in the nineteenth century and Droog have experienced in the last couple of decades, it is difficult to make a living from making high-quality design unless one sells spectacular things to the rich at a premium. Only a couple of years after opening, the Las Vegas store was closed. Now, in Amsterdam, the Droog store is still open, and a café and even hotel means we can all go and experience Droog, but it is not the force it was at the beginning of the century.

Ramakers and Bakker may have intended for the name Droog to signify a wry detachment or ironic stance on the part of the work presented, but as has been demonstrated, irony always takes place within a discourse. It *happens* rather than exists as some form of ontological constant. For irony to exist there must be what Hutcheon describes as a 'discursive community', in that both sides must understand the codes for the trope to function. As she suggests, 'the complexity of the potential interaction of the interpreter, ironist and text in making irony happen has to be part of any consideration of irony as the "performative" happening it is'.[79] Therefore, the meanings of the work presented change as it passes through time, as it moves through history and the discursive community alters, in this case to the point where the apparent irony is stripped away and its darker qualities become enhanced.

In this way, the disjunctive and ambiguous designs presented by Droog can be seen to have been more involved with a surrealist uncanny, the return of the repressed, the irrational and emotional residue of life, than they were any form of dry humour. Yet Droog's products were always meant to be actual use-objects and Ramakers's justifications of its output have consistently stressed the relation of the organization to the market.[80] It is perhaps for this reason that Droog has been presented as humorous and ironic rather than critical, as such. Yet in the tactics adopted by those who were taken up and promoted by the organization, in the disjuncture and messy uncanny qualities of the objects, it may be that a form of subversion can be detected which has more to do with cosmic irony, of the unintended consequences of life, than any programmatic assault upon the ideological material culture of consumerism.

It is within this context that the development of emotive design, as objects that play upon the irrational residue of life, must be understood. Yes, the development of the market in such design can be traced (as it is in Chapter 4). However, it must be accepted that this has taken place within a broader context of social change characterized by a shifting relationship between subjects and objects as the technologies of reproduction have expanded and fundamentally altered our experience of the world. What then is interesting is how the emotive tendency has arisen in a world that has come to be disenchanted by rationalist scientism in design, at just the same time that consumer capitalism has been operating to re-enchant it through the fetishization of the things we buy to make our lives meaningful.

In attempting to understand how emotive design has come about, therefore, the story of Droog serves to reveal some of the key tensions at the heart of the development of this tendency. To really make sense of the emergence of design work that plays upon, and with, emotion without trying to harness it to other ends, however, it will be necessary to tease out the fundamental tensions at the centre of such practice whilst seeking to place it in its cultural and historical perspective.

2

Framing design art

Two old tables have been used to make a base. Upon this has been placed another, creating a form of frame. This has then been screened around by lace curtains and topped-off with sheets and blankets braced by string guys which extend out to be held by rocks, as when camping on hard ground. Within the chamber there is a mattress. It is a private, shrouded space. The entrance to this is then defined by the carcass of a wardrobe, the back removed and its doors open, allowing access to the interior, creating a threshold. Here sits a chair with its back legs sunk into the floor of the wardrobe. The seat wavers in indeterminacy, it at once suggests the act of entering just as it seems to stand sentinel, guarding. The whole is a strange thing. It is evocative. Though it is not clear what it is as such, the assemblage of elements, its scale and shape are suggestive of other forms of room or space. It seems to invoke other structures: the den, a gypsy caravan, a funeral coach.

If you had seen this object at the V&A exhibition, 'Telling Tales: Fear and Fantasy in Contemporary Design' in 2009, you might have examined the label to discover that in this show it was titled *Linen Cupboard House*, though more recently this has been translated as *Linen Chest House* (Figure 15). The text would have made clear that it was the work of Dutch creative partnership, designer Jurgen Bey and architect Rianne Makkink, under the name Studio Makkink & Bey. If this was all it told, however, you might not be any the wiser. At the entrance an information board set the context for the exhibition as a whole:

> In recent years works like this have been described collectively as Design Art, a catch-all term for objects that are somewhere between art, craft and design. They are mostly self-initiated works – personal statements or manifestos, made by designers as unique pieces or in limited editions. Rather like art, the objects in this exhibition are generally traded through galleries. Yet unlike sculpture, they retain their role as functional objects, even if their usability is often subordinated to their symbolic or decorative value.[1]

Figure 15 Studio Makkink & Bey, *Linen Chest House*, 2002. Courtsey of Studio Makkink & Bey

So here, rather concisely, the curator of the show, Gareth Williams, situates Studio Makkink & Bey's piece for us. It is a 'personal statement or manifesto' that exists 'somewhere between art, craft and design'. It is something that might be traded as though it were art, yet it retains its role as a functional object, even if its 'usability' has been subordinated to its 'symbolic' qualities. The show presented a collection of this type of design, including Wieke Somers's *Bath Boat* previously discussed in the introduction, work by Tord Boontje, and strange and highly decorative pieces from a range of other designers, many of whom were or had been associated with Droog.

Makkink and Bey's odd little house stood at the entrance to the 'Forest Glade', the first room of the exhibition where it sat in a stylized woodland setting. In the next space, 'The Enchanted Castle', were similar pieces that were of a more domestic bent: highly expressive use objects by the likes of Antwerp-based duo Studio Job that seemed to allude to deeper meanings than we usually expect from chairs and tables. Finally, in the 'Heaven and Hell' section were housed dark and disturbing objects that spoke of mortality and hidden desires.

As the most significant exhibition of this kind of work by this point, the curatorial team used the concept of narrative and storytelling to give a coherency to the collection. This made sense for the development and presentation of a museum show. Although referred to as Design Art (a term that had gained a certain currency but was falling out of favour even as the exhibition was presented), given that the work shown made a claim to be functional, the provision of a context operated to emphasize the nominal 'usability' of such design.[2] That is, such a device was necessary if the 'Design' part of the phrase was to be important, since the alternative, to place the pieces on plinths in a white cube space, would be to overemphasize the 'Art' part of the conjunction.

Narrative as a theme certainly makes sense in terms of delivering museum exhibitions, in that it gives context to objects that are at least nominally domestic use objects.[3] Recently, this manner of framing design with content has been used in the Crafts Council show 'Twelve Tall Tales', curated by Onkar Kular in 2016 and 'The Learned Society of Extraordinary Objects', curated by Danny Clarke and Carl Clerkin at Somerset House in 2017. Yet, in such circumstances, the concentration on storytelling, though effective, can tend to overemphasize this very quality of the work, to bring to the fore its communicative dimension and spectacular nature.

One thing is certain with this kind of design, how it is framed will have quite a profound effect upon the way in which it is comprehended and folded into the lifeworld of those who encounter it. What field or context it is presented as being part of will serve to define how it is understood. To come across something in a gallery is very different to being offered it to sit at to eat a meal. Similarly, a technique, usage or material that in one set of circumstances is entirely appropriate may seem out of place in another. Therefore, this chapter sets out to position such 'Design Art' in relation to the discourses through which it flows, and against which it must be understood. In order to do this, it will be necessary to position such expressive and emotive design against the functionalism and rationalism of modernism in design and its legacy. It will then be worth pausing for a moment to ask how such design can be said to operate in relation to art as a set of practices and a social phenomenon. The entangled issues of authorship and agency in design will be addressed, to see how the practice of making useful things with content has developed against a certain background defined to some degree by debates within art. Yet, there are issues here that are also proper to design as a field of practice concerned with actual use and the intimacy of experience that such a mode of living with objects implies. Such concerns will, therefore, lead to an examination of how work such as this can be understood as performative. Recently, some confusion has developed around this term. In the age of social media, this word has come to mean 'done as a performance', which more properly would be represented by the word 'performatory'.[4] In linguistics, 'performative' has a more precise meaning, which also has a quite profound political dimension, in that it refers to an utterance that does not just represent the world, but alters it in its operation. Thus, when applied to the furnishings of our lives, such a concept provides an important insight into how we relate to the material things we encounter.

This then calls for an exploration of how this happens, not least in terms of the embodied and affective way that we encounter useful things. To understand this emotional relationship to design it will be necessary to show how such reciprocities between people and things develop in the field of everyday life. The implication is that as the nature of the everyday changes, as it has done profoundly in the last thirty years or so, so the nature of such relationships has altered. This is not least because of the way in which what was once called 'the media' has expanded to encompass this very daily life almost in its entirety. However, given that the first thing we notice about such works is really that they are so noticeable, it seems pertinent to begin by examining why these seem to be things that have 'something to say'.

Meaningful things

As Williams notes, designed objects such as those shown in 'Telling Tales' are clearly intended to communicate something beyond the nature of their usability. A few years ago, work such as this would have been easily dismissed as so much postmodernism. As a reaction to the perceived sterility of modernism, postmodern design drew upon historical styles and references, happily attempting to erase distinctions between high and low culture, whilst relying on techniques of exaggeration and parody to work with hegemonic narratives of style and class.[5] As was noted in the last chapter, postmodernism played with codes to create effects such as irony or pastiche. To do this it operated semantically, at what might be described as a semiotic level. As the optimism of modernism came to be superseded by a diffuse sense that all had been done and everything said, what was articulated was so often placed in ironic quotation marks, suggesting a distancing from the content. The work of Droog and those that followed, as has been discussed, is different in that it is less ironic than it is disjunctive and uncanny. Yet, at the root of postmodernism in design was the principle that everyday use objects can be meaningful in terms of content rather than simply by dint of their usefulness. In the catalogue to 'Telling Tales', Williams suggests that the postmodern approach had a direct relationship to the work in the exhibition, arguing that much of what was presented seemed to 'embody' postmodern thinking, particularly in terms of how it manipulated conventions of understanding. Yet, he also noted that whilst postmodernism was concerned with the symbolic qualities of objects, the work seldom engaged with emotion, remaining as 'cool intellectual exercises'. The work of the more contemporary designers exemplified by the work shown in 'Telling Tales' is then described as 'much more emotionally hot'.[6] This illustrates how Williams as a critical commentator had identified a key quality of such work, that it engages at the level of the emotions rather than primarily operating at the level of conscious decoding.

As was noted in the introduction, much of the critical commentary on the use of emotion in design practice conducted this century has tended to cast the emotive as essentially instrumental, as something to be manipulated to enhance an object's usability. In the work presented in 'Telling Tales' and what has followed in a similar vein, emotion and affective reaction appear to be operating in a different manner. Rather than utilizing emotive qualities to allow for the better practical functioning of the object, or to enhance its meaning to particular ends, work such as this appears to be playing upon emotion. That is to say, it is not using emotive reaction to make the product more appealing or easier to use. Instead, in such design it seems that emotion is being worked on and through as an end in itself. In this way it is employing the formal and allusional playfulness of postmodernism, but with a certain seriousness as to what this means. Throughout the development of design as a field of professional activity, there has been a tension between the need for things to function on a practical level, and our emotional reaction to what we use to live our lives. Recently, the latter has been instrumentalized to serve the former, and an examination of how and why this has come about serves to show how any other attitude to the emotive qualities of everyday use objects might be seen as problematic. Yet, such an investigation does also seem to reveal how emotion actually underpins the whole area.

Function-*ing*

To the engineering minded, it might be difficult to see what problem is solved by a piece such as Makkink and Bey's marvellous den. For a certain kind of design tendency, doing something as efficiently as possible is what matters. Yet, the problem-solving paradigm is actually the manifestation of a particular conceptualization of the role of design that has evolved in specific historical conditions. As a central concern of modernist thought and practice in the early part of the twentieth century, the debate about the nature of the role of function was at the heart of the search for an ethics of design.[7] The rapid modernization of the world had produced in Art Nouveau (or Jugendstil, or Style 1900, depending where you were), a design style that was to be a florid last gasp of romanticism. After the devastation of the Great War, a new seriousness was required; a new objectivity that could produce rationally worked-out schemes of thought and production to allow for the construction of a new world. In Europe, organizations such as the Bauhaus sought out the rational basis of making and manufacture. In America, the Scientific Management of Fredric Winslow Taylor was being enthusiastically applied in the rationalization of industry. Time and motion studies were employed and a ruthless division of labour instituted to make the process of production as efficient as possible.

For designers, at this time, the emphasis on function was the guarantor of seriousness. This was then the reinscription of a current in design that has underpinned the making of goods for use: that things should first and foremost work, and that how this can be achieved can be determined by systematic investigation of the problem. In this sense, functionalism is a belief that problems can be solved through the application of reason, which is a way of regarding the making of things that has run as 'an unbroken thread through design thinking since the Enlightenment',[8] but which found its fullest expression in modernism. What this approach did in design was to open up a space whereby efficiency was paramount. For the modernists, this project had a defining ethical dimension. For those that came after them, however, the main legacy of this emphasis was to create the circumstances in which consumer capitalism could use the lever of rationality to establish the conditions in which all other values were to be subservient to the efficient production of profit.

For the enlightened souls of the nineteenth and early twentieth centuries, reason, based in the objectivity and empiricism of the scientific method, was seen as a progressive force that was supplanting superstition and mysticism. The apparently manifest gains brought about by the technology that such an approach made possible seemed to prove the primacy of such a philosophy. The German sociologist Max Weber described this triumph of scientific rationalism as the 'disenchantment' of the world. No longer was life to be understood as controlled by mysterious forces, characterized by a belief in religion and supernatural explanations of phenomena. Instead, the ascendency of scientific thinking meant that, in principle at least, all things could be mastered by calculation.[9]

In this way, those who subscribed to such a view believed that the ascendency of reason meant life had been definitively demystified by science, and the sway of imagination subordinated to the instrumentality of rational thought. Thus, as the design critic Aren Kurtgözü notes, this calculating disenchantment of the world meant meaning was coming to be regarded as transparent and ultimately available to explanation, that there was thought to be no 'opacity that resists knowledge', within 'the realm of objects'. So, given the rise of such an ontological perspective, design discourse responded by asserting 'the primacy of functional, utilitarian ethics and aesthetics'.[10] In this way, what came to be known as functionalism, that is to say a credo based on the idea that form follows function, a prospective use which can be ultimately known and calculated for, was constituted as a project that both depended upon and existed to guarantee a certain transparency and stability of the world of things. If this philosophy then found the height of its expression in the 'efficient' design of the late twentieth century, it was at the Bauhaus that its modern manifestation in design was first determined.

Marcel Breuer's 1925 *Model B3* chair, later to become known as the *Wassily* chair, takes the essential structure of an easy chair, but it is as though the mass of Victorian upholstery has been hollowed-out to leave simply volume delineated by lines of tubular steel. It is spare and economical. The metal gleams, the linear tensions of the struts beat out mechanical rhythms against each other as the light plays upon them. The webbing is tight. The angles are correct and the proportions satisfying. It appears to subtract all that is not absolutely necessary for the act of sitting, to the extent that the user seems to almost float in the space an armchair usually takes up. It is a large thing, its footprint being the same as that of the traditional version, but its construction means that it gives the impression that it fills up very little space. It looks like an efficient tool for sitting at the same time that it is a coolly elegant piece of furniture.

This was one of the first products to emerge from the Dessau Bauhaus and it played a part in establishing the school's reputation as an institution pioneering a functionalist approach to design. As one of the earliest domestic products to exploit the qualities of tubular steel, it is said that Breuer took inspiration for its design from observing the construction of his Adler bicycle.[11] This was arguably because such a vehicle, particularly at this time, would have exemplified a machine that represented an almost perfect marriage of form and function: nothing is there that does not need to be there for the efficient fulfilment of the machine's purpose, at the same time that what is there is absolutely honest as to what it is made from and what it does.

At this time, one of the key objectives of an institution such as the Bauhaus was to establish design as a serious method for rebuilding the world. Part of the way this new seriousness was signalled was through the disavowal of ornamentation and decoration. In his influential polemic *Ornament and Crime*, first published in 1908, Adolf Loos, who later went on to work at the Bauhaus, famously argued that 'the evolution of culture is synonymous with the removal of ornament from utilitarian objects'.[12] This was to introduce a moral imperative to aesthetics and the styling of objects as to their functionality; that the removal of ornament to emphasize the functional nature of design was to somehow become more civilized; that an ascetic lack of ornament or adornment was more morally sound. This was in part because ornamentation was seen to be primitive, in that it appeals to the senses rather than reason. Breuer's design, as part of the ascendency of utilitarian functionality, was thus an assertion of design as a rational exercise for pragmatic purposes, rather than any form of emotional practice. In this way, Breuer's chair can be seen as an attempt to make a disenchanted object. The fripperies of ornamentation are stripped away and all that is left are the 'facts' of its existence. This was the application of instrumental reason to design, but as is becoming clear, this was anything but a dispassionate exercise.

The social rhetoric of function

The form of the *B3* has to a large degree been determined by the material qualities of tubular steel and the technical capacities of the equipment used to bend it at the time of making. It is clear from actually sitting in it that questions of ergonomics and position have been considered. It is a comfortable chair, clearly one that has been made to sit in as much as look at. Breuer's decision to effectively leave the mechanism exposed, to show how the chair is formed and held together, however, was as much based on aesthetic considerations as any practical problems associated with the physical act of sitting. The newness of the materials from which it was manufactured and the stark look adopted were intended just as much to symbolize and express a modernist faith in the machine future – as a place where people would live, use furniture, sit down – as it was for any utilitarian reasons. As a sitting device, this chair was no more effective or functional than the upholstered version it was meant to replace. Yes, it was meant to be easier and cheaper to mass-produce, but at this point it was still very much a prototype that had been handmade.[13] In this way then, it operated as much as a suggestion or a proposal as to how furniture might be in a truly modern world as it did as any practical solution to a problem.

Modernist functionalism made a claim to be concerned with the logic and grammar of design in the service of usefulness. However, this in itself is a rhetorical statement through an object. Rhetoric is language that is meant to persuade. Rhetorical design is thus the creation of functional objects that do not just do what they need to in utilitarian terms, but that also put forward an argument through their materiality.[14] Here then is the centre of the problem with such 'functionalism': the objects created were meant to be first and foremost rational and dispassionate solutions to the problems of life. Yet, in doing this, they were also engineered to communicate this world view to the user. They were not just being functional, they were also appealing to function as a symbolic quality of the object based on forms which were perceived to embody the spirit of the machine. This was thus the expression of an essentially romantic belief in the moral superiority of functional objects, or perhaps more accurately those that displayed a functional aesthetic.

We do not need a chair, table or sideboard in an absolute sense, rather we use one because it fits in with a certain manner of living. In this instance, the goal of Breuer's chair was not simply to facilitate sitting, it was to allow the sitter to both sit and feel themselves to be doing so in a chair that does nothing but speak of function. As the design historian George Marcus points out, functionalism was actually as much about aesthetics and symbolism as it was concerned with the practical functioning of designed objects.[15] Thus, even in the apparently disenchanted clarity of a Bauhaus chair, we see how design is necessarily and inevitably about creating a material point, about *saying* something by making something, and that this cannot be avoided by denying the emotive qualities of what has been created. As the design theorist Richard Buchanan has observed, the designer is never just making an object or a thing, rather they are 'creating a persuasive argument that comes to life whenever a user considers or uses a product as a means to some end.'[16] In this way, Breuer's chair was an example of the provisioning of functionalism as a creed with the tools for achieving a certain sort of life as much for narrative and emotional reasons as for rational or technical ones.

The modernist employment of functionalism was as much a poetic approach to how the world should appear in the symbolizing of a new life with new values as it was a practical attempt to realize a functioning and functional utopia. In this way, function, as it is manifest in modernist design practice, is essentially a romantic idea or defining myth. Therefore, speaking very broadly, the objective of modernism in design, as exemplified by a chair such as Breuer's *B3*, was not function as the basic satisfaction of utilitarian need with regard to the individual thing, but rather this was superseded by the overarching purpose of the object. The final cause, the teleological goal of Breuer's chair, is not sitting as function but modernist design as mythology: the creation of a milieu that both looks and feels modern, or what Baudrillard describes as 'the functionalist myth', the vision of the possibility of a completely functional world.[17] This is, therefore, to suggest that the purpose of modernist design was ultimately the construction of a uniquely modern subjectivity, a way of reacting and being in the world; that ideas such as functionalism were above all facilitators in the pursuit of this end. What we may be seeing in work produced more recently, where practitioners seem to have absorbed Buchanan's message that designed goods always take a position, is not just a reaction against functionalism, as such, but the use of rhetorical methods for other ends.

In Shklovsky's sack

A piece such as *Linen Chest House* is certainly not a modernist object. It is not a functionalist piece of furniture meant to make life 'easier'. Nor is it simply a postmodern gag, a play on signifiers for the viewer to decode. In some ways the narrative allusions of the piece, its archaic materials, and the ad hoc nature of its construction, seem to be playing not to the confrontational anti-modern tendencies of postmodern design, but rather appear to be operating in multivalent ways in the manner of contemporary art. Given that for a while such work was referred to as Design Art, this might then suggest that such work can be examined and understood as a new form of art, one which operates within the field of design. However, to ask whether such material *is* art, in a categorical sense does not seem very productive. To examine where, how and why such design may be seen to borrow from the techniques of art may then be a more useful starting point.

In his 1925 essay 'Art as Technique', the Russian formalist literary critic Viktor Shklovsky argued that 'the purpose of art is to impart the sensation of things as they are perceived and not as they are known'. This emphasis on the relationship between art and perception was important to him because of his belief that the habitualization of life renders it impossible to see the world around us with any degree of clarity, as he argues that as perception becomes habitual it becomes automatic. Therefore, he suggests that we actually only apprehend objects and recognize them through their main characteristics, that we take the generalization of the thing because we have encountered it so many times. In this way, he argues, we perceive only its outline and 'we see the object as though it were enveloped in a sack'.[18] This automatization of the object takes place because it allows for the greatest economy of effort in perceiving it, yet this can mean that if things behave as we expect them to, they may not even appear present to us at all. Thus, for Shklovsky, 'Habitualization devours work, clothes, furniture, one's wife, and the fear of war'. He, therefore, concluded that art can operate to rescue the sensation of life from this oblivion; that a central function of art is 'to make one feel things, to make the stone stony'. This was then to be achieved through the technique of what he calls *ostranenie*, or estrangement, a method that was meant to revivify the sensorial experience of the world.

The act of defamiliarization was intended to increase the difficulty and length of perception in order to prolong it, to make it richer and more productive. This is a tactic that is to be discerned in the work of Droog designers in the 1990s, and arguably is a defining quality of the work of those such as Maarten Baas, Studio Job, Nacho Carbonell and the like who have followed. They make strange things that do not fit into normal schemas of furnishing and interior design, they create an oddness in the domestic that causes us to stop for a moment and take in what has been done. A key way in which this is achieved is in the production of an emotional reaction in the user or viewer that is not instrumental in its intention, or based solely upon authorial intention, but which serves primarily to lend the object presence and effect in its own right as it persists in the world. Certainly one consequence of this is that such estrangement appears to have been done for a reason, that such work is not just a response to a perceived need, but instead is a statement about the world, and any such utterance of course then implies that there is an author who is speaking, even if it is through a table or a peculiar chair.

Authors of possibility

On their website, Makkink and Bey tell the following story about their creation: 'An old and dozy, redundant linen cupboard in a dusty attic, wanted to be a sleeping cabin. Together with forgotten folded sheets, blankets and an old table it morphed into a garden canopy: a Linen Chest House'. They go on to suggest, in line with Williams's reading of such work, that 'the installation tells a modern fairy tale about daily objects that have been dismissed as meaningful objects. All parts of the final alliance have kept their former value and connotation, they still point out where they came from'. They then go on to argue that the parts, though 'written off', now that they have 'morphed into one' so 'they gain back a new kind of charm, an accumulation of implied perceptions'.[19] It is interesting to note then that they describe the piece as an 'installation', aligning what they do with artistic practice.

One thing that is striking is the fact that Makkink and Bey are claiming a certain level of authorship over the piece. Through the telling of their story so they frame for the viewer what the work means. We shall return to the content and its implications in a moment, but it is worth pausing for a moment to consider what is implied when designers act in this way in relation to what they produce. This then is part of a shift that took place in the first decade of the new millennium whereby some designers seemed keen to assert themselves as the authors of their work, beyond having manipulated the technical processes to bring it into being or simply applying an aesthetic gloss to a functional object. Pieces such as *Linen Chest House* or Reinoso's *Spaghetti Bench* (see Figure 7) seem to drip with significance and invite interpretation, and as Makkink and Bey demonstrate, the producers of such work seemed happy to comment upon the meaning of what they produced.

This mirrors a situation that arose in graphic design around a decade or so earlier. As Michael Rock observed in his 1996 essay, 'The Designer as Author', graphic design developed as a profession that was more concerned with the communication of messages rather than their origination, yet increasingly commentators in the press and academia were discussing such design in terms of what the person who had made a particular image was 'trying to say', at the same time those who had made such things often appeared desirous of being regarded as having authored what they produced. At the centre of this in graphic design, of course, was meaning. That is to say, at this time in both the academy and in wider public discourse, meaning, the semantic or semiotic content of the work, what it denoted and connoted, was a key issue. What such designers wanted credit for was the putting in, so to speak, of meaning to a message – not just its communication. As Rock notes, authorship as a word 'has a ring of importance: it connotes seductive ideas of origination and agency'.[20] Yet, paradoxically, it was the decentring of the authority of the author that gave rise to graphic designers' ability to claim such origination.

Part of the reason that the issue of how signs were to be decoded and messages inferred was so pertinent in the late 1990s was the way that so much popular postmodern theory had destabilized the idea that the author was the point of origin for meaning. In 1967, the French theorist Roland Barthes published the essay 'The Death of the Author'.[21] In it he argued that the person who created any work was not the sole source or arbiter of what it meant. At the time this was a necessary corrective to the dominant model that held that the truth behind any work could be ascertained by sufficient knowledge of the author and their intentions. It was also a recognition of a developing understanding, perhaps best exemplified by the work of Marshall McLuhan, that the medium itself served to define the message.[22]

Barthes was not arguing that the intentions of the author did not matter (the title in French is a playful twist on the famous story of *Mort d'Arthur*, but this lightness is rather lost in the English translation). Instead, he was recognizing that rather than a single unitary author being the source of all meaning there are many other agencies that must be taken into account in the way that any text (which is anything that is being 'read' and understood as meaningful) signifies. Barthes ends the essay with the famous dictum: 'the birth of the reader must be at the cost of the death of the Author.'[23] This, however, does not place sole power in the hands of the decoder as is often suggested by the wilder fringes of postmodernism (or rather more often in its poorly informed detractors). Rather it recognizes that it is in reading that signification takes place, as coherence is generated from a decoding of the palimpsest of meanings that have accreted in the thing being read.

This implied that if the author was dead (or playfully deposed, depending how you look at it), then this allowed a space where 'mere' designers could come in and stake a claim to also be the ones defining the content of what was produced. It would not be the *only* meaning, but this did not matter, plurality and decentred truth being all the rage at the time. This was in graphic design, however, a medium that has traditionally dealt with communication. How then did this become applicable to the design of furniture and domestic products?

Well, the general absorption of Barthes's message into the curricula of art and design schools through the 1980s and 1990s meant that there was a pervasive sense that not only was there no central author, but that authority itself was no longer something that could be imposed on passive subjects; that meaning was constructed by collaborative agencies, and a range of actors could and would be responsible for its constitution. That is to say, the death of the author seemed to authorize new forms of authorship. In design schools across Europe and America students working in three dimensions were becoming free for perhaps the first time to take on the role of author, since the central seat, the law of the father, had become vacated. This does not mean they could take up the reins of such central authority, they could not immediately adopt the role of the author-father who defined 'What Things Mean', but they could certainly enter the game of saying 'here, what this means is…'. This is a role that the makers of furniture and domestic products are increasingly taking on. That such designers are now often working collaboratively, sometimes in partnerships at other times as collectives, does not then defuse the authorial nature of such practice. It is not the voice of the individual that is of import here, but that those creating the work have come to feel empowered to claim their own statements and interventions.

So, in such a situation the makers of physical objects are becoming more confident in trying to communicate through what they create, through the making of everyday things that are 'about' something. However, in graphic design, such meaning is generated in a way that is analogous to that of reading. The form of what is presented is decoded to produce significance. What is being 'said' is parsed to produce a narrative sense of what something means. This will depend upon a meeting of what the producer has put in (be they one person, a partnership, a collective or a company), and what the consumer brings to the piece.

With graphics this is essentially on the level of a semantic action. It is about the interpretation of symbolic codes. With physical objects there is another dimension. We do interpret things visually and relate to meanings in terms of symbolic schemas and the play of signification, indeed this is the methodology that postmodern design worked through. Yet, arguably it is not a process of reading that is primary in understanding what a physical use object means, but the act of use itself. That is to say, we do look at the things we use and read them, to some extent, but we also experience such objects at a bodily level in their functioning. It is in this way that the performative nature of furniture and designed goods becomes particularly pertinent.

Given that we inhabit everyday life, we often do not notice the structures and protocols that pertain to it. The objects we live with in the everyday have a profound effect in structuring our sense of our selves. They effectively create the infrastructure that allows us to live, but then shapes how we might operate within it. As the political theorist Louis Althusser observes in his analysis of the action of ideological reproduction of the conditions of production, 'an ideology always exists in an apparatus, and its practice or practices. This existence is material.'[24] That is, it is through the material world that we are constituted as particular subjectivities. This is then achieved through the act of interpellation, whereby ideology functions in such a way that it recruits subjects among individuals (and as Althusser notes, it recruits them all) by the act of hailing: his famous 'Hey, you there!' cried by the police officer, where the guilty response of acknowledging the call ('they mean me!') acts to constitute the subject. Similarly, the furniture and furnishings we live with interpellate us, they act to encourage or disallow certain ways of being, specific forms of life.

Consequently, the things we live with in the everyday can be understood as performative, they do not simply express life, but change it. Here the term 'performative' is derived from the linguistic designation outlined by the philosopher of language, J. L. Austin, whereby, as was noted previously, it refers to a statement or utterance that does not simply describe the world but actually affects it; it is a speech act which performs a function, such as when a judge pronounces sentence on a convict, or a priest declares, 'I now pronounce you man and wife.'[25] As the philosopher Jacques Derrida states, a performative utterance does not refer to something that exists outside of language. Rather it transforms a situation and actually creates an effect through its operation.[26] It is a statement that does not describe but actually enacts. Judith Butler transferred this concept from the linguistic to the social realm by noting how a cultural construct such as gender does not exist as a fixed given that we adopt, but rather is a role that is continually performed and thus generated through iteration.[27] In design then, one form of performative operation is the emotive, that which actually builds or intensifies emotion, not as an expression of what the author has 'put in' to the work as such, but as a feature of what the work *does*, what it emerges as, through its operation in the world.[28]

Things created by practitioners working in three-dimensional design have what can be described as 'affordances', physical formal qualities that either facilitate or discourage certain actions, movements or postures.[29] In his analysis of the way we interact with an environment, the psychologist James Gibson observes that we never simply find meaning in any given context, nor do we fully impose it from without. Rather understanding emerges from interaction with that which we encounter. So, compellingly, all meaning is to be found 'in between' people and what they meet in the world. In this way, because they shape such artefacts designers are authors of possibility. So far then, this follows the cognitivist model propounded by Norman and others of this position. In his earlier work, Norman seemed content to ascribe such relations as essentially relying on a meeting between the reactions that are 'wired-in' to human neurological systems, and the simple matter of the designed world.[30] More recently, he has begun to temper this with a slightly more nuanced cultural understanding of how we relate to manufactured things, but the basic principle still stands.[31]

To think about the performative nature of objects is to see such relations as more ideologically determined. That is to say that by creating an object with a range of particular potentialities, and thus the disallowance of other uses and relationships, so those who make such things are defining the limits of any experience that can come from the artefact, they create the conditions in which the performative function of the object will play out. This then is not the absolute prescription of the meaning of the thing, but rather the author in such a situation is creating the nature of the circumstances in which meetings of subjects and objects can take place, it is to craft contingencies, thus to some degree directing what *can* be felt, but not determining it. How this takes place is not then in the sole control of the author, since the parameters of what is possible (or even conceived of as possible) is a political issue.

Things with agency

Given that Makkink and Bey seem to be claiming authorship of the piece, it may then seem curious that their story about it actually casts the components, the cupboard, the sheets, blankets and so on, as the acting agents. Though it may seem patently absurd to suggest that any object 'wants' to be or do anything, it may be that this object's creators in telling their fabulous tale are actually tapping into a deeper truth about the way we interact with objects. Whilst inanimate matter clearly has no will, and cannot be acting with agency in a sociological sense of exercising intentionality, it may be that we can see objects operating to express agency, in that such things can demonstrably be seen to be the conduits through which power dynamics are played out on the material level. Although we may regard the acting subject in the form of the designer-maker as being the author or source of the artefact, in actuality it will always have been created and constituted in the form that it is by a collaboration of forces acting upon each other. This is the point of Barthes's observation: there are always more agencies than one working to generate the form and meaning of a piece of work.

The historian of science, Bruno Latour, in outlining what he refers to as Actor-Network Theory (ANT) stresses the way that objects do not just act to express or convey human intention, but to the extent that they act performatively can be seen as having agency.[32] Madeleine Akrich's concept of products as having 'scripts' encoded into them, developed from ANT, then proceeds to provide a methodological tool for the study of design, as it begins to allow us to conceptualize such a relation between production and use through form.[33] This is because through its material manifestation any artefact can be said to contain a kind of metaphorical instruction manual (the script), which keys the user into how it is intended to be used. This is the palette of possibilities encoded into the piece by the designer-author. A chair, for example, has legs that maintain the seat pan at a certain height from the floor, it has a back against which the sitter can rest. Therefore, its formal script suggests this act. This methodology is useful, as design historian Kjetil Fallan observes, because the physical scripts of the object can then be related to the broader 'sociotechnical script' in which it is implicit. According to Fallan, the trope of the physical script, therefore, 'consists of those properties of the product's physical form and interface that try to tell the user about its intended use', whilst 'the socio-technical script has more to do with the transportation and transformation of a product's symbolic, emotional, social, and cultural meanings. This also is partly related to the artifact's physical, formal, aesthetic qualities, but the socio-technical script includes much more than the artifact itself'.[34] So what is here called the 'sociotechnical script' can also be understood as the wider social narrative into which the object fits, and as Fallan then concludes this is not to suggest a dichotomy between the physical script and the sociotechnical. Rather it is to observe that these elements can be understood as entangled and reciprocal. Affective experience depends upon form; form exists within the larger social narrative of which we are a part.

Just as the maker cannot ever be fully cognizant of the scripts they are coding into the piece, it should also be noted that there is no guarantee that the script will absolutely determine the role that the user adopts. People can often choose to misuse or subvert the scripts and the object may be displaced into a setting that was never envisaged for it.[35] However, the manner in which the subject relates to the object, as they 'de-script' it, in Akrich's designation, will certainly happen *in relation* to the scripts encoded by the designer and the wider social narrative in which it is situated. Material form will either facilitate or baffle particular affective encounters. If we are to regard objects as acting agents it must then be necessary to conceptualize how the scripts coded into objects, both intended and unintended, are actualized in the world.

Making sense of things

In its use of elements such as old furniture and lace, a piece such as *Linen Chest House* appears to be working with a vocabulary that is self-consciously unmodern. It is the 'old and dozy' and the 'forgotten' that come together in this installation. Similarly, Remy's *Rag Chair* from a decade before (as discussed in the previous chapter; see Figure 6) used this method. Whereas Breuer's B3 employed the most technologically advanced materials of its time to signify its modernity, so Remy's chair used rags to situate itself outside of such a flow. Rags can happen any time, old furniture and linens can be brought out from the cupboard at will. Such components thus rely less on grand rhetorical gestures, such as an appeal to representing a new way of life for all, and instead seem to emphasize contingency and the specificity of things coming together in a moment. This then is not the grand narrative of a movement, or even the lesser collective act of storytelling suggested by Williams. Instead it seems to be a more intimate action of invocation, of the offering up to each person who interacts with the work of a moment in which their emotional reaction, as a personally determined pathway, can and will emerge in relation to the artefact, the 'new kind of charm' that Makkink and Bey describe, which comes from 'an accumulation of implied perceptions.'[36] With perception of course comes emotion, but notice the way in which such a reaction depends upon implication, this is then much less precise than stimulation, and it corresponds to the idea that emotion is culturally determined rather than simply an effect of preset bodily reactions.

The idea that there are basic, recognizable emotions can be traced back to one of Charles Darwin's lesser-known works, *The Expression of Emotion in Man and Animals*, in which he argued that emotion was a universal part of human nature, a feature of our makeup that transcends culture, whereby how somebody is feeling is registered in physical changes in the body.[37] This model is based on the principle that there are a series of basic emotions: happiness, sadness, anger, fear, disgust and surprise, which can be mapped on to specific facial expressions and bodily reactions. From the 1960s experiments were conducted which seemed to support this idea, often using photographs of actors apparently demonstrating the appropriate expressions.[38] Therefore, in this model, emotion can be tested and measured by recording such physical markers.

What can be called the 'basic emotion' theory suggests that there is a bodily emotional mechanism that underpins behaviour, whereby everybody, everywhere, regardless of sex, age or personality, experiences emotion in broadly the same way. Thus, as the neuroscientist Lisa Feldman Barrett notes, this should mean that there is a specific somatic 'fingerprint' for each emotion, a collection of measurable bodily reactions that equate to these basic emotions, at the very least. Yet such a marker has proven difficult to find. That is to say, it is demonstrable that when people are feeling emotions there are physical changes, but these seem to be different for each individual, or at least appear to be culturally specific, and do not in any recognizable way correspond to classical notions of the way a particular emotion should manifest.[39] Thus, the fact that there is a physical dimension to emotion has tended to make those examining the phenomenon believe that the psychological can be read in the biological, when it seems that it is not as straightforward as this.

The embodied nature of emotion can be conceptualized through the concept of affect. This is to propose that in the first instance there is a corporeal experience of the world, a sense of sensing something, so to speak. Thus, in such a schema, affect is not emotion; it is the material from which emotion is formed. According to James Russell, affect in its most basic sense has two features: arousal and valence. Valence is a simple registration of whether the experience feels negative or positive. 'The pleasantness of the sun on your skin, the deliciousness of your favourite food, and the discomfort of a stomach ache or a pinch are all examples of affective valance.'[40] Arousal is then a registration of how calm or agitated you feel. Thus, these two spectra can be represented as axes on a circular, or 'circumplex', model that allows for the classification of affective states as negatively or positively valenced, and high or low arousal. This Russell calls 'core affect', and the implication is that it underpins our experience of emotion.[41]

When we feel something, we then need to make sense of what we are sensing, so to speak. Based on the ideas of Magda Arnold, who argued that the understanding of emotion is essentially contextual,[42] appraisal theory suggests that emotion is experienced when something changes in the environment, when the intensity of our arousal or the quality of the valence alters.[43] The idea is that we 'appraise' or judge the alteration in state and assign it a particular quality to it. Emotion is then a reaction to the modulation of affect. This is important because we are then making sense of affect. As the psychologist Richard Lazarus observes, if all emotion is based on appraisal, if emotion *is* appraisal, then this must be understood as being acknowledged and interpreted by the self in relation to the environment.[44] In this way, emotion can be understood as the registration of change; it is a quality of our movement through time and space.

One model of appraisal theory suggests that initially affective experience triggers physical responses.[45] Inside the temporal lobes of the brain is an almond-shaped structure known as the amygdala. Part of the limbic system and at the end of the hippocampus, this is the control centre for our reactions, and arguably the seat of emotional processing in the brain. Its role is to assess stimuli and dictate responses to it, to conduct appraisal, so to speak. Thus, upon registering a change in conditions, the amygdala sets off a range of physical reactions: glands are instructed to secrete, the heart rate may rise, muscles may contract, sweat can raise to the surface of the skin, as we ready to make sense of the effect that is being felt and act accordingly. Arguably what we then do is say, 'why am I feeling like this' and we then ascribe meaning, we name the emotion to allow us to comprehend how we feel. The neuroscientist Antonio Damasio therefore posits that emotion can be understood as essentially physical, in that subjective emotional experience emerges from somatic experience, yet how that will be then assimilated and made use of by the acting subject will depend upon the social context in which they are experiencing a particular encounter.[46]

To feel a pounding heart on the way to a job interview feels like nerves. A similar reaction when stood next to somebody we find attractive can mean something very different. Such mechanisms have developed to attenuate us to context, to make us hyper-evaluative. Though this may in itself be overly reductive as a model, it does seem more interesting and productive than the assertion that there are simply circuits for definable emotions that are triggered by certain conditions. Rather, particularly in relation to design, it seems useful to consider that what we call emotions are actually a register of the relationship between inside and outside, an effect of experiencing change and trying to make sense of it. Part of this process will then be the naming or labelling of emotion.

Feelings are complex. We seldom feel only one emotion in a pure form.[47] Even anger, which is surely one of the clearest and most universal of emotions, is not usually present on its own. We are mad and sad at the same time, or furious and embarrassed ('why am I acting like this?'). We usually experience a confusing mix of feelings, which we must disentangle, and make sense of. This is then to bring sensation into language, it is the naming of feeling. In this regard the cultural theorist Sara Ahmed talks about the sociality of emotion. As she notes, the everyday language of emotion is based on a presumed interiority of emotion, that there is something inside us, within the body, that constitutes 'feeling', and this is a form of belonging or possession, in that 'I have feelings and they are mine'.[48] This then is a very consumerist notion of emotion. It presupposes an individual who 'owns' their experience, a figure that is coterminous with the body. Ahmed critiques this 'psychologized' model of emotion to observe that far from being purely internal matters, emotions can be understood as 'social and cultural practices'. That is to say, yes emotions are experienced internally, but they are not simply determined by a body as unchanging physical fact. In this way, affect is not just a psychological term, it is a political category that is concerned with the human relationship between an inner and an outer world.

Affect can be understood as intensity. In recent years, authors such as the philosopher Brian Massumi and the theorist of embodiment Erin Manning have built on the work of Gilles Deleuze and Felix Guattari's conception of affect, itself derived from that of Baruch Spinoza, as something that is not contained by, or possessed of, the individual, but is instead an effect of movement, of the interplay between things as a coming into being.[49] As Massumi notes, 'intensity is the unassimilable', in that in its pure form it cannot be fitted into our schema of experience. It needs to be worked on, fed through the system, before it can become part of the landscape of our lived experience, part of our personal world in any meaningful way. In this sense, what we call emotion is the assimilation of the experience of intensity, that is to say that 'change is emergent relation, the becoming sensible in empirical conditions of mixture, of a modulation of potential.'[50] Thus, it is in change that affect becomes emotion, as we bring the sensation of altered circumstances into social meaning. It is this level of evaluation, the bringing of affect into language that we call emotion. It is the naming of the intersection of intensity and quality as an embodied subject. We bring together the strands of the feeling in the moment to weave them into the shape of happiness or sadness, fear or anger or anxiety; but these are deeply and intrinsically cultural concepts. Thus, a part of feeling will always be comprised of embodied contextual knowledge; physical being as history. As Massumi observes: 'Emotion is qualified intensity, the conventional, consensual point of insertion of intensity into semantically and semiotically formed progressions, into narrativizable action-reaction circuits, into function and meaning.' Emotions are the story we tell to make sense of feeling, they are 'intensity owned and recognized'.[51] Emotion is thus what can be assimilated of the affective, named and made meaningful in relation to our experience of the world, and what we believe we already know. This is important in design because our experience of manufactured things will always be a negotiation between the affordances of the object, and the role we encounter it in. With highly wrought things such as the pre-millennial products of Droog and the later works of those such as Makkink and Bey, the work of the pieces, so to speak, takes place within such interstices.

Thus, reactions to what was once referred to as Design Art are not easily definable because much of the work is happening is not of a semantic nature but an emotive form. Thus, such experiences are complex and hard to name, because emotions always are. Recent developments in neuroscience have shown that the idea that emotion is simply an uncomplicated physical phenomenon of the individual inherited directly from our ancestors is an absurdly reductive way of thinking about our feelings. Yet, as early as 1936, Bertolt Brecht noted, 'Emotions, instincts, drives are generally presented as being deeper, more eternal, less easily influenced by society, but this is in no way true. The emotions are neither common to all humanity, nor incapable of alteration, the instincts neither infallible or independent of reason, the drives neither uncontrollable or spontaneously engendered and so on.'[52] This then seems particularly true of our emotional reactions to design, since the use of things will always be a cultural practice. Yet in recent years this has not been the emphasis.

Rationalizing emotions

As Pieter Desmet, one of the key writers coming from the cognitivist school of emotion and usability in design, notes, for those who study such things, core affect theory, linked to the concept of emotion as based on appraisal has been very attractive because it provides a simple way to organize understanding of the affective nature of products. As he notes, the irritation felt for a malfunctioning computer, the pleasantness of a warm bath, the exhilaration of ice skating, the sadness of the memory of a broken crystal vase, all can be neatly plotted on the circumplex model.[53] Classified, codified, measured and accounted for. Thus, in attempting to render the concept of affect useful to designers, Donald Norman proposed a tripartite structure of how we relate to objects on an emotional level.[54] In doing this, he adapted a model from cognitive psychology which suggests that we experience the world at three levels of information processing: the reactive, the routine and the reflective. Thus, in this schema, the reactive accounts for simple 'programmed' responses, such as reflexes, or fight-or-flight behaviour. This is said to be biologically determined 'hard wired'. It is taken to be 'pure' affect, in that it is not emotion, as such, in that it is not elaborated or appraised, it is essentially regarded in this model as unmediated bodily reaction.[55] Routine is then taken to be just that: deeply ingrained behaviour, that which has been done many times. The reflective level is then said to be the 'highest' layer of experience, because this is understood to be where consciousness resides and cognitive skills such as planning and problem-solving take place. Norman has then mapped these strata onto a model of affective product experience. What he describes as 'visceral design' supposes that we see the world and react to it immediately and in an unmediated manner. This is then overlaid with 'behavioural' experience, which is based on expectations, and allows for an approach to design that is engaging with this level of consciousness. Finally, 'reflective design' is understood to be that which has been created to appeal to us on a fully conscious level, where apparently rich and properly human emotions are experienced that relate to higher concepts such as self-image and social status.

What this way of thinking about design and emotion does, however, is actually create a form of hierarchy of rationalism in relation to the experience of products and designed goods, in that it essentially suggests that there is the purely physical, which has no decision making in it, which is in contrast to the other end of the scale where we are really wholly conscious of our reactions and thus properly applying reason. In suggesting that everything we do is tinged with emotion,[56] Norman implies that the reality of human experience is reason, which is somehow inflected by the effect of emotion, at the same time the affective is cast as a form of nature in opposition to human consciousness.

Because there is tendency to regard affective response as somehow being reductively bodily, genetic and 'hard wired', so emotion, which is derived from affect, is often thought to be somehow 'raw' natural, and somehow animalistic, whilst consciousness is cultural, and more fully human, in that it is at the very least available to reason and rational reflection. This then falls into a dichotomizing of experience into that which is of the body, which is then contrasted to that which pertains to culture and thought. Emotion is thus cast as physical and subjective, reason as cerebral and objective. At the same time a subtle but persistent gendering is applied, as subjectivity is mapped onto the female, and masculinity is characterized as objective and reasonable. As the anthropologist Catherine Lutz observes, 'the contrast between emotion and thought goes under several other rubrics including the more academic and psychological affect and cognition, the more romantic and philosophical passion and reason, and the more prosaic feeling and thinking.'[57] In each of these constructions, the former is mapped onto that which is 'only' personally experienced (and is therefore frivolous), whilst the latter is characterized as objective and thus serious and of value. The emotional is determined as the optional supplement of the rational essential. As Lutz continues,

> One of the most pervasive cultural assumptions about the emotional is that it is antithetical to reason or rationality. Both a moral and an amorphous concept, rationality is generally used to talk about actions and ideas that are sensible, that seem sane or reasonable, and that are based on socially accepted ways of reasoning about problems. Rationality is closely related to intelligence, which in Euroamerican thought is defined as the ability to solve problems, particularly those whose assigned parameters are technical rather than social or moral.[58]

So, though it may be possible to rationalize feelings, to identify their cause and function, it is not usually the case that emotions will be seen as being part of reason. Instead, emotions are regarded as disruptive of the more serious and 'useful' rational response to the world. As Lutz concludes: 'To label someone as emotional is often to question the validity, and more, the very sense of what they are saying.'[59] As reason is understood to produce a practical vision of the world from which can come order, predictability and the optimization of possibility, so emotion is characterized as blurring any clarity in experience and thus productive of only disorder, dysfunction and chaos. The modelling of emotion as irrational then leads to its cultural designation as essentially disruptive, unproductive and feminine, whilst problem-solving is seen as rational, useful and masculine.

Yet, what we actually see in the fact that emotions exist in the interaction between the inside and the outside, the self and the world, is that emotion is a register of the nature of such relations. As the scholar of emotion Keith Oatley says: 'Emotions occur at the junctures of our inner concerns with the outer world; they are evaluations of events in terms of their importance for our concerns. This importance derives jointly from genes, individual experience, and society. The human system of emotions is the map of our values.'[60] There is a sense that emotion is a bodily experience that does not change, yet at the same time there is an inference, from commentators such as Chapman, that the shape and nature of emotion will always depend upon the individual's life experience.[61] This can be resolved by observing that emotion can be understood as changing over time, yet since it is a bringing into culture of affect, it must alter with the historical alteration of social relations. Recent discussion of emotion in design has been a project of disenchanting design, to render it less mysterious and more available to quantification. The corollary of this has been to primitivize affect, to posit it as essentially pre-rational.

Yet affect is not sealed off from reason. Affect is present within rationality. It is part of the overall experience of the world. Yet affect always overflows the rational. Intensity, and therefore affect, is always more than emotion, it always exceeds it. There is necessarily a residue of affect that cannot fit neatly into the receptacles we call emotions, yet this does not mean that affect is raw and unvarnished. It will always be determined historically. What it does suggest is that there is persistently a part of our experience that is always unnamable, unquantifiable and unavailable to reason. This does not devalue it, quite the contrary, it makes it a tremendously valuable part of experience, but one that can only be approached obliquely.

The revolution in everyday life

If there is a persistent criticism of work such as *Linen Chest House* or the other objects on display in 'Telling Tales', it is that this is the only situation in which they can exist: as exhibits in a gallery, or as memes in wider cultural circulation, that any pretence to functionality is just that, a fiction that allows a certain type of design-based art practice to exist. This then was what underpinned the discourse of Design Art, that such work only survives in its spectacular manifestation, as material with representational value. However, arguably the work really only really becomes theoretically productive when we begin to consider what it might mean for such work to take on a more everyday quality as actual use objects. One of the most interesting things about the Droog experiment in its early days was the insistence that these really were domestic things to be sold, bought and used. With limited-edition pieces such as those shown in 'Telling Tales', this proposition is diluted (for reasons that will be explored in more detail in Chapter 4), yet even their nominal designation as use objects points to the thrilling possibility that such things can take on a Shklovskian role in everyday life, whereby their strangeness and disjunctive emotional qualities can serve to extend the moment of perception, and mundane things begin to reveal their enchanted nature.

It is in the routines and rituals of the hardly noticed that much of existence is constituted. Even significant and life-changing moments take place in the landscape of the mundane, what has come to be termed 'the everyday'. The design theorist and cultural commentator Ben Highmore describes the everyday as 'the landscape closest to us, the world most immediately met' which is constituted by 'those most repeated actions, those most travelled journeys, those most inhabited spaces that make up, literally the day to day'.[62] In this way things appear to recede into the fabric of life, the space of habit, what the sociologist Pierrre Bourdieu has called 'habitus'.[63] Underlying the philosophy of modernism, there has often been an implicit suggestion that good design should do this: that it should essentially be invisible, that it should simply be expressed as 'function', as though this were to strip it of meaning.

Beneath the concept of functionalism, therefore, is the proposition that the things we use in everyday life must primarily be valued for their efficiency. That first and foremost good design should be based on clarity, effectiveness and fitness for purpose.[64] As has been noted, this is then a conceptualization of what is useful to us which has been gleefully co-opted by those who would sell us as much as they can to keep the wheels of industry turning. Yet, such an instrumental approach to the nature and value of the making of useful things disregards the opposite feature of everyday life identified by Highmore: its marvellous character. As he notes, 'To see everyday modernity as boring or relentlessly routinized is to capture only one side of its general articulation.' This would then be to miss the way in which the everyday can also be seen as strange and mysterious.[65] The everyday is both mundane and fabulous, tedious and extraordinary, and the 'everyday offers itself up as a problem, a contradiction, a paradox: both ordinary and extraordinary, self-evident and opaque, known and unknown, obvious and enigmatic';[66] this is, therefore, to identify a dialectical tension at the heart of everyday life. This is the setting in which we perforce emerge as subjectivities, as selves, and this is then the productive space in which emotive design can operate, in that it works with (and often in contradiction to) a structure of mood and reaction which we often hardly even perceive enveloping us.

As was noted in the introduction, the kind of work exemplified by Droog and shown in 'Telling Tales' can at one end of the spectrum very much be seen as spectacle. The objects are very mediagenic, and to a large degree they exist to be seen. In the 1960s, Guy Debord argued that the first stage of the financial economy coming to dominate social life was a process whereby '*being* had become *having*'. This he then contended had culminated in a 'shift from *having* to *appearing*' whereby all ownership, all use, must derive its logic and ultimate purpose from appearances.[67] He thus concludes that this had culminated in an all-encompassing spectacle, which had become 'the ruling order's non-stop discourse about itself'.[68] This discourse is, however, not only manifest on the level of visual spectacle, it is also a very material experience, and for the Situationists this represented a profoundly alienating experience. However, if Debord's conceptualization of the everyday as dominated by spectacular experience appears somewhat insubstantial, the Marxist thought upon which it is predicated was resolutely materialist in its concentration on the effects of living in a commodity culture. It is then in this register that the other end of the spectrum functions, whereby emotionally laden and content-heavy domestic design has the possibility to become part of everyday life. This then is where things become really interesting.

In Marx's terms, the things we live with can be regarded as commodities because they have both use value, what they are for in a practical sense, and exchange value, what they can be exchanged for in monetary terms.[69] In the logic of the market everything has value in relation to money, in that all things in a capitalist system can be exchanged in this way as an abstract representation of something's worth. This means that, from a Marxist perspective, there is a definite equivalence to all commodities, in that they can be exchanged for money, no matter what their putative use value.[70] For Marx, this value is then derived from the human labour exerted in the production of commodities. He suggests that because of the ultimate exchangeability of all commodities for money, the real source of their value, human labour, is obscured and cannot be seen. Therefore, value is perceived in its fantastic form as a relation between things rather than people. This is then to apprehend the world of objects as essentially alienated: as the result of forces that are not human and changeable but somehow external, natural and intrinsic to the world of things rather than human action.[71] Just as life becomes disenchanted, so the commodity becomes fetishized.

As Don Slater observes, Marx, in using the term 'fetish', draws from Ludwig Feuerbach and Emile Durkheim who discuss the way in which religion projects or externalizes human powers and social values onto an independent God or totem, thus meaning that the object world is endowed with a certain power.[72] This, therefore, not only points to the way in which a culture based in the exchange of commodities confers a certain latency to the object; it also, through the employment of a word associated with 'primitive' religion, suggests a certain mysticism is involved in the subject's relation to the things they encounter in a commodity system. In order to understand the everyday more fully, however, it is necessary to look to the way in which this effect was conceptualized in the wake of the upheaval of the Russian Revolution for, as Roberts observes, the detailed theoretical elaboration this category underwent at this time 'largely shapes the content of the concept through the twentieth century, pulling other uses of the "everyday" towards it'.[73]

The Hungarian philosopher Georg Lukács, for example, argued that the commodity structure that Marx interrogated in such detail in the first chapter of *Capital, Vol 1* wholly permeates society, not just in terms of economics but in the very fabric of everyday action and thought. The commodity, he argued, is the 'central structural problem of capitalist society in all its aspects' being the 'model of all objective forms of bourgeois society, together with all the subjective forms corresponding to them'.[74] Therefore, from this perspective, in the same way that commodities in the arena of production took on an essentially alienated form and became fetishes that then appeared to be separate from the social processes of their creation, so any reified conception of the object as an unchanging given can be said to obscure the sociohistorical processes which had allowed it to come into being.[75]

To counter the ruthless quantification of life through the action the commodity form, Lukács argues that it is necessary to understand how we relate to quality, as he suggests that 'all the subjective and objective phenomena in the societies concerned are objectified in qualitatively different ways'.[76] This must then be resolved through an understanding of how both the object and the subject are constituted in a culture where the commodity is the universal structuring principle. As Stuart Sim notes, Lukács believed that art as an autonomous category, located between the individual experience (the here-and-now) and the universal (the essential) could act to reveal the structural workings of a culture. Not simply through an understanding of the intentions of the artist, but through the subtexts that cannot help but be coded into the work in its creation.[77] Given that art, in its institutionalized form, has now largely given up this role, it may be that design is moving into the position vacated.

Novi Byt

It is very difficult to escape the way that the commodity form shapes the nature of our society and the material experience of the everyday. For the Russian Constructivist thinker, Boris Arvatov, the phenomenon of the everyday arose as a result of the development of capitalist modes of production and the concomitant tendency for individuals to consume things that are primarily characterized as commodities. For him, writing in the early twentieth century, this shift from an economy whereby production was centred upon the home to a culture which depended upon the products of industrial production was crucial, because in such a situation the consumer no longer has 'direct physical contact with the production of material values' which means that subjects tend to have contact only with the forms that things take in the sphere of consumption.

For the Constructivists, their revolution was to be made manifest through what was termed *novi byt* – the new everyday life. In his 1925 essay, 'Everyday Life and the Culture of the Thing', Arvatov argues that material forms of culture represent an essentially conservative force known as the everyday (*byt*). Thus, understanding the tendencies of material *byt* meant being able to intervene in them to effect change. It was, therefore, a study of things and their operative capacities that was to be at the root of any revolution in everyday life. This was because:

> The commodity nature of bourgeois material byt constitutes the fundamental basis for its relation to the thing. The thing as an a-material category, as a category, as pure consumption, the thing outside its creative genesis, outside its material dynamics, outside its social processes of production, the thing as something completed, fixed, static and, consequently, dead – this is what characterises bourgeois material culture.[78]

Therefore, Arvatov was proposing that the social and cultural narratives of consumer-capitalist *byt* serve to shape the physical form of the things with which we live. The products of consumer capitalism, which have come to dominate our lives ever more since Arvatov undertook his analysis, tend to come to us as apparently completed and fixed in their function. This is, therefore, a political economy of design whereby the user is conceptualized as a perfect consumer of the completed product. This was a theme picked up by Theodore Adorno and Max Horkheimer in their analysis of mass-culture and the effects of mass production. However, in their hands the consumer is rather reduced to a dupe of the system, passively taking in the culture manufactured for them.[79] For Arvatov, this analysis of material culture was intended to be a more practical intervention, which would actually begin to equip subjects with a way to resist the deleterious effects of bourgeois *byt*.

Given that the structure of commodity exchange can be demonstrated to be a fundamental ordering principle of consumer culture, how is the relationship between the subject and the object constituted in this process? In Cartesian terms, the world can be divided into subjects, which are regarded as pure reason or consciousness, and objects, which are defined as external to the subject and constituted as matter, which is devoid of reason or mind. In this way, the material world is declared to be a mechanism separate from Descartes's Cogito, mind or self; it is disenchanted and deemed to be a field of knowledge that can be mastered by human reason in the form of science; understanding of the material therefore becomes a question of epistemology. However, as Slater notes, such a vision of the world is profoundly alienating because 'If the world has become pure object to human subjects, how can they ever be at home in it?' Slater's response it to observe, drawing from Hegel, that 'the relation between subject and object is in reality dialectical and interrelated, not external and mechanical. It is a relationship of mutual constitution of subject by object and object by subject'.[80] This was at the basis of Arvatov's analysis and it suggests a way in which our relationship to objects can be reconceptualized. Not as the fixed relation between a discoverable authentic self and an external world of objects, but as a dynamic relationship whereby subjects and objects generate each other in their reciprocal action.

Living in a world that appears complete, where all we are asked to do is be consumers, seems to limit the possibilities of action to almost nil. Arvatov argued that the realization that the very materiality of life, *byt*, is acting upon us opens up this space as one of radical action, in that changing the everyday is to alter subjectivity. Examining the extent to which emotive furniture and domestic products develop the possibilities of incompleteness, of authored possibility and emergent affect, then gives us a way of understanding how such an approach to design may be fruitful, beyond simply creating baubles for the rich, in that it can render visible the subject–object dialectic that can be said to underlie our relationship to all material things in a commodity culture.

Moving objects

To understand that furniture (or any other category of thing) is in motion, in both time and space, is to recognize its volatility and the broader nature of change. This is to understand history not simply as the recounting of what has happened, but as an attempt to recover existence as sensate experience, affect, which takes place in time and space. With an object such as Makkink and Bey's *Linen Chest House*, there is a tendency to say, 'Yes, but what is it? What is it for? What does it do?' The answer to these questions is of course that it is a Linen Chest House: a useful thing with emotive qualities. As well as allowing its user to achieve something, it also provides the possibility of the emergence of a certain kind of emotional experience, not to make something work better, or to improve it as a product, but for its own sake, because feeling is valuable in itself.

Works of design such as Studio Makkink & Bey's *Linen Chest House* are certainly meaningful things, but it would be a mistake to assume that they are mere vehicles for an agenda determined by those who have authored them. Since designed objects are performative, in that they do not just reflect or represent the world but are functional parts of it, they have an ideological function, in that they cannot help but operate within the political structure in which they have been created, and in the normal operation of things designed goods serve to facilitate the perpetuation of the status quo. In present circumstances it should then be remembered that such normality is the rapacious consumption of commodities, which appear complete, finished, whose only role is now to be consumed.

With the development of design as authorial practice, designers have been using the emotive qualities of objects to explore the range of what useful things can do. In the past, the tendency has been to see the emotional in design as an instrumental category, something that can be manipulated to help serve what is perceived as the primary purpose of things. In the discourse of modernism in design, the guiding principle was one of functionalism, that things should be first and foremost efficient. This approach was then co-opted by consumer capitalism in the pursuit of the production of the ultimate efficient object: the docile yet constantly craving consumer. Though the emotive objects discussed here are currently generally only available to the rich, their radical unfinishedness and ultimate incompleteness thus offers the possibility of another approach. If such a perspective can come to infect the everyday then there is the real possibility that a space will open up for the creation of a new everyday life, Arvatov's *Novi Byt*, whereby the things with which we interact can become something more than the sterile pseudo-characters of consumerism's dream time. Now that designers are embracing the mediascape, so another dimension is added to their practice. Designs can move through the channels of culture more accessibly than ever before, and so the nature of use and ownership will come to be bent into a new shape. Whether this is then productive, or simply represents another turn of the spectacular kaleidoscope of consumer culture remains to be seen. One thing is certain, however, even as we move into a digital culture, so we will remain embodied creatures (even as what this means changes), and this will serve to determine how we can and do relate to the things we create.

3

Viscerealities

Furniture is necessarily resonant of the bodies it is made to serve. A chair will echo the human frame it was meant for. Tables are the height they are because people sit at them. A bed, through its affordances of size and shape and horizontality, speaks of the recumbent human form. Yet this is not just a material congruence. The relationship between bodies and design that resides in the domestic interior is also highly charged in terms of the level of transference and interplay that can and does take place between bodies and matter. It is comforting to be with your own things, to be at home and surrounded by that which has been marked by a shared history. Yet, when confronted by the residue of others' lives such evidence of life can be unsettling, greasily uncanny.

When a chair becomes old and soiled by having been used for many years, for example, if they are not our own marks, the stains and smears of life can be troubling in a way that affects us more than can be accounted for by a simple dislike of dirt. Unless there were very compelling reasons, few of us would get into a bed that had been used by some unknown other. This is not only because of worries about 'catching something', but because the intimacy of the thing exceeds its uncomplicated material presence, because it would not be possible to be comfortable in such a situation. We are often less troubled by our own filth or perhaps that of a loved one, but it can only take a slight shift of perception for such personal traces to become unsettling. In recent years, then, it seems that those who make such things have started to become interested in the way that furniture can move us in this way.

Consequently, this chapter begins by showing how emotive design has drawn from a particular form of artistic practice that developed in the 1990s, a time when the body as a site of experience was a particular concern to creative practitioners. Through an examination of how such work operates on the symbolic level, here explored through the powerful driver of disgust, the intention is to show how objects are implicit in the negotiation of the boundaries of who we are.

The suggestion then is that in an age where we are encouraged to see objects as powerful, as the index and focus of our desires, at just the same time that our own bodies are presented back to us as matter to be maintained, mastered and perfected, so the reciprocities and feedback loops set up by such congruencies come to define our sense of agency. Thus, by considering how a concept such as comfort is much less a quality of things than something that exists in encounters between people and the designed goods they use to live, the intention is to show how furniture exists at this boundary. Through a complication of the nature of the framing of such practice, the discussion then moves on to what the consequences may be when the questioning and exploratory nature of such techniques are transplanted from the gallery and comes to be more immediately implicated in the material actualities of everyday life.

Embodiments

The art of the latter part of the twentieth century often presented everyday objects *as* bodies. In 1998, the artist Tracey Emin exhibited a bed that she had spent several days inhabiting, smoking, drinking and suffering a broken heart. Around the bed were cigarette butts and bottles, a pair of old slippers, soiled knickers and condoms. *My Bed* was criticized because it was just this, a bed, spread around with the abject material detritus of an unhappy phase of one person's life. Though the body of the person is present in its absence, all we are left with is the object, a mute thing, a part of the everyday that has become animated. In Sarah Lucas's 1999 piece, *Cigarette Tits (The Idealized Smoker I)*, the wood and metal stacking chair, by the simple addition of a bra (which holds orbs sculpted from cigarettes), becomes a woman's body (Figure 16). This is an effect that Lucas makes full use of in her art: the thing becomes the human form and in this way the transference that is apparent in our fetishization of both bodies and consumer goods is made visible. Chairs, tables, an old mattress, through the simple manipulation of such forms with the addition of bits of food and scraps of clothing the schematic nature of how we think of bodies, particularly female ones, is represented.

Of course, in part, this tactic sprang from the availability of materials. Just as with young designers, skips are good places for poor artists to find what they need to express themselves. This was then because of material abundance, the simple availability of things. This created a palette that allowed for the reflection of, and reflection upon, such a cornucopian availability of manufactured goods. Yet, this

Figure 16 Sarah Lucas, *Cigarette Tits (Idealized Smokers Chest I)*, 1999, bra, footballs, cigarettes, chair, 78.5 × 50 × 54 cm. © Sarah Lucas. Courtesy of Sadie Coles HQ, London

was not the only reason that such artists used furniture to examine how society represents women's bodies. That this should take the form of a meditation on the processes of objectification and commodification was fitting given the extent to which such effects were becoming apparent in consumer culture. At just the point in history that we were being incited to think of ourselves through things, so just this form of consumption, and the mass disposability it necessitates, created the possibility of an art that replaced the body with collaged detritus. Just as we are encouraged to see ourselves, and each other, in things, as things, so such montage takes this on as subject matter.

Taught in the same schools as artists and exposed through popular culture to the heavily mediatized art of the time, designers began taking on the techniques of art, at the same time as they investigated similar themes and problems. However, if the body is a theme in art, in the design and making of furniture and domestic objects, it is a central concern. When acting within the discourse of art interventions that dealt with issues of embodiment could be semi-distanced comments on this situation because of the autonomy that modern art established for itself over the previous hundred years. As Theodore Adorno notes, throughout the twentieth century, fine art carved out a paradoxical position whereby on the one hand it could seek to be autonomous, separate from society, kept apart in white cubes, on plinths, behind ropes.[1] Yet, this was done, in Adorno's model, to allow art to comment upon and relate to the knotty problems of the politics of everyday life. Thus, in its autonomy, it could engage in politics. However, to actually make something to be used by people in the passage of everyday life, which is essentially not autonomous, not distanced, and thus inextricably part of everyday life, suggests a more complex relation between form and content.

In the 1990s, the developed West entered a new phase of plenty, whereby manufactured goods were so abundant and so available to common people that the lifestyle that any individual yearned for could be sculpted, at least in facsimile, from the elements made available at the likes of IKEA, Target and DFS. Material prosperity allowed by the engineered economic bubble of the 1990s and early 2000s meant that people in developed countries could express themselves through things as never before. By shopping we could buy furnishings that reflected who we saw ourselves to be, whilst whole industries of advertising and marketing flourished as we were persuaded of the rightness and importance of doing so. In this way, consumer goods, which had long been fetishized, began to be incorporated into the self more fully than ever before, to the point where we began to almost merge with the things we own.

With technological development not only have we been able to consume more material things, what we live with has become more complex, and the boundary between us and what we use has become less defined. From pacemakers and cochlear implants to digital assistants and online avatars, where the apparatus ends and we begin is less and less apparent and easy to read. Discoveries in the field of genetics have rendered the building blocks of life seemingly more transparent, making existence apparently less mysterious and more scientifically legible. Developments in neuroscience have quite radically opened up the mind to observation and exploration that would have amazed the psychological theorists of the early twentieth century. Many people now carry with them devices that record their levels of activity and vital signs, to make the body a quantifiable entity. Such revelations would then appear to be the triumph of reason, a definitive validation of the calculative mindset.

Yet it does not feel like this. If anything, the stable categories we have depended upon seem to be coming unstuck. As the literary theorist Sianne Ngai notes, in the stage of capitalism that can be said to define our 'contemporary moment', the emotions we feel 'no longer link up as securely as they once did with the models of social action and transformation theorized by Aristotle, Thomas Hobbes and others under the signs of relatively unambiguous emotions like anger of fear'. That is to say 'the nature of the sociopolitical itself has changed in a manner that both calls for and calls upon a new set of feelings, ones less powerful than the classical political passions, though perhaps more suited in their ambience'.[2] Thus, to such ends, she suggests that emotional states such as anxiety or irritation are the dominant feelings of our time, and there should be a vocabulary of social emotion that suits this. Given the bodily nature of emotional experience, or perhaps that should be the emotional nature of bodily experience, the way in which our bodies are changing must be giving rise to new nexus of feeling: new emotional conditions.

A hundred years ago, to get on a jet liner and cross the oceans would have been beyond the wildest dreams of most, yet now we haul our hunter-gatherer bodies off the transatlantic plane and complain of a sense of dislocation and depletion. We sit for hours and hours in front of screens, and then say we feel alienated. Perhaps we need new vocabularies for these things. Indeed, as we exist in unprecedented circumstances and are required to adopt novel attitudes, so we need fresh ways of understanding our emotional states.

The intensification of the importance of physical objects, their sheer presence as signifiers of personal worth and meaning through the action of consumer culture, also means that there is an increasing transference happening in relation to bodies and things, which is a theme that furniture is supremely suited to address. The absorption of this preoccupation into the practice of design is then clearly apparent in some of the work produced in the first couple of decades of the twenty-first century. The following discussion consequently examines how contemporary furniture designers are working with issues centred upon embodied experience, emotions such as disgust or feelings such as comfort, to trace the way in which these concerns are being handled and employed, to see how and why such work can deal with what it means to be a person in the world.

You/me/it

The functional things we use are to some degree prosthetics: they allow us to extend ourselves into the world. As the design historian and theorist Judy Attfield notes, 'design, whether tools, clothes, houses, cars, toothbrushes or gadgets' can be understood as 'supplementing the body and co-extensive to it'.[3]

A chair allows us to sit in a certain manner. A lamp makes it possible to read as the daylight fails. The table keeps the coffee cup to hand. However, with useful things, because we are often so intimate with them, this is not a one-way process. As we push outwards, so the world exerts a pressure as it yields. We feel the things we use. The proximity of furniture and the way such possessions are constantly returned to mean they are implicated in our sense of selfhood. As we extend out into the world, so what we encounter comes to be folded into who we are. For the sociologist Maurice Merleau-Ponty, writing from a phenomenological perspective, this then represents a form reciprocity, whereby body and world bend towards each other, and the body is itself both an object and a lived subject.[4]

This dichotomous yet reciprocal state is essential to our sense of ourselves as embodied creatures. We understand ourselves to be both self and object at once. Yet, this sets up a fraught boundary. In psychoanalytic theories of selfhood, the process of 'introjection' refers to the way in which we include other subjects in our sense of who we are.[5] When trying to define ourselves, we often think of our relationship to family and friends, workmates and even enemies. When we form attachments to other people exchanges take place in our behavior, we bend a little to them, we take on their traits, they take on ours. The relationship is forged in give and take. In a world where material things appear to possess the qualities of subjects, so perhaps the term 'material introjection' could be said to name the mechanism whereby the objects we use become part of our sense of identity.

In the age of internet mobility and the apotheosis of consumer culture, the process whereby we negotiate the boundary of the self has come to be extended beyond base emotional security, as the physical and psychological relationship between people and the designed objects they use becomes more complex, reciprocal and highly wrought. In this way, the prosthetic qualities of objects, their power to extend us into the world, is balanced by their tendency to become included in our sense of who we are, what we believe matters and how we behave. As the sociologist Tim Dant says, 'Material objects act as a conduit that extends the agency of the body and the person into the world while also providing a channel from the world back into the person'.[6] This means that what functional material objects achieve for individual subjects, what things do for people, cannot be uncomplicatedly practical or nakedly functional; nor can they be simplistically symbolic, straightforwardly communicating particular meanings. Rather such practical and social functions are necessarily tangled up with the physical and emotional configurations that we live out in the process of being an embodied self.

To live in a body can be a disgusting experience. For all the glory of the body, the pleasures it can provide and the marvels of its operation, there is a side to being an embodied creature that can be downright horrid. Blood, mucus, feaces, that which should be inside coming out; bits stopping working, parts growing, sagging or falling off, all can serve to remind us of the monstrous qualities of being a physical entity. As the historian Tiffany Watt Smith notes, if there is a candidate for an emotion that seems to support the possibility of there being universal basic reactions underpinning our affective relationship to the world, then this must be disgust. The very bodily reaction of disgust seems to verify its essential nature. As Watt Smith observes, 'everyone seems to make retching noises and sticks out their tongues when they are disgusted; everyone wrinkles their noses.' This then seems to map into a functional model of emotion: this reaction operates to protect us from that which would corrupt the body. Yet, as Watt Smith explains, there are actually different kinds of revulsion. Our main experiences of disgust are based on reactions to food, body products and sex. Core disgust is our reaction to that which might poison us. Contamination disgust is the name for the feeling experienced when we fear being infected.[7]

In an age that seems to be increasingly antiseptic, the sense that something from the outside can contaminate is very strong. This is the feeling that the Indonesian product designer Denny Priyatna is working with in his chair titled *the appalstered 1: disease*, of 2017 (Figure 17). Though safe to sit on, and soft and comfortable, these pieces are revolting in a very visceral way, that is to say they

Figure 17 Denny Priyatna, *the appalstered 1: disease*, 2017. Courtesy of the designer

are disgusting. Yet, this is not to invoke some inevitable bodily reaction. Though, as shall be discussed, disgust is a universal human sensation that is indeed embodied, how this comes to be registered, to be recognized and assimilated, is a process of acculturation that speaks of the political nature of object–subject relations.

In Priyatna's pieces the actual furniture forms are archetypal, but the manner by which infected skin is invoked is powerfully affecting. Priyatna suggests that the intention was to critique the culture of bodily perfection.[8] What these certainly do is disrupt the simple fetishized desire we have for furniture. Here the smooth skin of the commodified device has become malignant, it is the rupture of the unsullied surface of a commodity for sale. To find this in a standard furniture shop would be unthinkable, because there everything must present as unsullied by life, virgin and without infection. This is not least because what we seek reflected in our furnishings (at least when we buy them) is an idealized self.

For the psychoanalyst Donald Winnicott, the transitional object is a feature of child development, whereby the inanimate thing becomes a way for the child to negotiate the letting go of the mother and the establishment of an independent selfhood.[9] In this way, the blanket (or other such object that a child carries around for security) becomes what Winnicott calls the 'not-me', the 'other', which serves to help establish the boundaries of the self.[10] For the psychological theorist Julia Kristeva, this boundary is then policed using the concept of the 'abject' – whereby that which transgresses, infects or corrupts, reminds us of the object nature of the body, which then speaks of the fact of its meat and the inevitability of death. For her then, this sets up a complex relationship whereby we establish this 'not-me' in objects that surround us through the processes of disgust.[11] Yet this is not a neutral, natural process. Rather it is revealed as deeply political. As Sara Ahmed notes, what she describes as 'disgust relations', the where, when and how of what we are disgusted by, are established by what is seen to be culturally acceptable and desirable. Arguably, then, such relations are formed through the way that these conditions are articulated, what Ahmed refers to as 'the figurability of disgust', which is determined by the way such emotions are represented and culturally worked through.[12] In applying prosthesis, in using things to extend our reach, we do not then simply act upon neutral matter to achieve our ends. The things we use become part of who we are. They infect us with the world views worked into them; they affect us and alter how we can and do act.

Familiar fetishes

In the early twentieth century, Lukács examined the relationship between people and the things they use in consumer culture. Where Marx had talked of how commodities came to be fetishized, seen as powerful and acting agents, so Lukács argued that at the same time people came to see themselves as objects. On the level of production, work was becoming more mechanized. With the introduction of the moving assembly line in 1913, Henry Ford had helped to usher in a new age whereby workers were increasingly beholden to the machine. Combined with the effect of time and motion studies introduced by Taylorism, which broke tasks down in to ever smaller steps, so those making the things for sale were invested less and less in what they produced. In terms of consumption, workers were now increasingly able to buy and use goods that seemed to arrive in their lives fully formed, complete, the origins of which they knew little. From the 1920s onwards, as industrial capacity increased, so people welcomed more consumer goods into their lives. These washing machines and fridges, carpets and vacuum cleaners, chairs and tables appeared to make life if not always better, then certainly fuller and more efficient. In such a situation, these objects started to look very powerful, to have agency. At the same time, people were required to increasingly fit in with the demands of things. As Stuart Jeffries notes, 'Fordism's new industrial revolution changed production, consumption, culture and thereby what it was to be human.'[13] Things started to look a lot like people, just as people were starting to look a lot like things. This process is called 'reification'.[14]

Reification is apparent in our relationship to the things we use, not least in furniture and domestic products because of their closeness. A fundamental principle of consumer capitalism is the idea that it is through the consumption of commodities that we act and become. If you want to be beautiful, buy Givenchy. If you want to be sophisticated, buy an Eames chair. We treat the things we use as though they contain the human qualities of subjects, and in this way, they are animated in relation to us as consumers. This perceived relationship is then played out in the home. In the latter part of the nineteenth century, the heavy and physically dense furniture that began to crowd Victorian parlours was not just made up of devices that would allow their owners to sit, eat and interact. They were also avatars, parts of the self-externalized, that not only proved their keeper's taste but also mitigated for a certain form of life on a practical level, and in this way, they were materially and ideologically performative. As philosophers of the Frankfurt School noted in the 1930s, the development of mass production was only possible because it also produced the masses, people with a subjectivity, an internal cosmology of affect and mental processing, that suited the things being made.[15] Curiously, what then helped produce these subjectivities was people's very proximity to consumer goods.

In that design presumes a user, so to some degree it generates this figure through design. To sit in Breuer's *B3*, as discussed in the previous chapter, is to get a strong sense of becoming the 'modern' person imagined by its maker. As you lower yourself into it, the piece reveals itself to be remarkably comfortable. The seat is well angled, and the tensioned material gives in a satisfying manner. Yet the chrome gleams. Where you touch the metal with your skin, the feeling is of bicycles, or an operating theatre, not the comfort of the consumer's living room. In this way, it is not an easy chair. If you are hoping for the coziness of the parlour, you will be disappointed. To this end, it is an uneasy chair. It is the throne of the modernist, where even sitting is to be doing: being modern.

Similarly, to lie on Le Corbusier's and Charlotte Perriand's 1928 chaise (Figure 18) is not a comfortable experience for bodies more schooled to the slouch of contemporary furniture. To use it you must recline in a fairly fixed position, more on Freud's couch than the sofa. The body lies like a precision tool at rest, a device on its stand. According to Le Corbusier, it is 'the true machine for resting', built, he tells us, from 'bicycle tubes'. Though he suggests that the inspiration was 'the western cowboy smoking his pipe, his feet up above his head, leaning against a fireplace: complete restfulness', it is the efficiency of its operation that is emphasized in its form.[16] Such a piece is meant to be symbolic, communicative, there is a material rhetoric here, but this extends beyond the visual into the experiential, in that through the making of such pieces a

Figure 18 Le Corbusier and Charlotte Perriand, *Chaise Longue*, 1928. The Museum of Modern Art, New York. © Photo SCALA, Florence

particular self was being imagined into being, not just symbolically conceived, but also made at the level of actual affordances and embodiment through use. For the modernists a brave new world was being created, and new people would live in it. These would then not only be serviced by such design, but created by it.

Modernism, therefore, masked its own content with the claim to have none, to be concerned only with function. Throughout the twentieth century, mass production meant that, in the developed West, people had more things than ever before. As conditions changed so what had previously appeared as a capacity proper to people, that is the ability to act and change the world, came ever more to seem to reside in things. Thus, objects came to appear more powerful, to have agency, as they took on the qualities of acting subjects in our lives. Yet the rhetoric of modernism was that it had created a universal language, one way of making things, one way of being. This paved the way for a mechanized and standardized mode of emotion, one produced in a very definite manner, through a mechanization of affect.

Certainly, modernism has gone through modification and reappraisal since its inception in the interwar period. Yet, what is notable is the way that its fetishization of mass production and functional efficiency has been taken up in mainstream modernity. This is now how our environment is manufactured, and so, ultimately and intimately, it is how we are engineered. Work such as Priyatna's applies to furniture a methodology more derived from art than functional modernism or its legacy. In this what might be expected to be a universal emotional reaction, that of disgust and revulsion, rather than producing a standardized affective response, can instead be seen to represent a figuration of this emotion that opens up a space of play in which multiple reactions, and therefore various possibilities of self, are set in motion. This baffling of the natural order of mass-produced embodiment, of the standardization of self through consumption is then a feature of work that exhibits the emotive tendency, which works with emotional reaction for its own ends.

The uncanny valley

In Studio 9191's *Skin Chair* of 2014, the designer maker Gigi Barker has created a piece of furniture that looks and feels like skin (Figure 19). The silicone from which the surface is formed is skin toned and mottled-like flesh, and the piece has been made in such a way that the give of the cushioning yields to just the right degree to read as though it were fashioned from fat. Here we have a male

Figure 19 Studio 9191, *Skin Chair*, 2014. Courtesy of the designer

body reflected upon by a female practitioner. Barker spent time with the model, drawing, taking photographs, getting to know his embodied self. What has resulted is a belly to be sat on. It is in some ways a jolly body part, lolling on its own. Yet, the impression is of something that has grown. This is both endearing and horrifying at the same time.

Barker's chair is a bit too lifelike to be comfortable. This is particularly the case because of its smell, the most evocative of all the senses. The piece has been rubbed with the aftershave that the model wore.[17] This takes it from being the body-styled chair into a more liminal zone. The narrative content of the piece is that of a chair inspired by the body; we can discuss the inspiration and talk about the model, the sketching process and the manufacturing. However, to actually encounter such a piece is not to only intellectualize it; it is to *feel* it. In such emotional experience, there will then be narrativized meaning, but there will also be a residue of physical sensation, qualities of the unnamable that shows the deeper dimensions of the world we inhabit. In an art work this would be disturbing, but the distancing effect of the gallery or art world frame would render it comprehensible, controlled enough to be dealt with. With furniture, however, the nature of such bodily figuration is different.

Throughout the twentieth century, it was not just at the level of production that people were becoming alienated. As has been noted, mass production depends upon mass consumption, and the goods and services that people had to buy into were coming to be increasingly moulded by consumerist desire. If

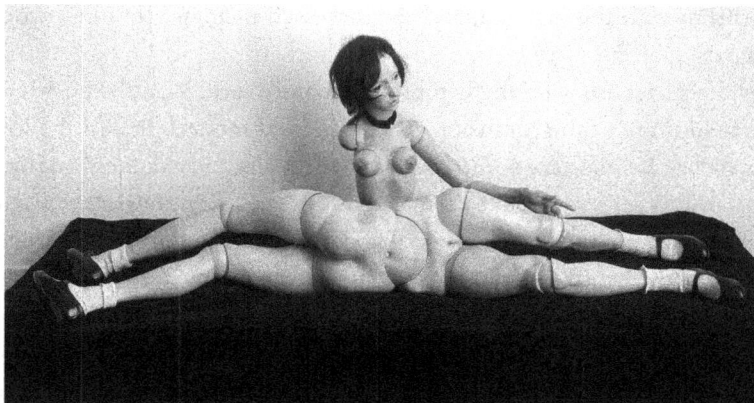

Figure 20 Hans Bellmer, *La Poupee*, 1934. Private collection. Sculpture © 2019. Photo Josse/Scala, Florence. © Photo SCALA, Florence

the modernists were experimenting with creating ideal forms of the body, then commercial design was catering for the one already there. Similarly, in a world of rampant consumerist desire, artists could not help but react to and interpret this new landscape of bodily relations.

When the surrealist Hans Bellmer made his dolls in the 1930s, he was clearly creating objects of erotic exploration in a form that made sense then (see Figure 20). From the perspective of the twenty-first century, they appear horrifying. Strange paedophillic devices that betray a male desire that dehumanizes and sexualizes the female body, simply reducing it to a doll, at the same time that real fear is present. Though Bellmer's particular obsessions are clear in the work, it would be a mistake to overly personalize the effect, to reduce it to one man's perversion. For what is visible in Bellmer's dolls is the logical extension of an effect whereby women's bodies were perpetually presented to men as objects for their satisfaction, and women were encouraged to perceive themselves in this process. This is the body as thing to be consumed, but as we have seen, the thing is always a little stranger than it appears on the surface. What Bellmer does, of course, is present us with this. Not as direct critique, but as an effect, in which we somehow become complicit through looking.

In robotics and human simulation, the uncanny valley is the point at which artificial humans start to appear disturbing. Apparently, we can stand things that look like caricatures or dolls, but once they start to look too human we find it disconcerting, causing feelings of eeriness and revulsion.[18] This is true of Bellmer's strange sexualized creatures, of course, but into the twenty-first century the sense of uncanny humanity is changing because of our intensified relationship with the material, and the increased incidence of our encounters with quasi-subjects.

For the surrealists working before the Second World War, the body was the ultimate location of the confusion and paradox of modern life. In the work of artists such as Bellmer, the body is both a site of desire and a point of mystery and horror. In this sense, the naked female body at the beginning of the twentieth century represented sexual desire; sexual desire spoke to the men making most of the art of the irrationality of life, how we are driven by needs and forces that are beyond our control and, indeed, hardly known to us. This was then an appeal to the fallacy discussed in Chapter 2, whereby it is posited that there is a visceral rawness to feelings that can be contrasted to the rationality of the mind. Emotion often feels like this – that a force is acting upon us, that we have no choice but to react as we do. However, though we may not perceive it, there is of course a great deal of cognition in affect, in the structuring of what is even noticed, just as there is the effect of the affective, of the unnamable in experience, in conscious life.[19]

What we perceive is not the force of affect, but its translation into the social, where experience becomes emotion. This is the territory that emotive design such as that of Barker inhabits; it is not pure affect, it is feelings owned, translated, made tangible, whilst also retaining the shadow of that part of affect that cannot be assimilated. What design that plays upon emotion does is very visibly manifest forms of affective relationality. It works with the uncanny and evokes the unnamable. This does not allow us to 'understand' such emotion better, but it begins to obliquely bring it into play through a tangible language or material figuration that can be shared in its physicality, which does not reduce emotion to words, but which can retain the multivalence of experience present in sensate, embodied existence.

The emotive nature of design operates as a dialectics of emotion. In such work, both fear and desire are operative. For the surrealists this was always true, and this is perhaps one of the most important features of the more interesting examples of such design work, that the very ambiguity of life can be rendered available to consciousness, rather than being tidied up so that prevailing models and linguistic structures neatly apply. In art, there is a whole canon of theory and a material apparatus that facilitates (and to some degree neuters) this effect. In design, in the practice of making useful things, this has still to be established. There is a tendency to assume that the uncanny valley in human simulation will be overcome by the improvement of technology. What seems more likely is that we will begin to develop the emotional vocabulary to allow us to deal with quasi-humans. As we change, so the actual emotions we experience alter. To feel an emotion is to know complexity. This is not least because we experience something that is, in part at least, always unknowable, and certainly unquantifiable.

Feeling feelings

As was noted in Chapter 2, throughout the latter part of the twentieth century, there was an effort in the field of psychology to cast emotions as universal and identical across cultures. This was achieved through an attempt to demonstrate how emotions are bodily; that reactions such as facial expression can be shown to be the index of particular ahistorical emotional states. This is an example of biological determinism that seeks to establish the independence of the entity that is the body, a scientific identifiable and quantifiable fact, an object that exists in opposition to the vagaries of culture and social change. In more recent times, the development of cultural neuroscience has challenged such a position by suggesting that emotion can be better understood as the social dimension of physical experience.[20]

How the embodied nature of emotions is conceived of and spoken about has changed radically over the ages. Famously the seventeenth-century philosopher Descartes divided the self into mind and body. Following this, Thomas Hobbes suggested that to experience a sensation, that is to say notice a change in temperature or to see a colour, is not so much to gain knowledge, but to be affected by alterations in matter. In this way, our contacts with the outside world are simply affirmations that the body itself is a material thing, a physical entity. Thus, for men of science such as Hobbes, such phenomena could be studied as physical effects, as laws of science, but crucially only if the emphasis was on empirical observation from the outside, through the application of intellectual reasoning. It ignored empirical observation from the inside, and in this way reason came to push feeling to the margins.[21]

Until the early nineteenth century nobody really had emotions. Of course they felt things, they experienced the world and were subject to affect, but people did not call them emotions before about 1830.[22] Yes, people felt up or down, angry or reticent, but they were not characterized as 'emotions' as such. How we speak about what we feel matters, as it helps to serve to outline their form. How things are 'figured' in Ahmed's terms, how they are defined, referred to, named and shaped serves to delineate what we think things are and what they can do.

The characterization of emotions as something within us, possessed by the individual experiencing them, is the product of a certain historically specific worldview. Before the coming of the Victorian age, people spoke of 'passions' or 'sensibilities'. The rise of the concept of emotion is thus congruent with the developing importance of the individual throughout the nineteenth and into the twentieth century. This naming, the giving of conceptual form, is important, because it starts to show how it is not simply the nature of different feelings and ways of reacting that change, but the wider schema of meaning and power that alters over time. There is a tendency to suggest that the body is a finished fact – a given from genetics, the 'hard-wiring' of emotions, the reality of the gut. Yet, as Benjamin notes, 'During long periods of history, the mode of human sense perception changes with humanity's entire mode of existence. The manner in which human sense perception is organized, the medium in which it is accomplished, is determined not only by nature but by historical circumstances as well.'[23] In this way, as our mechanisms of perception alter, so do our emotions, as expressions of social and cultural discourse.

In his work on the action of power through the body, what he refers to as 'biopower', the philosopher Michel Foucault suggests that we are essentially constituted as bodies by political processes. Through his analysis of the development of medicine, the study of the history of madness and an examination of the way in which sexuality has changed over time, Foucault examines how bodies have been talked about, referred to, accounted for, and thus constituted. He suggests that an entity such as the body has actually been brought into being through the mechanism of discourse, which he describes as an organizing principle that not only orders the phenomena of which it speaks, but actually produces it in terms of the way in which it is, and can be, conceived of.[24] He contends that how something is referred to both shapes and expresses the way it is conceptualized. This, he argues, organizes and constrains what can be thought or enacted in relation to it.[25] He then goes on to discuss how certain institutions and technologies operate to either validate or disallow such circulations.

Consequently, for Foucault, the body (at least as we understand and conceptualize it) is the product of certain material practices in particular historical circumstances, which are then articulated in precise forms that either facilitate or prevent types of action and modes of being. Thus, even if we are to see emotions as 'bodily', they will still be 'strategic formations' that result from the operation of discourse within particular technological regimes.[26] That is to say, we feel things in a bodily way, but the nature of these feelings, and how we name and express them, how they are figured, will depend upon social forces. Given the emotive capacity of furniture, because of its intimacy with the body and its social significance, this is then a site where such dynamics can be worked through.

Our first home is a body. What do we remember of the womb? What do we bring with us into life that was first learnt or experienced in-utero? One of the problems is of course that we cannot know. As has been discussed, there is always a quality to experience that overflows explanation; indeed, there is necessarily an unnamable part of being that is linguistically and conceptually unavailable to the self. This is not an inability to find the words, but that an actual part of selfhood is beyond what can be articulated. If a large part of our emotional experience is bringing into language the raw matter of experience, the naming of what we are feeling, then it might seem that this is the genesis and process of emotion. But part of what we feel and experience is always that which is beyond semantic expression. In the early part of the twentieth century the surrealists were fascinated by this – not as a puzzle to be completed or resolved, but as a valid register of being in itself. This then is a methodology that has revived in a world of uncannily animated things.

Atelier Van Lieshout is a studio established in Rotterdam in 1995 by sculptor, painter and creative provocateur, Joep van Lieshout. Formed to counter the idea of the artist or maker as authorial genius, the group acts as a collective to realize works that are difficult to categorize, but which clearly reflect upon the material discourses of art, design and architecture in the exploration of more conceptual themes. In the 2008 piece *Womb House* (Figure 21), the occupant is provided with all that they need for life. We are used to the modernist legacy of the machine for living in, with its hard angles and technological systems. In this fantasy house we are presented with its antithesis: the soft machine.

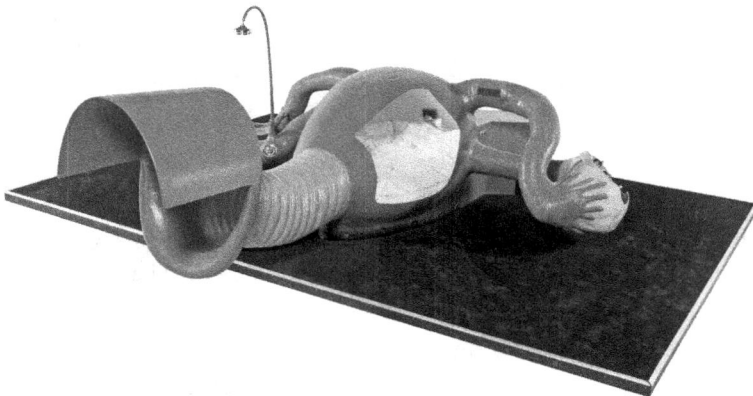

Figure 21 Atelier Van Lieshout, *Womb House*, 2008. Courtesy of Atelier Van Lieshout

Though the realization of it here is cartoonish, and has the crude almost amateurish finish that is the trademark of much of the material that emerges from the studio, the sense the piece evokes is still that of the biological. It becomes pertinent now because of how the home is changing. In the early twentieth century, it was possible for Benjamin to critique the bourgeois home of a generation before as the etui, or case for the middle classes, because its solidity, both figuratively and materially bore this comparison.[27] The stout walls and formal arrangements of the middle-class house at this time formed a hard carapace around life that was dictated by formal rules, even within the intimacy of the home.

Since both functionalism and surrealism can be said to have been concerned with the effect of the things we encounter, they can be positioned as dialectical counterparts. Both are philosophies of the object, yet as the sociologist Scott Lash notes, functionalism can be identified as an essentially extensive attitude to the human relationship to things, in that it was an attempt to engage with material reality through set categorizations.[28] Surrealism, by contrast, can be understood as an intensive reading of things, as mysterious and always subject to an irrational residue that exceeds our knowledge of them. As Hal Foster states:

> Functionalism is about discipline: it breaks down the domestic body into functions and assigns them to antiseptic spaces; the result is often a house type with scant allowance for history, sexuality, the unconscious. Surrealism is about desire: in order to allow it back into architecture it fixes on the outmoded and the ornamental, the very forms tabooed in such functionalism, associated as they became not only with the historical and the fantastic, but with the infantile and the feminine. In effect, against the 'machine for living in', surrealism presents the house as hysterical body.[29]

In the early 2000s, the home was once more pierced by the flows of communication. In 1997, the first version of the IEEE protocol 802.11 was released, which made domestic Wi-Fi a viable proposition.[30] Since this time, smartphones, tablets, and myriad other devices have been developed that rely upon the wireless connectivity of the home, which allow us to be both here and there at the same time. Far from being the retreat from the outward-facing expressions of life, the home, the room, even the bed has become a space for projecting outward (here is my lovely life; here is my dinner; here I am relaxing in my bathroom in my bra and pants), and for receiving the world (that person you met two years ago at a party is showing you their dinner; a work acquaintance's roses have flowered; the president of the United States of

America has said something horrifying). In such circumstances, the retreat to the womb seems sensible. It is to become removed from responsibility. It is to be ultimately cradled and coddled by the environment. Sometimes we yearn for the comfort of the womb.

Sitting comfortably?

Yet, what do we mean when we talk about comfort? Is being comfortable an emotion? Take sitting in a chair, for example. How do you actually tell if you are sitting comfortably? Here the concept of comfort appears to offer a point at which the material qualities of the chair and a certain emotional state intersect: matter and subjectivity interact. When asked what most people would want from a chair, what a chair's central functions are, most people would include comfort as a priority: that a chair should *be* comfortable. Yet, it is not absolutely clear what this might mean. The design critic Galen Cranz notes that there is no single universally accepted definition of comfort, and goes on to suggest that we have a problem with the concept because it may be that what she designates as its two components, support and freedom, are sometimes 'in conflict'.[31] Yet, even here she is actually making assumptions about the nature of sitting comfortably, about how comfort is experienced. In this model, the overarching idea of comfort is being conceptualized as an absolute quality of the object, that the thing will be comfortable or uncomfortable because of the way it has been materially engineered. When Cranz states, 'Most disconcertingly, what ergonomics researchers recommend – support of the sit bones, not cutting under the thigh, support for the lower spine, etc. – never translates into chairs that all human beings describe as comfortable,'[32] it is telling that this should be 'disconcerting' as this demonstrates not just the dominance that the mechanistic ergonomic discourse of subject–object relationships has had, but also its limits. As the sociologist Elizabeth Shove and her colleagues note in their study of design and everyday life, when defined as a quality of action rather than a physical attribute, comfort has to do with much more than simply the qualities of the object. It is 'to do with things,' but also crucially 'conditions and circumstances'.[33] What then is clear is that sitting cannot be discussed as an abstract experience; we are always talking about the experience of being an embodied self, sitting in a specific chair in a particular place at a certain point in history. As Witold Rybczynski notes in his book *Home: A Short History of an Idea*, comfort is a cultural trope, which changes as society changes. As he states, chairs are comfortable because they support the biology of the human frame, but also because they accommodate 'the postures of the time'.[34]

'Posture' is a lovely word that clearly points to the issue at hand: it could be taken to be an engineering question, one of seat heights and angles of recline, yet it also of course has another meaning. Posture also refers to how one poses, in both physical and social terms, as a form of posturing or the adoption of a role, it is concerned with how we administer the self in a Foucauldian sense. Particular types of chair, therefore, allow not only for different kinds of sitting in a mechanistic way, they also allow us to appear to be a certain sort of person as we adopt a pose, and as Rybczynski notes, different times require changing postures.

To sit in a chair is to enter into a relationship between form and function on an affective level. That is, in sitting we inevitably feel something about the nature of the act depending upon the type of chair used. The plastic monobloc chair is made by extruding molten polypropylene into a mould at 220°C, creating a product which comes out in a single piece, hence the name. Millions have been made since they were first introduced to the market in the early 1980s and a new one comes off a production line somewhere in the world every seventy seconds.[35] Originally designed by Vico Magistretti in 1967,[36] now over one hundred companies worldwide produce versions of the one-piece plastic chair which share the central characteristics of legs, a seat and a back but which can differ in minor variations, such as the shape of the back splat and the presence or not of arm rests. It could be described as the definition of mass production: it is cheap to make, easy to transport, profitable for its producers and functional for its users; it is light, strong, stackable and washable. In many ways, it could be seen as a triumph of the legacy of modernist design; it is a solution to a problem that fulfills a need simply and efficiently. It also effortlessly expresses its functionality through its form.

The *Plastic Chair in Wood* is exactly what its title describes (Figure 22). Whilst taking part in a residency at the Contrasts Gallery in Shanghai in 2008, Maarten Baas contracted local craftsmen to hand-carve a facsimile of a plastic monobloc chair in elm. With this transposition, the richness and elegance of the material and (by implication) the method by which it was fashioned seems to jar with a form that speaks so forcefully of standardization and mass production. Here the nature of the material (wood) and the method of manufacture (hand-carving) have been made absolutely subservient to a shape that derives from the formal predicates and limitations of another material (plastic) and another method of manufacture (moulding). It retains the same form and almost exactly the same

Figure 22 Maarten Baas, *Plastic Chair in Wood*, 2008. Courtesy of Pearl Lam Galleries, Shanghai

utilitarian function, yet through transposing it into wood its communicative or signifying function has been recognizably altered, as has the nature of its performativity based on the affective reaction of the user. As the material has been changed, so its place in the emotional register of its users has been altered, and not just because it means something different in a narrative sense.

The form speaks of reproducibility, of commonness, whilst the material and the way in which it has been made communicate a definite singularity. Design critic and promoter of sustainability in design Stuart Walker has argued that if the intention is to make objects which may have an enhanced emotional resonance in order to promote a certain longevity, a sustainable approach depends upon a certain congruence between the conditions of use, the method of making, and the materials employed. In this object, Baas is doing the exact opposite, in that, in Walker's terms, the 'various elements are not integrated into a unified whole, and a dissonance is created because of this lack of coherence'.[37] This disjuncture between the method of making, the form and the materials therefore has an effect upon anybody encountering such a piece on the level of semantics. However, Baas's intervention should not be simply seen as an aesthetic one, or be seen as working only on the level of semiotics. To sit in the wooden chair will be a qualitatively different sensory experience from using the plastic version.

Not only will the touch and feel of Baas's chair be more sensually pleasurable than that of the monobloc, the give and torque of the structure will be different in each case. The two versions of the same form can in this way then be said to inhabit markedly different places in the perceptual economies of our experience of objects. This illustrates the way in which we ascribe meaning and value to our material culture and suggests that through a piece such as Baas's the affective and emotional experience of using such an object will be markedly different to that of the mass-produced thing from which it has been derived, not just in the way it appears, but also in the way that it functions on a more practical level and on the plane of its physical effect. In such an object, therefore, the disjunctive action of the design enhances the affective qualities of the object through dissonance, whilst a new emotional relationship is established.

It could be suggested that the monobloc chair simply and efficiently solves the problem of comfort. However, from the experience of being in such a chair, it is quite apparent that sitting in it is a dynamic experience: it is about movement. On a physical level, the quality of comfort is constantly being sought out and mitigated by the sitter as they experience the chair. Yet, until the process reaches a point of discomfort, it is unlikely that they will be aware of this. Similarly, we feel comfortable in a chair if is suited to the posture we wish to adopt: this is true not only of physical postures but also social ones. In just the same way as we materially negotiate comfort, then, as a semi-conscious process, so we socially mitigate comfort through the way in which we interact with these things in the arena of everyday life. Yet this is also an historical experience. Just as somebody sitting in a chair does not remain motionless throughout but moves and shifts, distributing weight and allowing for gesture, so historically speaking we are always seeking out furniture, the apparatus of living, that suits our required pose. Yet the codes of posture, both physical and ideological, are altering through time as we experience them. It is, therefore, not a surprise that comfort should be concerned with conflict as it is a point of constant negotiation between a self-conscious subject, social discourse and the materiality of the world. Comfort exists in the relationship between narrative, affect and form.

The *Perished* collection of 2007, created by Antwerp-based designers Job Smeets and Nynke Tynagel working under the name Studio Job, is an ensemble of a table, cabinet, screen, bench, chest and lamp made from inlaid tropical hardwoods (see Figure 23). Inspired by illustrations seen in the New York Museum of Natural History, the skeletons of animals and birds range decoratively across the surfaces. On the front of the chest the skeleton of conjoined twins completes the symmetrical pattern formed by the bodily remains. The decorative

Figure 23 Studio Job, *Perished Screen and Chest*, 2007. Courtesy of Carpenters Workshop Gallery

effect is intended by its creators to be reminiscent of Art Deco, a luxury style that subsumed any of the political concerns of modernism beneath a more decadent sensualism. It is hard to escape from the symbolism of the use of essentially unsustainable materials to comment upon the death of species. The pieces are also, according to their authors, meant to recall Flemish art of the sixteenth and seventeenth centuries, which was replete with images of skulls and dancing skeletons, reminding the viewer that in the end death always triumphs.[38]

Having met at the Design Academy Eindhoven in 1996, where Smeets studied product and furniture design and Tynagel graphics, they began working together seriously around 2000. Smeets has never made any secret of his desire to be regarded as an artist and consequently the fact that little attention is paid to usability in their work is perhaps understandable. Tynagel seems to be more serious about what they create being functional things, asserting that these are useful objects, which is why they make chairs and tables and vases.[39] Yet, the communicative quality of pieces such as those represented by the *Perished* collection appears to completely subsume any consideration of comfort, either on a physical level with the bench, or a more social register with the other pieces.

They say that through the use of the skeleton motifs that are both 'violent and innocent' the work reflects the times in which it was created, which they claim are 'extravagant and violent'.[40] Thus, in the work of Studio Job the subject matter often takes on an illustrative quality, whereby even the 3D work can be regarded as looking like pictures given depth. Consequently, the work appears to be a surface comment on a subject, a semantic gesture similar to that of postmodern techniques. It also seems to rely on a certain irony, a detachment that suggests a distance that precludes actual people actually sitting on it, or such work ever really being part of people's lives. In this sense, this is furniture that works with comfort – but as with Emin's bed, it is present in its absence. Through the three-dimensional realization of Tynagel's drawings, a form has been arrived at that arouses but does not seek to comfort.

Comfort is then as much social and symbolic as it is practical. In terms of ergonomics we might expect Baas's *Plastic Chair in Wood* to function in much the same way as its plastic model. The elm from which it has been carved will be warmer to touch and its greater rigidity will eliminate some of the annoying torsion which is such a feature of sitting in the monobloc, but its essential formal qualities, its seat height and pitch, the shape of the back and the like are identical. However, if we extend the idea of being comfortable in the chair to include its broader social life there can be said to be marked differences between the two types of object.

For example, should you be offered Baas's chair to sit in, would you feel comfortable if everybody else was lounging in easy chairs? Your posture would not be the same, you would be at a different height; you might feel exposed and out of place. Alternatively, through being higher than everybody else you might perceive yourself to be in a superior position, which may or may not be comfortable, depending upon what you required from the social situation and how you understood the narrative as being played out. Similarly, if offered a seat in one of Priyatna's *disease* chairs, could you be comfortable? In a material sense such an object is just the same as an easy chair from IKEA, but in terms of how we might feel about it the figuration of emotion that takes place between subject and object would be very different.

The uncanny temporality of things

How do we recognize a chair? From a common-sense point of view, the answer would seem to be that a chair is an object that allows us to sit down. It is something that holds the body in a certain posture. However, to what extent has design history, or even anthropology or ethnographic approaches, really considered the act of sitting in a chair, that is to say *being* in a chair? Design history, certainly, has often regarded the chair as more an object of contemplation than a site of such being.[41] Where sitting has been considered, it has tended to be from a technical or ergonomic point of view that stresses the qualities of a chair as a more or less efficient tool.[42] Yet sitting is a form of material interpellation, one whereby we negotiate an important part of our lives. That is to say sitting is much more than simply a material act, it has definite emotional and cultural dimensions that must be considered when attempting to understand how the nature of any given chair will affect the user.

Robert Stadler is an Austrian designer who studied at the IED school of design in Milan. From 1992 until 2008, he worked with the Radi Designers group, which he co-founded, producing both limited-edition gallery pieces and more mainstream industrial design. In 2001, he established his own studio, through which he has been producing work in which he attempts to blur the boundaries between design and artistic practice. In his evocatively named *Rest in Peace* chair of 2010, he has nibbled away at an aluminium facsimilie of a monobloc chair to create a patina that speaks of the action of some creature or disease. This is disturbing not least because such chairs are usually made from plastic. As the design critic Tom Fisher notes,

> Plastics cease to be pristine, and become evidently worn, in a particular way. They do not patinate; they gather dirt rather than 'charm', and then may elicit particularly strong feelings of disgust. When they are no longer an acceptable element in humanized nature, they perhaps are doubly *un*natural. They are not trustworthy because they seem to make an issue of the margins of our bodies, and the manner of their ageing draws our attention to their margins.[43]

So, in Stadler's piece his intervention into the monobloc has rendered what appears to be wholly naturalized through ubiquity, 'doubly unnatural' by deliberately compromising its pristine nature and eliciting the sense of disgust that Fisher identifies. In doing so, therefore, the uncanny qualities of the object are stimulated as it becomes less innocent, less 'trustworthy' because of the way its passage through time has been accentuated and exaggerated through the apparent attack on its material qualities, its abjection. We know that plastic does not decompose naturally, yet Stadler has produced an 'artificially rotten' chair.[44] This is, therefore, an attack on our perceived boundaries between categories in relation to the bodily, our sense of the correctness and mutual exclusivity of particular physical states and modes of being that are played out in the abject.

Plastic is not meant to rot. If it is seen to do so it is disturbing, it is the temporalized break down of the material. Our understanding of how objects pass through time is constructed through, and depends upon, the material affordances made available to us by the way we live. As Lash and Lury suggest, 'Mass products draw in the public at the level of the senses, and lead to the restructuring of the very conditions of experience, subjectivity and the body.'[45] Stadler's piece thus has this uncanny effect on the level of a material disgust which accompanies such visceral transgressions; it is also a social anxiety which is stimulated, as the new thing we are offered, the piece of high design exhibited in the gallery or presented in the showroom, seems to be of a different order to that which we expect and demand. The things we buy are meant to be shiny and new, pristine and with the promise of a new life. To sell rotten things is then to disturb this.

In such a situation, the apparent sequentiality of time is a key underpinning prerequisite for the consumer mode of subject–object conjunctions. One of the absolutely essential tropes upon which consumer capitalism depends is neophilia and the veneration of the new. As Susan Buck-Morss notes, for Walter Benjamin, this endless craving for the new represents modernity as 'the time of Hell' which deals not with 'the fact that "always the same thing happens" … but on the face of that oversized head called earth precisely what is newest doesn't change; that this "newest" in all its pieces remains the same. It constitutes the eternity of hell and its sadistic craving for innovation.'[46] One thing we think we know is that these newest things should always be pristine and intact when we buy them. Yet, Benjamin detects within the craving for the new a certain death-drive that fetishizes the almost immediate decay of the aura of novelty implicit in consumption. For how long can a new chair remain new?

As many commentators have observed, the things we consume are now seldom made to age well. Therefore, it has been suggested by those such as Jonathan Chapman that if design is to be more 'sustainable', it is necessary to engineer objects in such a way as to make the materials and methods of manufacture appropriate to aging.[47] In Benjaminian terms, this could then be a call to invest such things with an aura that makes them sufficiently appealing to endure. Yet, this is then to engage not only with methods and materials but their relationship to a conception of change and the passage of time. As the philosopher Andrew Benjamin has observed, 'The complexity of the problem of the relationship between time and aura stems from the fact that solving the problem necessitates making substantial claims about the way in which the relationship between time and being has been structured.'[48] Therefore, any attempt to render the object more or less meaningful to achieve specific instrumental ends, such as any enduring appeal that Chapman has argued for, will necessarily be contingent upon the nature of the ideological apparatus being intervened in. It will depend upon what is being sustained, and how this relates to how we understand time.

If Studio Job's *Perished* collection refers to death in a semantic sense, then Stadler, rather than creating a more sustainable object, has fashioned a thing that speaks of decay and therefore death in more visceral manner. In making the *Rest in Peace* chair artificially abject, he has created an allegorical object, a *momento mori*, which rather than looking forward actually appears to be a foreshadowing of its own decline and disintegration. It is a paradox of our culture that our craving for the new contains within it an intimate knowledge of its dialectical opposite, which is not oldness but decay. When Walter Benjamin argues that novelty always remains the same, he is observing the tendency, constituted by relating to things as commodity forms, to flatten everything into equivalence where the ur-moment of the object is that of its display and initial consumption, the taking possession of its pristine state. This then homogenizes the very act of existence as we appear to be held in a stasis point of commodity aesthetics, even as we feel we move into each new part of the sequence. The plastic monobloc exists as a trope of constant potential newness: cheap enough to always be available. Yet, this very quality is what allows it to collapse into abjection, as it appears to have little value in time. Stadler's chair by contrast has been made temporally singular by its simulation of decay. It ceases to be available to homogeneous time and the apparently sequential nature of the thing and becomes about duration. It is not simply another tick of the clock, another iteration coming off the production line, one more homogeneous event in the endless dream-state of consumption. It is this thing, now at this moment that shall never come again.

The *Rest in Peace* chair gives the sense of being an object that through decay is coming to the end of its life. This is then disturbing because it suggests ending, *per se*; it is a material expression of how moments in human time are not reversible. At the beginning of the twentieth century, the philosopher Henri Bergson introduced the concept of duration (*durée*) as a term to describe the human experience of time as intensive and not available to be quantified as discrete elements within a homogeneity. Our conceptualization of time as an undifferentiated medium through which we pass, he argues, is actually a product of a very particular representation of time and temporality. He states that to conceive of human experience as duration means to be entirely 'rid of the idea of a homogeneous medium or a measurable quantity'. And from this he concludes,

'By carefully examining our consciousness we shall recognize that it proceeds in this way whenever it refrains from representing duration symbolically.'[49] Indeed Bergson's response to the problem of Zeno's paradox, whereby a flying arrow can be said to never reach its target because each element of distance can be eternally halved, is to state that motion is indivisible. The problem only arises when motion and time, that is, duration, are mistaken for the spatial metaphor that underlies them.

The objects that we live with are in motion, both in space and time. To understand how we relate to objects is then to see how we move with and encounter them. In this sense objects do not endure as such, but are experienced as duration. This concept of duration is important because, as Bergson argues, 'What is duration within us? A qualitative multiplicity, with no likeness to number; an organic evolution which is yet not an increasing quantity; a pure heterogeneity within which there are no distinct qualities. In a word, the moments of inner duration are not external to one another'.[50] If our inner sense of duration is made up of moments which are not external to one another then the external world is made up of objects (or phenomena observed by the subject) which do not endure, because they are constantly changing, because they are emergent. That is to say the persistence of objects in the world is a construct, a way of seeing things rather than an apperception of a reality to be grasped. It is therefore in the nature of movement, and how we emerge in relation to things, to furniture, to the everyday things that furnish our lives, that any political understanding of such conditions must lie.

Stadler's chair does not then shock us into realizing this. It does not bring this into consciousness as such. Rather it changes the repertoire of postures that may be adopted in the process. It creates a reservoir of subjectivities that may be taken through such a relationship. It is of course problematic that it will generally be experienced in a gallery. This means that the narrative content is amplified, its spectacular register highlighted at the expense of its more intimate functioning, which can only be experienced in its semantic sense, not in its affective dimension. Yet this can still be powerful.

The plastic monobloc chair exists in the form it does because it is a material expression of an attitude to objects and their physicality based on what we believe time is and how it can be inhabited. It is made from a precious and finite resource, oil, over which wars are fought, yet such is our sense of a progression into empty time that this can be used up with hardly a second thought. The monobloc, therefore, does not reflect or symbolize our sense of consuming the moments of our lives, of selling our time for abstract value in a putative future to buy goods which promise newness but contain decay: it is of the same order, it is the same thing. As Bergson argues,

> In place of a heterogeneous duration whose moments permeate one another, we thus get a homogeneous time whose moments are strung on a spatial line. In place of an inner life whose successive phases, each unique of its kind, cannot be expressed in the fixed terms of language, we get a self which can be artificially reconstructed, and simple psychic states which can be added to and taken from one another just like the letters of the alphabet in forming words.[51]

So, the endlessly equivalent nature of the commodity form is not simply mirrored in the nature of our existence. The seemingly continuous interchangeability of things existing in time comes to constitute the self and any sense of the inner life of the subject in a material world, just as we come to find this in the quality of our experience. Technologies of power serve to establish the conditions in which the self is formed. Stadler's chair then refuses this and baffles the well-worn reactive circuits we have developed. This does not then liberate us to perceive the abject quality in the fetishized newness of the commodity, but it does perhaps open up a space where something different can happen. This is because newness is a static concept, it is an imagined point that the commodity takes on in its biography, as it transitions between states. Decay by its very nature is dynamic. It is not so much a state as a process. This then suggests that, without our motive force, or even our sanction, things are *doing* things, and this can be a bit disturbing.

Body horror

We can read the patterns and historical specificity of disgust in the furniture we use. The psychologists Paul Rozin, Jonathan Haidt and Clark R. McCauley argue that this emotion has developed beyond being a rejection response based a fear of actual infection, and has become a cultural mode of reaction that extends to incorporate social phenomena.[52] Though our feelings about disease and death may be based in a fear of contamination on a practical level, that dead things bring germs, there is also unquestionably a cultural horror of the truth of death: that we are living creatures, embodied and undeniable, who will die. Gareth Williams asks whether, as humans, this is not our unique gift and curse: the ability to objectify death, our own and that of others. Yet, it seems that there is a reason that this has generally not been an issue that has been addressed by design. There is a fear of this ending in our culture. So this index of disgust can be read in our relationship to the domestic goods that we rely upon. The modern home is scrubbed of its animal qualities. The surfaces of modernity are all very wipe-clean. They are hygienic. Everything can be rendered pristine: scrubbed of death. Thus, any play upon our sense of being contaminated upends the sanitized appeal of the showroom and offers a more complex relationship to the thing.

As well as expressing a fear of contamination or infection, there is also a form of disgust which psychologists term 'body envelope violation disgust' that is based upon a reaction to the very base horror of an open body.[53] To be confronted with the open body, the boundary transgressed, is to be faced with viscera. A burst or slashed piece of furniture is one of the most abject objects we can encounter in daily life. This is an effect that designers have played with at different levels of consciousness. In Nacho Carbonell's *Skin* series, first shown in Milan in 2009, there are echoes of Bey and Koning's *Kokon* furniture of a generation before. Again furniture has been wrapped in fabric, but now it is looser and more tactile. The exterior can be compromised, the smooth covering of the interior transgressed by placing things beneath the skin. The designer suggests that this allows for a 'hide and seek' interaction with the pieces. Yet, where long loops of material have been placed beneath the surface and they tumble from the gut of the table, there is a certain disquiet, a feeling of the insides coming out that plays to a very deep fear. Similarly, in Priyatna's *damaged* (Figure 24), the body of the furniture again resonates with our flesh. In the slashes there is horror, but since such things fascinate, we cannot look away.

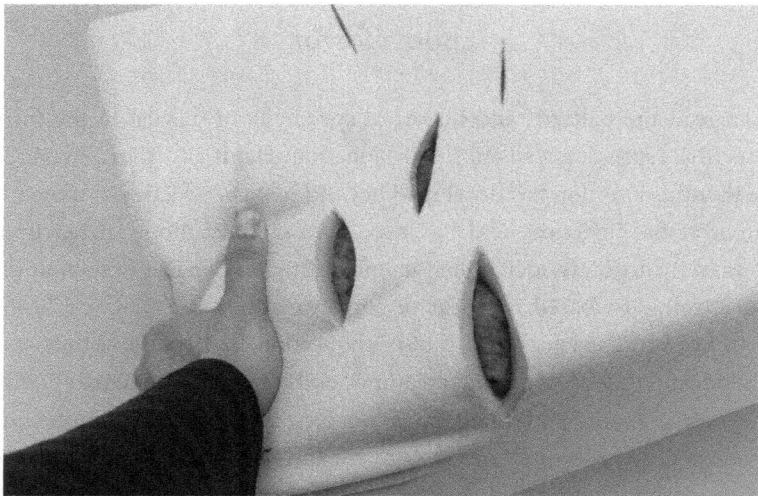

Figure 24 Denny Priyatna, *the appalstered 2: damaged*, 2017. Courtesy of the designer

Content as function

Julia Lohmann's *Lasting Void* is a resin and fibreglass cast of the interior of a calf, which was first shown as part of a collection of stools created by contemporary designers at the Kreo Gallery in Paris in 2007. Lohmann presented a statement to accompany the work, explaining that the piece had been made by casting the void left when an animal's organs are removed, which she notes is a form that exists for a 'transitional period' during which the creature becomes a product, 'the animal transmutes into meat'. According to Lohmann, the object was, therefore, meant to challenge 'our established emotions, classifications and prejudices towards animals'.[54] Thus, though the piece was presented alongside other stools that were simply opulent-designed objects, here, as author of the piece, Lohmann was asserting a discursive or critical function for the work, that it would cause those who viewed it to reflect upon the nature of death in meat.

That this was not always what the viewer saw was then demonstrated by her fellow exhibitor Alessandro Mendini, who sent a letter to the gallery, also copied to *Icon* magazine, in which he stated that he could see 'no theoretical, aesthetic, methodological or anthropological reason which justifies the idea of immortalizing a dead animal's last breath, in order sadistically to propose it as an item for everyday use, directly expressed in its suffering.' He notes that sometimes in the art of those such as Hermann Nitsch or Damien Hirst, such usages can be employed in the service of denouncing or even representing such horrors, and speculates that this may be the 'sensitive area where Julia is working'. Yet, he notes that Lohmann had also somewhat light-heartedly discussed the nature of stools in use, and this therefore troubled him very much.[55]

Lohmann responded by saying that in consumer culture, whereby relationships are mediated through objects, the designer has a responsibility to equip what they make with 'emotional and ethical functionality', in order that such work should cause those who encounter it to reflect upon 'how we lead our lives.'[56] This assertion, which was noted in the introduction to this book, seems to be quite a claim: that designers can actually equip everyday use-objects with such functionalities. Whilst Lohmann's intervention with *Lasting Void* seems far from cynical and pointless, it is not clear that it was entirely unfair of Mendini to react in the way that he did. Even though the designer did not quite turn the torture of a dead body into entertainment, as he suggested, she did turn the index of its interior into a stool. To some degree, she was therefore stimulating a level of disgust in the viewer. It should hardly then have been a surprise that somebody should react in this way. The narrative content of the piece was actually disjunctive with the emotional content. This is partly because the actual object is rather beautiful. It is only when we hear what it is that any level of disgust kicks in. That a designer had appropriated the form of the viscera of an animal is a shocking act (surely part of the re-sensitization that Lohmann sought). In her reply to Mendini, Lohmann made it clear that art was not the game she was playing, that this is not the discourse in which she was operating. She is adamant that design was her concern. Yet she seems to have wanted the design she had made to do some of the work of art.

As has been discussed, in art its very presentation *as* art creates an autonomous space, a frame which allows the work to act as both reflection and commentary on the subject. The art critic Arthur Danto makes the point that it is the setting in which we encounter cultural practices that allows us to make sense of them. He uses the example that a man standing on the street making elephant sounds and barking like a dog would be thought mad, but to perform the same act on a stage would provoke a different reaction.[57] In this way, he argues that setting places what we encounter, it frames it, and art has evolved some very specific methods of managing such contexts. Gareth Williams has suggested that Lohmann was appropriating the role of modern artist, as an independent mediator and commentator on the human condition. Yet in fine art this happens in specific, quite rarified conditions. Also, within these parameters one thing that is clear is the extent to which the author must abandon any hope of absolutely determining the reaction of the viewer. If the designer begins to use the horror of the interior as a mechanism, if it is to be part of the semantic content of the piece, then there must be some expectation of powerful reactions on the part of the viewer/user. If this is done in the context of art, if the piece is presented as an autonomous art work in an art-world context then such a response is channelled into reflection upon the meaning of the work in these terms. However, when something is presented as useful, it occupies a different space of signification and connotation, because it contains the suggestion that it will be integrated into lived experience. When a designer offers up a design work for contemplation, it is not a representation, they present a piece of the real world. It is a figuration, but this is a performative utterance, it changes the world rather than just representing it. The suggestion of use moves it from a realm of the free interplay of signs into one of actualité, of functionality. This then means that it is very difficult for designers to use their work to make didactic or direct political comments, as Lohmann appears to wish to.

Heavily authored design has content. As well as what it does, it has what the author believes it is 'about'. As conceived of by Lohmann above, this then suggests that certain qualities can be incorporated into the piece that will have a specified effect upon the viewer or user. This then might be seen as an extension of Akrich's concept of the script, that a certain series of affordances and cues can be encoded in the work, to then be de-scripted by the user. However, when this process is concerned with the best way to use a stool in a practical sense, it looks relatively straightforward. If we approach an object with one flat plane, from which extends a base or legs, the script is easy to read. When the script is concerned with ethics or emotions, it might be harder to decipher, and the context in which it is offered is significant. If the author wishes to shock the viewer into some form of realization, then this will need to be carefully constructed, since if the framing goes awry meaning can come adrift. If, on the other hand, such placing is not taken into account because it is not the 'point' of the piece, this does not absolve the work from any effect it creates.

Hair highway

Discourse matters. Where we encounter something, within which frame or context, will to some degree determine what we can get from it. The particular economy of experience and affect that it moves within will make a difference. *Hair Highway* is a project by Alexander Groves and Azusa Murakami, both graduates of the Royal College of Art (RCA) in London who together go by the name Studio Swine. As part of the work, a set of beautiful objects have been made from a strange translucent material embedded with fibers. These strands are human hair set in resin in shades of red and a golden-brown amber, in a way that seems to mimic tortoise shell. The panels formed have then been cut and shaped into a vase, a perfume bottle, a jewellery box and the like. The objects are iridescent and beautiful. The physical things are then accompanied by a meticulously constructed and artfully produced film, directed by Juriaan Booij and edited by Sally Cooper, which shows the hair markets from which the material was sourced, and the making of the designs.

The first hair piece that Groves and Murakami created was a pair of glasses for a student project. Groves suggests that their initial impulse was to find a material that could replace tortoise shell. 'Hair is one natural resource that is actually increasing globally,' he said. 'We knew that China imported the most amount of tropical hardwood from slow-growth forests across Africa, and we wanted to explore the possibility of using Chinese traditional crafts with a sustainable material.'[58] So, here the narrative is concerned with the sustainability of materials. This places the discussion firmly in the discourse of design. To be sustainable is an admirable quality to be striving for in this field, so this appears to be a virtuous endeavour. But this is a design project that uses human hair without any apparent self-reflexivity and this makes it more than a little creepy, whether the authors intended to inspire this feeling or not.[59]

Hair is liminal. It is of the self, but it is not quite a body part proper. It exists at the boundary between the individual and the outside world. To use such a material is thus an appeal to the abject, whether this is intended or not. The novelist Siri Hustvedt is correct when she notes that such ambiguity is central to the meanings of hair. Referring to Mary Douglas's thinking, she notes that substances that cross the body's boundaries are signs of disorder – they have the power to disturb.[60] Hair is also powerfully connected to ideas of presence and absence, it has been associated with mourning, loss and longing. To keep a lock of someone's hair has been to keep a part of them, a special connection through the indexicality of such matter.

In these circumstances, it seems to be somewhat disingenuous to suggest that the use of hair in a design for a functional object is a neutral act. This is not least because of where this resource comes from. It is poor people that sell their hair. As the anthropologist and historian of the hair trade Emma Tarlo observes, 'Long hair is a useful resource upon which women in different times and places have relied,' but as she goes on to explain, when their living conditions improve and they are less in need of the income, they are much less likely to sell it. They do so because they are desperate, and for the destitute selling that which is of the body is the last resort. As Tarlo notes, in China when the 2008 Beijing Olympics brought investment and new prosperity for many, the number of women selling their hair decreased dramatically, forcing hair collectors out into more remote areas 'in search of their crop'.[61]

The rectilinear jazz modern forms of Shanghai Deco were clearly suited to the panel construction of the pieces. This is a luxury style; it is self-consciously about display and opulence. Yet particularly in its Shanghai mode it was also about colonial wealth. As the novelist J. G. Ballard observes about the city of his birth, with its radio stations and newspapers in every language, Shanghai in the 1930s was 'a media city before its time, celebrated as the Paris of the Orient and the "wickedest city in the world"' – a place where untrammelled venture capitalism 'rode in gaudy style down streets lined with beggars showing off their sores and open wounds'.[62] Much as with Studio Job's *Perished* series, the *Hair Highway* work represents design that uses the hard surface of deco to allude to luxury and style, but which beneath such a façade a more disturbing quality can be discerned. With both duos this mixing of the discourses of art and design is deliberate, yet with neither is it clear that they are really aware of the effects of what they are doing.

Until the beginning of 2019, Studio Swine presented themselves as designers. After this time their website started referring to them as artists, and more recently reference to precisely what form of practice they are involved in has been removed. Yet, with the use of human hair in a project the category the product exists within matters very much. The discourses of art and design are different; one suggests criticality and distance, the other, unless managed very carefully, implies actual use and a form of material proposition as to how things should be. For a designer to use hair, which has been harvested from the heads of the poor, to make use-objects for the rich has at its worst something of the concentration camp about it. In 1729, Jonathan Swift wrote a pamphlet, usually referred to as *A Modest Proposal*.[63] In this piece, he suggested that the impoverished Irish might want to alleviate their economic suffering by selling their children to the rich as food. This was meant as satire to illustrate the heartlessness of attitudes to poverty. It is not clear that there is any satirical intention in Groves and Murakami's gesture. If a useful object made from human hair is presented as art, it will be understood as a reflection upon such practices, the distance implied by Adorno's autonomy will mean it can be a comment upon the world whilst still being of it. If it is presented as design, the usages and protocols of this field of practice will position the work in an emotional, and essentially political manner.

The assumption of actual use alters the discourse of power and meaning utterly. It is not a situation in which the rhetorical question 'what would this mean?' is being asked. It is the actual situation in which one person is using another person's hair to make a jewellery box, which at the very least seems cruel and insensitive to the lives of those from whom the hair has been sourced. As the designer and theorist Tomas Moldonado observes, 'When faced with the spectacle of cruelty, there are the following alternatives: condemnation, applause or indifference. The history of cruelty (or cruelty in history) teaches us that whenever condemnation, either for subjective or objective reasons, is not possible, sooner or later applause will come, almost always by way of a transitory stage of indifference'.[64]

Being embodied

We exist as embodied creatures.[65] If we do not take sufficient regard of this fact, then given our big brains there is the danger that we start to look like reasonable beings. Where design has started to be an authorial practice, it is understandable that the body and the political nature of our embodiment should be played out in this field. Priyatna's deliberately appalling furniture operates as it does because it invites those encountering it to sit. Even if you do not materially do so, the inference is there in a way that would not be the case with a more traditional artwork. It is one thing to experience disgust in a frame, at a distance, once removed, and then consider the nature of such a sensation. It is quite another to *be* disgusted by what you're sitting on.

In terms of materials and technique, emotive design has demonstrably drawn from art practices that came to the fore in the 1990s. The use of abject materials to stimulate a reaction in the viewer; the utilization of the allusional power of everyday things; reference to the resonatory and anthropomorphic qualities of furniture, all have been employed to destabilize our normally comfortable relationship with the products of mass production in this field. What the viscereal adventures of designers such as Gigi Barker or Attelier Van Lieshout show is that there is strong sense of our physicality that is just below the surface as we interact with things. They seem to demonstrate how the objects we use are much more than simple prostheses. They are the meeting of the self and the world, and in that conjunction is generation, not the action of the acting agent on the immobile, but flows meeting, melding and interacting in mutual constitution. In a work such as Baas's *Plastic Chair in Wood*, we are faced with the way we locate what suits us and why. We find things comfortable, or not, because they either fit us, or not. This is not as a consequence of ergonomically identifiable material qualities, but historically determined ones, that are themselves in motion. Not least we are moving in time, emerging into a world in tandem with the things that we make and use.

What we learn through confronting this then includes a realization of death, but not as a terrible fact, but as an understanding that can be liberatory as it destabilizes the apparent death grip of consumer capitalism and its perpetual novelty as played out in a sterile and manipulated now. In making disgusting things (or complicatedly comfortable things, for that matter), the flickering dialectics of the body and the thing are played out and are momentarily visible, the changing nature of the world becomes apparent, and we apprehend for a moment the physicality of the world of which we are a part.

As our embodied relationship to furniture seems to prove, since there is a fine line between desire and disgust, and emotion in as social as it is bodily, so what we experience exists in relation to these factors. Yet, in such a situation one thing is clear: there is a politics to what we feel to be valuable in our subject–object world. But where does this come from and how does it work? In order to tease these questions apart, it seems necessary to address this issue of value in design.

4

Valuing emotive design

In the video to her 1993 single *Rain*, Madonna reclines on a sleek silver chaise longue. The form undulates beneath her as its biomorphic curves echo the shape of her body. Though it is a static object, it seems to thrust and writhe as the light plays upon its hard yet somehow yielding surface. It appears to be a futuristic piece of furniture at the same time as its streamlined shape calls to mind the glamour of 1930s air travel. This is Marc Newson's *Lockheed Lounge* (Figure 25), the first version of which was created in 1986. There are fourteen of them in the world: an edition of ten, three artist's proofs and a prototype. It has been on magazine covers and discussed by critics[1] and it is in the collection of the Museum of Modern Art in New York. In 2015, it sold at auction for £2,434,500,[2] and Madonna has sat on it. You could be forgiven for thinking that it is the most important piece of furniture in the world.

The object upon which Madonna sits began its life in more humble surroundings, in a shed more usually used to make surfboards. Originally titled the LC1, it was constructed by creating a fibreglass-reinforced polyester resin core, which was then covered with small sections of aluminium sheet that had been hammered into shape with a wooden mallet. Each plate was then blind riveted into place forming a smooth skin. It was made for Newson's first solo show in 1986, at the Roslyn Oxley Gallery, shortly after his graduation from Sydney College of Arts. After the show he gave it to his mother. How then did this thing go from being something made in a shed to become one of the most expensive domestic objects ever made?

In our consumer culture, it seems that we have become so used to the idea that some things sell for far more than their apparent intrinsic worth that it does not seem strange. Houses, for example, which were once viewed primarily as a place to live, appeared to come free from their moorings and become generators of wealth, and until recently everybody seemed to believe that this process could only go on and on as the hidden hand of the market drove up their

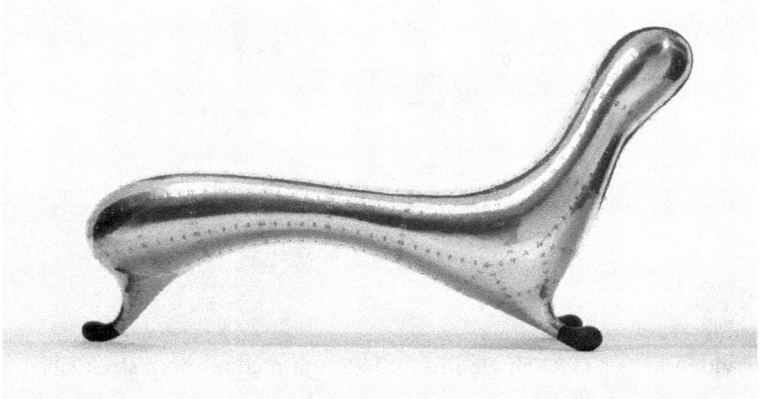

Figure 25 Marc Newson, *Lockheed Lounge*, 1990. Photography by Karin Catt. Courtesy of the designer

value. Similarly, in the world of furniture, the clear demarcation between simple utilitarian items and opulent status symbols has become blurred, as no longer is it materials or craftsmanship that determines what something is worth. Instead an artefact's status as a form of valuable design, as designated by a community of makers, dealers and collectors seems to be dependent more upon a series of opaque codes of taste and their place in the networks of the media, than it does upon any functional or aesthetic qualities.

This then is the cultural context in which emotive design has developed, as what we want is implicated in a complex economy of desire. Consequently, the first part of this chapter seeks to examine how the emergence of a new market for what Peter Dormer describes as 'high design'[3] has helped to stimulate the creation of certain forms of expressive and affective use-object, in order to determine how the form and emotional content of the work is related to the value ascribed to such things. It would be foolish to ignore the fact that a lot of the time people want these things because they are expensive, but is seems pertinent to ask why they should be seen as so valuable, and what other forms this takes other than the monetary register. The discussion then moves on to consider how the development of the market then relates to anything we may wish to call everyday life, since, if the practices described really are concerned with the making of use-objects rather than simply the creation of conversation pieces for wealthy patrons, it must be necessary to consider what it would mean to use such things, to live with them, and value them for what they do.

Who cares, as long as it sells?

Sophie Lovell, the ex-editor of the style magazine *Wallpaper**, suggests that the real difficulty critics have with the existence of design that is meant to be highly expressive as well as practically functional is that some people are 'willing to spend very large sums of money on it'.[4] In a way, she is right. One thing that must be accounted for when studying the appearance of this phenomenon is that many (though certainly not all) of the objects being discussed tend to sell for a lot of money. Why then would anybody be willing to pay so much for an apparently useless use-object?

When discussing how contemporary design has become 'militantly useless', the design critic and former director of the London Design Museum, Deyan Sudjic, refers to Thorstein Veblen's 1899 treatise *The Theory of the Leisure Class* to argue that this form of design represents conspicuous consumption, whereby for the leisured rich that consume them these are not objects that are primarily made to fulfil prosaic everyday functions. Instead, they are bought and owned in order to show the wealth and disposable income of those who can afford them; that their function is to exist as a needless extravagance or 'peacock tail'.[5] This is, therefore, to regard the ownership of such objects as a form of needless extravagance or exhibitionist excess.

Often we buy things to demonstrate that we know that this is what we should consume, in that, as Pierre Bourdieu notes, it is through the exercise of taste that 'one classifies oneself and is classified by others'.[6] The *Robber Baron* series, created by Studio Job, for example, consists of five monumental pieces: a cabinet, a mantel clock, a table, a standing lamp, and a jewel safe (Figure 26), all cast in bronze, each in a limited edition of five. However, despite being highly crafted pieces of design these could hardly be described as tasteful objects. Indeed, they appear to have been deliberately constructed to be the opposite of good taste. The cabinet is chunky and garish. The lamp is a skyscraper that is on fire and the jewel safe depicts a mocking clown face topped with a vase, which would be difficult to live with in any circumstances.

They have been deliberately designed to be so opulent and expensive that only those as wealthy as the oligarchs ostensibly being critiqued (or marketed to, depending upon the perspective adopted) could afford to buy the work. This has, therefore, neatly ensured not only the economic status of the furniture, since any potential purchaser would need to be very wealthy to own such things, but also their cultural position as something worth looking at, because, as Sudjic notes,

Figure 26 Studio Job, *Robber Baron* jewel safe, 2006. Courtesy of Carpenters Workshop Gallery

'money demands attention'.[7] This then confers on the owner a certain status as an individual so rich that they can afford to buy something essentially useless; just as they demonstrate their taste by knowing why such a thing is desirable.

This is one way in which these objects have come to fulfil a role previously reserved for art, that of a form of conspicuous display and demonstration of discernment by the wealthy. As Rolf Fehlbaum, CEO of Vitra, observed in 2009, one-off and limited-edition furniture has existed for some time. What has changed is the way in which a market for it has been established; as he states, 'the market developed when design in general became collectable for the people who are buying art. That is a phenomenon of the last ten years.'[8] This is to identify a shift in the status of design, in that the evidence seems to suggest that certain forms of everyday use-objects are coming to be consumed in the rarefied manner in which high-status art objects have been.

When considering whether this work can be regarded as important, as art might be said to be, whether it is able to 'push boundaries' or 'express the zeitgeist', Lovell's answer is straightforward: 'Who cares, as long as it sells?'[9] This is because she inhabits a certain economy of design, one where what is desirable is what goes for a lot of money. This is a world where design is something created and traded. The end user is a given: they are those who buy it. That is the final cause or purpose of the work in her world. The content of the pieces, what they might mean is not really the point, the purpose of the work is to be bought. Such economies then depend upon belief, what people feel about such work. How much is something worth? What people believe it is. How is this then established? Well, one way that the value of an object is determined is through the action of exchange in the marketplace.

Marketplaces

Those who control the market may not actually be able to establish particular values *per se*, they cannot just decide what something is worth if nobody will pay this, but they do have a lot of power over how value can be ascribed and afforded. As was noted in the introduction, the naming of Design Art has been attributed to the auctioneer, Alexander Payne, in 2001.[10] Despite the fact that it is quite likely that it was his employer, Simon de Pury, who actually suggested the title (he has also tried to create 'Game-Art' and other types of 'Art' to sell in the auction house), this attribution does point to the way in which the development of this type of furniture and the increased interest in it can be mapped in relation to its financial exploitation. Loic Le Galliard, co-founder of Carpenters Workshop Gallery in London, commented in the late 2000s that 'design art is a market that doesn't exist' in that 'market is a very big word' and the present field is 'tiny, tiny, tiny',[11] and there is little evidence that this field of economic activity has expanded considerably since then.

However, this market, small though it is, was established deliberately through the creation of a number of organizations and galleries dedicated to the manufacture and sale of such artefacts. In 1995, Murray Moss opened the Moss Gallery in New York's SoHo, selling work that he claimed to explore the 'ever-evolving rich dialogue between Industrial Design and Studio Art'.[12] In 1999, the Kreo Gallery in Paris was established by Didier Krzentowski. He set out to be what Lovell terms a 'producer-gallerist' or patron, gathering together what he styles as a 'family' of designers such as Ronan and Erwan Bouroullec, Naoto Fukasawa, Hella Jongerius and Jasper Morrison.[13] As was discussed in Chapter 1, Droog established a retail space in Amsterdam in 2002 in an attempt to capitalize on this market and then went on to expand more internationally later in the decade. In 2006, the Carpenters Workshop Gallery was established in London to sell this kind of design to the rich patrons who increasingly resided in the city.

Similarly, auction houses such as Sotheby's and Philips de Pury have also had a significant role in developing this market in the early 2000s. Yet, it would be inaccurate to suggest that the formation of the market has been entirely producer led, since it is also that people have come to regard design in a new way. Richard Wright of Wright auction house in Chicago argues that 'the collectors for design are changing. The influx of art collectors actively buying is a shift, both in their willingness to spend but also in what that signifies: design as the expression of the collector, not just quiet furniture that recedes into the room.'[14] Indeed, as Lovell notes, 'It is now far more fashionable to add polish to the personal identity with a house (or houses) furnished in a collection of contemporary one-offs and limited-edition pieces to match the art and the architecture.'[15] This is, therefore, to regard the work as having entered an economy of subjectivity and the expression of the self. This is then 'lifestyle' as a form of emotional landscape.[16] So the rich are doing just what we do. They are dressing the set of their lives with things that express who they are. They've just got more money than we have, so they can afford more exclusive stuff.

Limited edition

In the process by which objects such as these have come to be seen as valuable, one classical economic mechanism brought into play by those who produce and disseminate such artefacts has been the restriction of supply. The anthropologist Igor Kopytoff suggests that 'we take it more or less for granted that things – physical objects and rights to them – represent the natural universe of commodities', whilst at the opposite end of the spectrum 'we place people, who represent the natural universe of individuation and singularization.'[17] As was established in Chapter 2, this is not least because the commodity is understood to be essentially formed by a concept of equivalence: at its purest, all commodities are absolutely interchangeable and equivalent, in that they can be exchanged for money.[18]

At the opposite pole of our cultural schema, any given thing can be held to be unique; that this actual singular thing before us is the only representative of its particular passage through time and space to this moment. The exemplar of this, its quintessence, is then to be found in the individual person who is taken to be a unique product of their particular circumstances, biography and consciousness. These can, therefore, be said to represent two polar opposites: at the one end a world where everything is essentially the same and interchangeable; at the other a way of being in which each thing is its own singular entity.[19]

As he then goes on to note, neither of these absolutes are fully realizable. No social or economic situation could completely represent either end of the spectrum, since there can be no realistic possibility of everything being absolutely equivalent to everything else within one unitary sphere of exchange, just as there is no system in which everything is so singular as to entirely absent even the merest suggestion of similarity. They can, however, be posited as 'the two extremes between which every real economy occupies its own particular place'.[20] It is in such circumstances that the market for limited-edition furniture has developed; the pieces being sold having been deliberately engineered to appear as products that are in some way more singular than their mass-produced counterparts. One way in which this has been achieved is through restricting the physical supply. As Veblen argued, within this mode of conspicuous consumption, whereby commodities are consumed to display the wealth of those who own and use them, the presumed scarcity of particular consumables is one way in which value is ensured in our culture.[21] Thus, if in an abstract sense all things for sale are commodities and therefore common, one way in which this commonness can be mitigated is by restricting the practical availability of the object. The fact that the *Lockheed Lounge* or Studio Job's *Robber Baron* series have been limited in their editions has the de-facto effect of raising their value: this is one way that such things can become more singular, or rather move towards the pole of singularity. If the product were to go into mass production, its level of singularity would diminish, its scarcity value would decrease and therefore so would its monetary exchange value as a commodity.

Therefore, one way that the object can achieve a certain singularity is by the limiting of supply. It should be noted that as a commodity it will actually still partake of ultimate equivalence as exchange value, yet the restricting of supply gives the impression of distinction through an increased relation to the singular. This can happen at a series of different degrees of intensity. If the prestigious manufacturer Vitra, for example, were to produce an open edition that was still handcrafted and very expensive, this would have a much less devastating effect upon the object's singularity, and therefore its perceived value and how people feel about it than if IKEA were to stock a mass-market version at an affordable price. For example, in 2005, the Dutch designer Hella Jongerius was invited by the retailer to create large-run productions of her ceramics, the result being the *Jonsberg* vases which retailed in their stores for €34.95, thus making them accessible purchases for most people. Therefore, to own a *Jonsberg* vase is to have bought into the cachet of owning a Jongerius, it marks the owner out as a certain sort of person who knows something about design. Yet, its low price and mass availability through an outlet such as IKEA means that such an object loses its singular quality.

If everybody can have one, it is no longer exclusive. By limiting a piece to a specified edition, the value of the work is ensured to a set degree by the scarcity value programmed into the physical nature of the object and its actual existence in the world. Just as the diamond dealers DeBeers are careful to restrict the flow of precious stones onto the market in the knowledge that a glut would drive the price down,[22] so the designer and the dealers have insured against such a situation by declaring that only a restricted number shall be made. In this way these things become more desirable; just as through the process of singularization, objects are made to appear more human so that through the reification process what is lusted after seems less a thing and more like a form of individual in its own right. This singularity can then be parlayed into celebrity. In this way, spectacular design works like the relatability of the social media influencer; we think we know them. They have become part of our lives and, therefore, take on emotional weight and presence.

Gallery design

It is not only through physical scarcity and monetary price that a certain singularity can be achieved, as it is not exclusively through buying or owning objects that we engage with them. It is also through cultural exchange that value is established and regulated. Leonardo DaVinci's *Mona Lisa*, or Van Gogh's *Sunflowers*, may be some of the most valuable works of art in the world, but it is still possible to experience them in the original without having to buy them. If there were such a precondition, their almost 'priceless' nature (or high degree of singularity) would limit their availability to almost nil. Instead, they are made conditionally available to a wider public through a very restricted form of access. They are held in a very particular location, that of the prestigious gallery or museum where access is strictly controlled: visitor numbers are limited and opening times regulated. This is then an area that has been colonized in the constitution of the category of the spectacular Design Art form of emotive practice, as their value as culturally important items has been established.

These are things for which the claim is made that they are, to one degree or another, functional objects, a table, a chair, a bookcase and so on, but that are produced as either unique pieces or limited editions that are shown in gallery settings and sold at auction in much the same manner as art traditionally has been. In this regard, as Sudjic suggests, 'what is new ... is the huge increase in the size of what might be called gallery design'.[23] This should not be mistaken for the phenomenon whereby regular design objects get elevated to the status of classics, because they have become so iconic as to allow them to enter the gallery, rather this is to do with a category of object that because of its content, its intellectual and emotive qualities, makes sense in the gallery as a problem to be engaged with.

So, as well as appearing in gallery-style retail spaces, the type of design under discussion here is often shown in actual gallery and museum settings, and many of the more iconic pieces, such as Newson's *Lockheed Lounge*, are in the permanent collections of some of the most prestigious museums in the world. These objects are not simply being treated as expensive things; therefore, they are also clearly being related to as meaningful in a wider sense. They are being presented as culturally valuable, the determination of which then takes place through cultural exchange in the form of exhibition and reception in a particular context.

The furniture of the ruling elite has been shown in galleries and museums before, of course, but not generally as soon as it has been made. Traditionally, furniture and domestic products have not been deemed worthy of being exhibited as culturally important artefacts unless, that is, they had reached a certain age and therefore guaranteed their social significance, their economic value or their status as a classic of their type. In recent years, this has changed. Design, as a category consisting of objects that have ostensibly been created to fulfil functional requirements, such as chairs, beds and the like, has increasingly come to be seen as a form of cultural production that is worthy of being exhibited, analysed and discussed in a manner which was previously reserved for art.

This is certainly true of the manner in which Newson's creation has been made available to the world, for example. Though it was nominally created as a functional object, a chaise longue or day-bed, the very fact that there are not many examples in the world combined with its astronomical price tag mean that few people will have had chance to sit on such a piece, still less own it. It can, however, be experienced as an object and an original, but only in very particular circumstances. As has been mentioned, it is in the permanent collection of MOMA, and it can also be seen in Vitra's Weil am Rhein Museum in Germany, the Powerhouse in Sydney and the Pompidou in Paris, amongst others. What is important, however, is that it cannot be seen in your living room, and you cannot sit on it. That is a privilege afforded only to the likes of Madonna. As Bourdieu notes, this, therefore, represents a particular 'orchestration' of the relationship between the fields of production and consumption in the social construction of taste, whereby the objects come to attain a certain cultural capital.[24] In this way, therefore, these objects' position in a cultural economy of design can be seen, whereby objects take on a cultural role as carriers of meaning.

Through their movement in the media, they take on celebrity status. Not least, because they are consumed by actual celebrities, such as Kanye West, Brad Pitt and Madonna. Through our consumption of images of their consumption of the object, so a form of transference takes place, whereby the objects take on the glamour of those who pose upon it. Similarly, through association with the amplified emotive qualities of the furniture, its often cartoonish expressive qualities, its association with exclusivity, good taste, and glamour (and a definite darkness that is glossed over if not missed entirely), so these qualities rub off on those who are pictured doing the sitting, as their image is serially reproduced across multiple platforms.

Furniture has always been produced in series. This was as true of pre-modern forms of production and use, in the way that an archetype of a useful thing will be constantly reproduced because it always needs to be present, as it is of post-Fordist societies, whereby we literally live with technologically produced multiples much of the time. In art, it has long been common practice to produce several casts of a bronze from the same mould. Etching, lithography and screen-printing have also given opportunity to the artist to indulge to one extent or another in a form of mass production. Since Warhol, the extent to which art can be produced in a factory has been amply demonstrated, confronted and deconstructed. Yet, at the heart of the artistic discourse seems to be an anxiety as to the multiple's relationship to authenticity.[25] This is now a feature of the discourse of design, but such a conundrum has developed in historically specific circumstances different to those in which art had to confront this issue.

Virtually unique

Though Krzentowski of the Kreo Gallery maintains that the pieces he showed were not created as limited editions for marketing reasons, Lovell notes that such retailers are 'well aware of how much more desirable an object becomes when it is almost unique'.[26] 'Almost unique' is, of course, technically an oxymoron. Something is either unique or it is not. What becomes very interesting, however, is when we think of something as virtually unique. This is because the expansion of reproductive technologies means that the object can exist as both absolutely singular (in that this is a 'Newson' it is not anybody else's, only he does it) yet at the same time it can be almost endlessly available as a series of multiplicities.

If there was only one *Lockheed Lounge*, it could only be in one museum, or worse, one private collection. By creating an edition of ten, Newson has made the object multiple. On a material level, this means it can be in more than one place at a time. It is still the same thing because, with design much more than for art, the product is understood to be the original Newson (or Starck or whichever designer it may be), even if it has been produced in series. The fact that it is in a limited edition helps to guarantee exclusivity, but the cultural understanding of design and the way in which authorship is ascribed means that we are comfortable with the idea that there may be multiple editions of a single design. This means that it can both be on display in MOMA, for sale at Philips de Pury and in a private collection, all at the same time.

Not only can the event that is the *Lockheed* happen simultaneously in a (limited) number of places, but also what is in the museum and is thus deemed culturally important can be acquired, owned and used by a very small and exclusive group of people; and if it is culturally important, then so are they. By owning the object that exists in the museum, they therefore, by association, accrete its cultural capital. In this way, the artefact's place in the cultural economy of design helps to determine its position in the economy of selfhood and subjectivity in relation to the commodities that designed goods represent. How we relate emotionally to the piece will depend upon the extent to which we incorporate it into our lives. Some will only have the opportunity to consume the object as sign value, others will be able to sit on it and feel its pressure on their buttocks.

Crucially, with its relation to virtuality, that the *Lockheed* can be in more than one place at a time also means that it can move much more in the media; it can flow more easily through the channels of culture. Every time it is sold it is in the news. Each museum that shows it can use it in its publicity. The more of them there are, within the parameters of a certain prescribed exclusivity, the more they can be talked about. The object's multiple nature means it can exist as a reproducible series of events. We live in an age of hyper-mediation, whereby much of what we experience as real – the news, the things that are there to be consumed, even friends through social networking sites – actually come to us in the form of representation. Through such circulations, what indeed can be termed 'symbolic exchange', such objects then gather more weight, meaning and value. So, in our supremely materialist culture, the significance and emotional resonance of the things we consume has come to be determined not simply by their material qualities or physical use value, but through their circulation as signs in the media. They are written into the cultural narrative, they become part of the discourse. In this way, their value is determined by the action of symbolic exchange. This is particularly pertinent when discussing the development of heavily authored, content-laden design, as it exists as a phenomenon as much on the level of the image, through representation in magazines, websites and books as it does as a collection of material artefacts.

In the 1990s, Jean Baudrillard asserted that reality itself founders in the hyperreal of simulation, suggesting that we now live with signs with no referent in the real world, that we essentially exist within the circuits of mediation.[27] What then looked like exaggeration, in the age of the smartphone and the internet appears to be a conservative reading of the situation. In the endless technological reproduction of objects as signs, of things as virtualities, it is clear that their symbolic value, as established and maintained through representation, is as important, and indeed flows into and helps to determine, their existence as material objects. That this is then happening through a particular form of technological medium means that how it is occurring will help to determine the form of what is taking place. That is to say, through encountering such desirable and interesting things through internet interactions, we form a particular kind of emotional attachment. Thus, the technology is not just a channel for the experience, but it also serves to model the way in which such bonds are formed. As media commentator Javier Serrano-Puche observes, such interactions reveal the dominant role of emotions in our lives, as the technology can be demonstrated to be configuring the selves of the users who interact in this way.[28] Through the internet, we are coming to love things in a particular manner, in a certain form that this medium prescribes.

In this respect, it may be useful to compare Madonna to the piece of furniture upon which she sits in the initial example. Madonna is of course only one person. She is a real individual who you could go to see perform live or even shake hands with in the right circumstances. However, through the mass production and distribution of her music, it is possible to experience Madonna in an almost infinite range of situations. When the reproduction of her image and the other ways in which she colonizes the media are then factored into the equation, it starts to become apparent the extent to which the value which accretes to Madonna, and the way that people feel about her, is dependent upon not only her material presence in the world but also her virtual existence in the media. In this way, it can be argued that Madonna is not so much an individual but a brand, a collection of relationships and interactions, which circulate around a particular product.

In just the same way, Newson has established himself as a brand, with his specific objects being actualizations of this entity. When an individual consumes the *Lockheed Lounge*, either by actually buying it (should they be rich enough) or simply by viewing it (which is to consume its sign value), it is not just the object or its image that is consumed. Instead a certain relationship to Newson as a famous designer is established, for as Lash and Lury observe, the brand is constituted as set of relations, and for embodied beings with relations come emotions. In this sense, brands can be regarded as 'abstract objects', in that they 'operate as if they were interfaces or surfaces of communication',[29] and this is only possible because of the structure of distribution established in their mode of production, which in this case is constituted by their existence as limited-edition objects which circulate widely as multiples in the media. Yet, brands are also one of the primary ways in which our emotional response to products are ordered.[30] It is the mechanism by which the mundane and mass-produced is made into the apparently singular love object.[31]

It is not necessary to physically own something to have feelings towards it. Ramakers has argued, 'The mediatizing of our society means that "within everyone's reach" is no longer the same as "affordable for everyone". New products, whether expensive or cheap, are disseminated forthwith by the media.' She then goes on to ask, 'Why should actually have to own everything we find beautiful or interesting? Sometimes it can be enough to just to look at it or be inspired by it.'[32] This is to conceptualize 'within everyone's reach' in a very particular manner, in that the individual subject can only interact with the object within certain economies: in this way, use is then determined in a very specific form that equates representation with the economy of day-to-day material experience. This problem of the relationship between seeing and using is clearly worth addressing, but if for a moment these can both be collapsed into the idea of experiencing, then at least some of the mechanics of such a process can be seen.

Like live music, products are sold essentially as events, original multiples. Each gig in a U2 or Rolling Stones tour feels like a one-off event for the audience and may be a once in a lifetime experience for the individual, but for the band and the road crew, it is another night creating the same performance; it is part of a process whereby a product is manufactured continually. This does not make any iteration less authentic; the audience has still seen U2 or The Stones. Each night is an original multiple, with the audience experiencing it as authentic and emotionally fulfilling because they have had direct connection with the band in time and space. And, of course, with entities such as supergroups, the band is a brand. Consequently, interaction with the band as brand will come through multiple platforms. If a brand is characterized as an agglomeration of relationships then the possible ways in which an individual can interact with the brand are only limited by the communication opportunities available. If the gig is the actualization of the rock band, then the object is the actualization of a brand such as Newson. This was an approach deliberately pioneered in the realm of design by Ramakers and Droog and it has played a significant role in the way in which design has come to be regarded in contemporary culture.

An object may exist only as a one-off or as part of a very limited edition, but the proliferation of the channels of communication and the availability of platforms for interaction made possible by the development of the internet and communicative technologies means that though you may not be able to own an object by Newson, you can to some degree buy into it and feel you have a relationship to it through experiencing it virtually. As Benjamin observes, 'Technical reproduction can put the copy of the original into situations which would be out of reach of the original itself.' He goes on to note that technological reproduction, above all 'enables the original to meet the beholder half way … The cathedral leaves its locale to be received in the studio of a lover of art; the choral production, performed in an auditorium or in the open air, resounds in the drawing room.'[33] Similarly, the unique object, the material singularity, can become endlessly multiple in its virtual form and flow out into the world. We can meet it half way as it comes to us through the screen – which is now not even shackled to the domestic interior as we can take our interiority around with us.

This then has an effect on the material original. As Benjamin says, 'By making many reproductions it substitutes a plurality of copies for a unique existence. And in permitting the reproduction to meet the beholder … in his own particular situation, it reactivates the object reproduced.'[34] In such a conception, the original or material version of the object becomes another turn in the multiplicity of copies. The power of the mediated versions of the thing is derived from the value of the material original and its scarcity – however, this value is then dependent upon the multiplicity of copies that circulate in the broader mediascape. It is, therefore, in this way that objects such as Newson's chaise, or any of the other pieces under discussion here, are established in their value as part of a relationship between their singularity and their seriality as they circulate in the flows of culture.

Everyday things

Yet, it is not only on the level of exchange value that we give meaning to things. Use value still exists, despite the effects of consumer capitalism, and this is an aspect of our relationship to furniture and domestic furnishings that make them different to many other categories of thing that appear in the media. This then is a space that designers have been exploiting in an exploration of how use makes things valuable to us. Jurgen Bey's *Do Add* chair (Figure 27), made as part of Droog's *Do Create* series (2000), is an appropriated stacking chair which has had one leg shortened.[35] This means that if the chair is to be used, it is necessary to place something under it such as a stack of books or magazines. At first sight it appears absurd. Why would anybody want a chair that has been altered in such a way that it does not function properly?

The *Do* project was initiated by the Amsterdam publicity company KesselsKramer in 1996. Intended as an open-ended experiment in the

Figure 27 Jurgen Bey, *Do Add* chair, modified found chair, 2000. © Bianca Pilet

manipulation of the power of branding, an essentially 'empty' identity was created, *Do*, which existed as a collection of values and broad mission-statements concerned with the active participation of users rather than as an actual product range. The originators then anticipated that products or services could be developed that would express and manifest this. To such ends, Droog collaborated with the agency in developing the *Do Create* collection in 2000. The results were then shown at the Milan Salone del Mobile accompanied by large images, created by the photographer Bianca Pilet, which served to demonstrate the objects being used.

Though an exhibition of the work, 'Do Create on Location', then toured internationally, it is important to note that the objects created, through being presented as part of a brand and represented as being in use in the accompanying photographs, the underlying proposition of the objects' mediation is that these things were to be understood as existing in economy of design for use, rather than functioning entirely as representation, particularly since the central conceit of the work was the idea that it was only to be through the action of the user that the things would be 'completed'. This then is to some degree to employ the idea of the rhetorical user, as is often invoked in the critical methodologies discussed in the next chapter,[36] but in this case that should not suggest a fictional one, as such. Bey's object can actually work, if you found it in a café, you could make use of it, it would just require a certain form of interaction.

This approach of presenting prototypes, which are shown in exhibitions and disseminated in the media, only some of which then go on to be commercially produced, is typical of Droog's *modus operandi*. Since its first show, Droog has been as much a gallery of possibilities and a virtual shop window as it has been an actual facilitator of the commercial production of designed goods. Yet Droog is a business that sells and markets design, and the artefacts created for *Do* were intended to be products that could be bought and actually used. Yes, as a cultural object Bey's chair was mediated in its inception and it did not actually go on to be commercially produced as other objects in the range did. Yet the manner of its presentation means that it can be considered as a functional object, albeit one which exits on a material level only as a prototype.

Therefore, if we are to take Bey's ludicrous design seriously as an object of use, it must then be asked how the designer has intervened to alter its functionality and what effect this has had upon the way in which it might be used? That is to say, we must reflect upon what use would mean in such circumstances. In order to do this, it is necessary to conceptualize the way in which the *Do Add* chair exists as a material relationship between Bey as the designer, as author of the piece, and the end user, as the actor who actualizes the potential use inscribed into the physicality of the object.

One consequence of Bey's intervention into the chair, the shortening of the leg, has been to interact with the tendency discussed by Arvatov, outlined in Chapter 2, for things in consumerist material culture to appear seemingly finished or complete.[37] He has done this, in Akrich's terms, by altering the way in which the subject and the object can interact through changing the chair's physical script.[38] Yet, to what ends has this been done? The suggestion here is that Bey is not attempting to make the user conscious of the nature of the object and then reflect upon it as one might with a work of art such as Duchamp's snow shovel, or as a consciousness-raising piece of Critical Design as Anthony Dunne and Fiona Raby might. Rather, he has changed the way that the thing can be used, he has therefore altered the nature of this use and the place it can take in a wider sociotechnical script of usefulness.

The objects we live with are much more than simple utilitarian devices. We seek rational solutions to our needs, but the domestic objects we use are about much more than this. Somers's *Bath Boat* discussed previously (2005; Figure 5), for example, is actually a bath, a functional device for washing. It is, however, not simply an anonymous tool, it also has romantic and playful associations with floating and sailing that challenge any dictum that form must only follow basic utilitarian function, indeed it seems to suggest that fantasy is a necessary quality of the furnishings with which we live. By claiming to be, and not just represent, the functional elements of a house, things such as these illustrate how it is possible to materially alter the conditions of domesticity by providing an alternative version of the everyday, one in which objects may be much more than simply instruments which should recede as they allow us to lead a productive life.

As the design historian and theorist Louise Schouwenburg suggests, 'What makes conceptual use-objects so interesting is the tension between a certain disappearing into over familiar and reliable functionality while at the same time they make themselves subtly known by telling something about themselves.'[39] In late capitalism, the domestic becomes a gallery, just as the gallery has begun to draw upon the domestic and the everyday. However, this does not mean that the two have somehow merged or that there are no distinctions any more. A chair and a table may be shown in a gallery – but you couldn't go and live in it; the rituals of daily life may be played out in the gallery space, but only under certain circumstances.

Performative objects?

Bey's *Do Add* chair is certainly a performative object. The designer and commentator Kristina Niedderer has suggested that performative objects can act to raise consciousness, that in the baffling of straightforward utilitarian function it is possible to shock the user into a new form of mindset, that such interventions can cause us to think about our daily interactions with such things.[40] This would then be to understand performativity as a referring to the way in which the artefact could be said to act in an almost theatrical, more properly a performatory, sense, which would then be decoded by the user. It is to relate the concept to the use of alienation or shock tactics. Such an approach is discussed in detail in the next chapter, but it would suffice for the moment to say that this is not the way in which performativity is being discussed here. Rather the idea can be conceptualized in a different manner, as was outlined earlier, whereby it allows us to see the way in which an object such as Bey's chair can be said to be functioning in its relation to its place in the business of everyday life.

Performativity is a quality of all designed objects: it is not a specialized feature of some that have specifically been created to have an effect; it is a quality of all things as they function; it is concerned with the behaviour of objects, the totality of their actions and their power to animate subjects. As Judith Butler observes, in identifying ourselves as the one addressed in any interaction, recognition becomes constitution: 'the address animates the subject into existence.'[41] Thus, through their performativity, the things with which we live, far from simply reflecting some pre-existent selfhood, by a process of interpellation and incitement to discourse actually function to bring a certain form of subjectivity into being. Instead of being a specialized facet of a particular type of speech, or material activity as the speech act of the social, performative enunciations happen in ordinary circumstances, in the everyday. This is because performativity is at its most effective as an iterative form, one that emerges from the repeated processes of living with things as they enact their scripts in the everyday. That is to say it emerges from the repeated micro-modulations of affective response.

It is not necessary to alter a chair to turn it into a performative object. The simple fact of its existence means that it is affecting the user and acting to constitute their subjectivity, their sense of their place in the world, no matter what form it takes. So, if we take it seriously as a piece of functional design, rather than as simply a rhetorical object, a representation, or a visual joke, it can be seen that in the *Do Add* chair Bey is intervening in this process by altering the object's script, not to cause the user to reflect and decode the meaning of the piece as such, but rather to alter the affective potentiality of its functioning through the creation of an everyday use-object that is persistently incomplete.

Everyday play

Performativity is, therefore, an emergent quality of the relationship between subjects and objects, whereby entities act upon each other in their constitution. This should not be taken to suggest that the experiencing self is entirely constituted by discourse, material or otherwise, but that the intention of the subject and interpellation of the physical interact to create the tangible everyday world we inhabit. In this way, design is understood to be relational (a concept discussed in more detail in Chapter 6), in that it is brought into action by the participation of the actors involved. This, therefore, is to identify a point of intervention for the designer whereby the physical script of the object can be manipulated to affect its place in the broader ideological structures of the sociotechnical scripts in which it operates. That is to say form can be worked upon to alter the affective possibilities of the thing within particular cultural narratives and constellations of meaning. When practicing the rituals and iterations of everyday life, we do so to a large part through the medium of objects. We may have motivations and we may give meaning and emotional content to life, but it is through things that we exist in the world in a material way, and we experience the physical world on the level of affect.

In 2000, Jan Konings, Bey's former collaborator, was commissioned by Liudger Drachten School in the Netherlands to create benches for the grounds. The resultant designs took the conventional form of the bench and altered the performativity of the archetype in different ways. In the example shown (Figure 28), the seat is so narrow and the back at such a strange angle that it looks as though it would be very hard to sit on it comfortably. With another the seat is tilted, again making it appear that the object would be difficult to use. Konings relates that when the designs were shown to the school board, there was some degree of consternation as the benches seemed to have been made wilfully dysfunctional and uncomfortable. When the children were introduced to the seats, however, there was no such reserve. They immediately began to clamber about and find ways to sit on them (Figure 29).[42] They recognized what the designer had done: through subverting the typical form of the bench, he had created objects with more open-ended affordances that allowed them to be

Figure 28 Jan Konings, bench for Liudger Drachten School, 2000. Courtesy of the designer

Figure 29 Jan Konings, bench for Liudger Drachten School in use, 2000. Courtesy of the designer

creative in how they were used. That is, he had made things they could play with, and play allows for new forms of subjectivity to emerge.

The unusual form of the benches meant that there was no obvious way to use them. The children were forced to experiment and improvise to find ways to allow the object to come into use. Konings did not construct a game for the children. As Ben Matthews and his colleagues observe: 'It is difficult to conceive of games without rules: games, in order to be games, must be played in a certain way. They have a structure.' Games definitively contain a (usually explicit) script in Akrich's sense, whereas play can be said to be much broader and open than the game, in that 'play also can be the *suspension* of goal-directed activity (whereas most games trade on ultimate goals, winners and losers, etc.). Play can be for play's sake'.[43] This then is an important point in understanding the nature of emotive design. The fact that play can be non-instrumental, for nothing but itself, identifies it as a significant counter to the efficiency and goal-oriented nature of culture in consumer capitalism. It is not simply a pre-figuring site where the revolution can begin: it is already a space where we are free. In just the same way, the emotive in design, the stimulation of emotion for nothing but itself, is not just a reaction against the endless deployment of affect for commercial ends, as in marketing and branding, or the demand that everything should be rationally efficient (and therefore lucrative) that the mass-produced legacy of modernism stipulates, rather it is an effect that attests to the fact that feeling things is intrinsically valuable because it is part of what makes us human.

A similar effect can be seen in a design such as *This Is Rodeo*, by Ika Kuenzel (Figure 30). Here the affordances of a saddle have been harnessed to a chair,

Figure 30 Ika Kuenzel, *This Is Rodeo* chair, 2007. Courtesy of Carpenters Workshop Gallery

which is unstable and pitches when sat upon. The nature of such sitting has not been absolutely defined by the designer; possibilities of play have been made available. Play is often characterized as existing in opposition to earnest and productive activity. As Warren Motte observes, such a relationship is characteristically advanced as being isotopical and balanced, yet can actually be seen to be hierarchical and ideologically laden, in that 'the "earnest" is invested with meaning, importance, and value, while the "playful" is relegated to the domain of the trivial, the otiose, the supplementary'.[44] In this way, it is asserted that the real business of living is work, efficiency and, by implication, rationalized productivity; play may then be allowed outside of this zone of activity, but only if it supports the more valuable field of work. Indeed, even the cultural historian Johan Huizinga, who did much to popularize the notion that play is a part *of* culture, not something which arises *in* culture, asserted that play exists in opposition to ordinary life.[45] This was contested by Jacques Ehermann, who argues that play and the ludic impulse must be seen as very much a part of the texture of everyday existence.[46] In recent years, play has developed as a dominant metaphor in contemporary design whereby it has tended to be associated with a form of co-design whereby the active consumer or 'prosumer', in Alvin Toffler's famous designation, acts to 'complete' the artefact through use.[47]

An example of this can be seen in Marjin van der Poll's *Do Hit* chair (2000; Figure 31), also from the *Do* series. Here the chair arrives at the purchaser's home in the form of a sleek steel box, accompanied by a sledgehammer. The new owner must then smash the cube into the shape of the chair. This means that the object is completed by one explosive act of phallic power, which is then never repeated. The user is required to interact with the design to finish it, but the options are limited and are actually little different to the co-opting of the consumer to complete flat-pack furniture. Thus, such a conceptualization of play can be said to still be very much within a teleological model of design as serving the needs of consumer capitalism as a sociotechnical script, in that the performativity of the object is still constructed in such a way that play actually serves the efficient functioning of the artefact through the involvement of the consumer as they react 'correctly' to stimuli.[48] Conversely, designs such as Bey's, Koning's and Keunzel's present the notion of play as being valuable in and of itself, in that the act of material interpellation acts to require the user to find, recognize and create scripts of their own, to emerge as a self, rather than be constituted as one.

With the playground furniture, rather than simply offering an opportunity to sit down and momentarily cease play, Konings has created things that offer

Figure 31 Marijn van der Poll, *Do Hit* chair, 2000. © Bianca Pilet

the possibility of sitting *as* play. He has not stipulated a way of sitting; the script is unclear, thus, the content of the interpellative utterance is ambiguous. Keunzels's piece operates in the same way and, similarly, the very ludicrousness of Bey's intervention means that the efficient affordances of the original chair are frustrated in such a way as to mean that the user is prevented from following the usual sociotechnical script associated with such things. They cannot adopt the conventional instrumental relationship to a chair; instead, they are required to become inventive in how it is used. In this way, such design works refuse the boundary between, and the mutual exclusivity of, the two categories of play and not-play.

Use values

If Madonna had sat on Lohmann's *Cow Bench*, it would have been a very different video. This may not seem impossible now, but in 1993, the *Lockheed Lounge* represented just the right mixture of elegance, exclusivity and fantasy to serve her image-projection at the time. The *Lockheed*, therefore, acted as an expression of an intersection of particular economies of design that was only to intensify for things made after the advent of mass internet use and the expansion of reproductive technologies. That is to say, all designed objects come to be ascribed a certain value as they move through particular mechanisms of exchange, and this can be seen to be writ large in the cultural event that is the *Lockheed Lounge*. The object has become a celebrity, it has character and a place in the emotional economy of things that mean something to us.

This is, therefore, the process whereby the strange and emotionally laden design of the early twenty-first century has come to be seen as valuable. Such objects are commodities (or can be discussed as such) and therefore it is necessary to understand how monetary exchange determines one form of value; they are also increasingly seen as culturally significant, not least because they are now worth so much in monetary terms. Also, these things have risen to a certain prominence at a specific time in history when we have an unprecedented access to cultural information whereby a form of symbolic exchange is possible, which means that this must be factored in. Finally, the way in which monetary exchange value, cultural exchange value and symbolic exchange value interact to construct the possibilities of the economy of subjectivity must be accounted for.

Pieces such as Bey's *Do Add* chair, or Koning's benches, in being presented as design, as functional things for use rather than being simply a visual joke or a one-off gag, actually suggest a way in which the designer can intervene in the object to alter its physical script and therefore its performativity. They cannot completely control this, of course, but they can affect it. With Bey's creation, rather than transmuting the object into art, as Duchamp did, or convulsing the object into a performatory thing, as Neidderer suggests, what Bey has created is an object which, as with Koning's benches, or Kuenzel's seat, necessitates experiment and play through the very ambiguity of its affordances and material script. In this way, the performative nature of the piece has been shifted from the realm of efficiency to that of the ludic. It is still a performative object, as all things are, yet in Bey's chair a clear act of interpellation, the café or dining chair which tells us to sit in a certain manner, has been rendered absurd by the negation of its practical functionality. The alteration of its physicality has changed how it can exist in the broader sociotechnical script. This could then be compared to practices that only require a fictional idea of use, where rhetoricality suggests a more cerebral engagement. But would this be as powerful?

The *Do Add* chair is an incitement to slapstick, bringing play into a conventional and often mundane relationship and opening up the range of possibilities for the constitution of subjectivity. Therefore, in a culture whereby things are presented to us as 'complete', the creation of a radically incomplete object is a refutation of the dominance of the finished commodity; it is a refusal of the sociotechnical script of efficiency. This is not through the sterile form of the prosumer, who is actually the user co-opted into an extended goal-orientated mode of consumerist manufacture, but through a command to create a way in which the apparently broken or baffled can be made to be useful again. Duchamp's intervention discussed in Chapter 1 was titled *In Advance of a Broken Arm*. Therefore, it is forever caught in a position prior to use in temporal terms. It is metaphorically stopped; it always remains 'in advance' rather than projecting into future use. Bey's *Do Add* chair tells the user to *do* something, both in its title and in its physical script as manifested in its affordances, yet since this is design intended for use there is a question any potential user must answer, either discursively or through action: after it has been altered in this way, how could you live with such an object? That is, it is presented as the potential for action, which is then actualized through use, just as the user becomes a new form of subject in the act.

In the financial designation of how much these things are worth, how they function in a practical sense is irrelevant. How they operate symbolically is pertinent, in that it feeds into perceived value, but in terms of the market this has little to do with what things mean to individuals and everything to do with how a general economy of significance is established. Yet, to understand the value of a piece of design in this way is to ignore its most powerful effect, that of its performative effect as a working use-object.

Many of the things we use everyday seem to actively require our passivity. They have a tendency to appear finished or completed. The tropes of efficiency and functionalism that underpin the production of objects in a commodity-based culture leave little room for the user to actually interact with them beyond a relatively fixed and somewhat static conception of consumption. Therefore, objects such as these can be seen to offer an alternative, whereby through the alteration of the object's physicality a space is opened up in which the user is still interpellated into a subject position (as it can be argued that it is not possible to step out of the process) but that this role is one in which they are stimulated to become *as active* as the thing that is hailing them. Thus, a definite relationship between use, meaning and action has been established. If this is to be further explored, it would seem necessary to understand how approaches such as Critical and Speculative Design have attempted to work through such problems through in practice.

5

Rhetorical devices and lyrical things

What has come to be known as Critical and Speculative Design is an approach to the creation of artefacts that is less concerned with making actual functioning objects and more centred upon the creation of propositions, fictional prototypes and scenarios that are presented to the public to produce a reaction and spark debate, or allow for further exploration of design as a practice. Recently, a great deal has been written about this subject, and the intention here is not to try to cover all of this ground.[1] Rather, this chapter is concerned with mapping out one small current in this rapidly developing field.

It is not enough to simply state the intended effect of a piece of work. Without getting into the minutiae of Barthes's discussion about the author's health,[2] it seems fair to suggest that at the very least any designed object must be set up to generate the projected outcomes. That is to say, if a work is to be defined as having the potential to disrupt the status quo, then it must demonstrably have qualities that are capable of doing this. Walter Benjamin argues that two key issues must be understood if we are to position creative work politically.[3] These are 'tendency' and 'technique'. His point is that what matters about what somebody makes or brings into being is where it can be located in the process of production, how it can be seen as relating to power and, therefore, what radical or progressive potential it might have. Thus, tendency is the political orientation of the work, what it is meant to do, and technique is the manner in which the author attempts to do this, their methodology and means. Crucially, Benjamin argues that the positioning of an author's output then depends upon the relationship between the two, how they interact to create the effect of the piece. When applying this to the field of critical and speculative practice, and placing this in a larger economy of emotive design, it starts to become clear that amongst the myriad different forms that are developing two types of technique are apparent, which relate to differing tendencies as forms of practice: that of a rhetorical methodology based on theories about logos, meant to persuade; and a more poetic approach, which does draw from the power of pathos, in that it is experimenting with affective responses to things, but that is less about persuasion than it is concerned with an altered idea of what use might look like.

When rhetoric is mentioned in the context of Critical Design, it is usually to refer to a putative or 'rhetorical' user of such imagined things. This is the idea that when designers create products that cannot be used, either because they do not actually function or because they are presented in an exhibition, that the viewer can imagine using them, or picture others doing so.[4] In this way, the 'user' does not really exist (because the thing cannot be used), so is established as a rhetorical device. However, the intention in this chapter is first to consider critical and speculative methods as rhetorical practice more fully. Rhetoric relies on three modes of persuasion: logos, ethos and pathos.[5] Logos is the appeal to logic, the suggestion that the person being addressed should consider the facts of the situation, observe data and come to a rational conclusion based on the facts. The word ethos comes from the Greek for 'character', and is concerned with ethics, the underlying beliefs and ideals of what is being presented, as understood to be expressing those of the author. Pathos is an appeal to emotion.

The contention here is that the critical form of design has developed as a response to the dominance in design practice of the rhetoric of user centredness and the consumer/user that this approach relies upon. Thus, by showing how different approaches to criticality and alternatives to the mainstream relate to rhetorical methods, the intention is to show how they function both within the discourse of design and in relation to the wider world. In the second part of the chapter, a different type of criticality and speculation is considered. In these works, that are more concerned with the use of artefacts and their deployment in everyday life, it is argued that a form of poetic practice is being employed. Though this approach also has its weaknesses, it is argued that in such practice there are exciting glimmers of possibility for what it may mean to be an author in design in the coming age.

Becoming critical

For those who came of age before the informational revolution, it can be difficult to explain to people who have grown up with smartphones, social media and Google Earth, that until very recently knowledge of the world beyond the immediately proximate was very hard won. In the 1980s, for much of the UK population, even near neighbours such as France and Spain could seem impossibly exotic. Just to see photographs of such places you would need to look at a book or a magazine, and if you could not access such things, you could not see the picture. A documentary might be on television, but if you were not in to watch it as it aired, you would miss it completely. A friend might tape it for you if they had a video recorder, but they would still need to be there to press record (all videos had timers; nobody knew how to work them). The world beyond what was closest was difficult to access and other cultures and ways of being were alien in a way that is now hard to grasp.

Neuromancer, William Gibson's 1984 genre-defining cyberpunk science fiction novel is set in an extrapolated near future where technology is being assimilated into the human body whilst consciousness flows out into the matrix. That a lot of the action takes place in an imagined future Japan was no arbitrary choice. Even now, for Westerners, seeing Japan for the first time can feel like having seen the future, particularly when experiencing the accelerated and cacophonous reality of Tokyo. When Anthony Dunne arrived there in the late 1980s, having just graduated in Industrial Design at the RCA, it must have been a profound culture shock. As one of only two non-Japanese staff working at the Sony Corporation's Design Centre in Tokyo, he must have felt like he was at the centre of a shift in what it means to be human. Here he would have seen a culture in the full flow of accelerated technological change, at the same time as the strangely familiar exoticism of Japanese culture and its ability to absorb technology into everyday life clearly had a profound effect upon his understanding of the nature of product design and the possibilities for its development.

It is still exciting to read *Hertzian Tales*, the book that came from Dunne's PhD, completed at the RCA after his return from Japan. Here, in the newly formed Computer Related Design (CRD) unit, he worked with Fiona Raby, who had studied architecture, and together they were founding members of the Critical Design unit within the CRD programme. The book based on his thesis fizzes with the possibilities of design in the face of the new electronic world. In it he argues that design can be a medium for understanding the profound changes in human culture that he saw happening, as electronic devices were becoming increasingly embedded into everyday life and woven into sociality and people's sense of themselves. He refers to the ideas of Ezio Manzini, in suggesting that the days of the design visionary were over, that a weariness with utopian thinking had set in and it was now the role of designer to imagine a range of alternatives, thus enabling a form of democratic choice between different futures.[6] Referring to theorists such as Baudrillard, and his examination of the way in which our relationship to technology and ideas about the stability of truth were changing,

Dunne suggests that 'like J.G. Ballard's writer' the designer 'no longer knows anything for certain' and 'all he or she can offer are the contents of his or her own head, where internal imagination meets the external world of reality'. Thus, the intention at this point was to 'mix criticism with optimism to provide the "complicated pleasure" found in other imaginative media such as film and literature'.[7] This was then to argue for a conception of the designer as an author, somebody who did not simply respond to a brief, but would set their own agenda and work out not just how to answer a question, but to establish what questions were being asked.

Fundamental to Dunne's critique in *Hertzian Tales* is a problematization of the user as the central focus of design. Until 1988, Bruce Archer had been Director of Research at the RCA. Pursuing the agenda of design as a systematic method, Archer defined research in the field as scientific and highly schematized process that was meant to produce the most efficient result by a concentration on the nature of the problem and the needs of the user. It was to a large degree this stance that Dunne was reacting against in his argument for authorial design. 'User friendliness', he argues, helps normalize the values embodied in products, and we 'unwittingly adopt roles created by the human factors specialists of large corporations'.[8] In *Hertzian Tales*, the user-centred problem-solving approach to design is characterized as the adoption of an instrumentally rational stance that seeks to service the needs of users, which in a world of corporations and monopoly capitalism functions to essentially construct the very subjects it was meant to serve.

It seems important in any assessment of Critical Design, to bear in mind that this was, initially at least, one thing they were being critical of. Though in *Hertzian Tales* and the later works Dunne and Raby are quite explicit that their tactics are not derived directly from Critical Theory, it is clear that to some degree their method owes a debt to the work of writers such as Adorno and Horkheimer, Lukács and Benjamin, in their refusal to accept the status quo and their adoption of a questioning attitude meant to change things. Similarly, the work of Shklovsky is directly referenced, and Dunne makes an appeal to the 'alienation effect' employed by Brecht to make viewers 'aware that the institutions and social formulae they inherit are not eternal and natural but historical and man-made, and so capable of change through human action'.[9] This early work in particular is clearly intended to make the viewer think about the 'affirmative' nature of the optimization process in design. Thus, Critical Design was, certainly at this stage, meant to be oppositional in nature.

In the 2001 work co-authored with Fiona Raby, *Design Noir: The Secret Life of Electronic Objects*, they outline a method that describes the creation of aesthetic prototypes and design propositions and proposals that are intended to 'ask carefully crafted questions'.[10] Rejecting the dictates of the commercial design world and the mainstream 'affirmative' design they saw around them, the methodology laid out by Dunne and Raby suggests that design need not only serve as a handmaiden to industrial production, as it largely had up until this point, but could also operate as a site of dissent and criticality. The intention was not to make straightforward useable products, but to create difficult, baffling propositions for everyday use objects that were believable enough to register as design, but strange enough to make people reflect upon the nature of what they were looking at. Thus, these were not meant to be objects intended for production, but instead they were meant to 'stimulate reflection'. In this way, they were intended to be 'products of the mind'.[11] And so they were clearly appealing to the way that design can function as an argument, as a provocation that can provide a basis for thought and logical consideration.

As is clear from the titles of the books, at this early stage the focus was very definitely upon electronic products and objects. This interest was prompted by a desire to understand how the coming age of technological devices was going to necessarily disrupt our relationship to the physical world and alter the nature of product design. Yet, at this point, for all their social focus, it is the physical device as radiating object that really seems to exercise them more than anything else. Throughout *Hertzian Tales* and *Design Noir*, one thing that is noticeable is the extent to which Dunne and Raby are concerned with the electromagnetic radiation that electronic products produce, a physical field that they call 'hertzian space'.[12]

Now, from the perspective of a culture that is almost entirely constituted by the interwoven threads of digital communication, it is striking the extent to which this aspect of the effects of technology is absent from Dunne and Raby's critique at this point. They appear more concerned with the thing, the nature of the electronic object itself and the human relationship to it, than the flows of culture that such devices facilitate. The constant references to the patterns of electromagnetic radiation and the bleeding fields of electronic products seem to represent a reinscription of the aura of the object. Their interest in such electrical phenomena seems, well, static. In a world that was becoming virtual, Dunne and Raby's approach at the turn of the century seems to have been very tangible, concerned with the matter of such developments. This is not to say that they ignore subjectivities, as the nature of 'conceptual products' is rooted in the way they fuse 'complex narratives with everyday life',[13] they argue, but there still seems to be something of an obsession at this point with electromagnetic radiation. That is, they say that if cyberspace 'describes what lies beyond the screen', then hertzian space 'describes what happens in front of the screen' in that 'it is part of the space our bodies inhabit, even though our senses detect only a tiny part of it'.[14] In an age where Wi-Fi is starting to come to be regarded as some kind of human right and we exist daily in a space that is entirely hertzian, perhaps then this is to remember that there was a time when this was not the case, when critics had to use things to point it out, and people were not so dependent upon it that alternatives might have been possible.

One of the first material experiments created by Dunne in the process that fed into *Hertzian Tales* was *The Pillow*, shown as part of the 'Monitor as Material' exhibition, an LG Electronics exhibit at the RCA in 1997. This was an LCD screen encased in a transparent resin block, which was mounted into a clear plastic pillow. Configured to pick up local environmental electromagnetic radiation given off by electronic devices, the lights in the piece were meant to 'reflect television signals, radio, cell phones, even viewers' electromagnetic fields, allowing the object to become a kind of window onto this invisible world'.[15] In an essay written with Bill Gaver, a fellow member of the CRD who had come to the RCA after a brief stint working as a researcher for Apple, they explain that *The Pillow* was to be understood as a new category of designed object, a 'value fiction', in that 'in much science fiction, ideas emerge from imagining impossible technologies in recognizable cultures. In a value fiction, ideas come from imagining possible products, based on existing technologies, and trying to understand why they would not work in our current culture.' They suggest that the reason that such a device is not realizable is not because of technical or economic factors, but because current cultural values would render it impossible. They then propose that 'insofar as the Pillow is perceived as impractical, this prompts questions about what we do think is practical or useful'.[16] They, therefore, suggest that the key question such an object raises is 'why not?' That is to say, this was dialectical practice, in that the form and the functionality of the exhibit were intended to show the inherent contradictions that such a piece of kit would present.

The object was meant to act as a challenge to the norms of design at this time, in relation to ideas of usefulness, and what practicality might be. Yet, the way it is couched is as though such relationships are essentially logical, that the response to such implausibility is a rational questioning. This then is an appeal to logos, to logic. It is to suggest that in encountering such disjuncture the main reaction will be one of reasoned questioning. This may take place, but arguably this will inevitably occur in the context of an emotional reaction. That is, in experiencing an affective alteration the viewer of any such work will necessarily appraise the nature of such a shift and interpret it as an emotional reaction, within which rational assessment will take place.

The approach adopted in the *The Pillow* was the methodology that Dunne first examined in *Hertzian Tales* and then elaborated in *Design Noir*: the creation of objects based on 'what ifs' rather than the making of things meant to solve problems. In a project such as Dunne and Raby's *Placebo* series, the results of which were presented in *Design Noir*, the intention was to attempt to take what they described as 'conceptual products' out of the gallery and into everyday life. Through the production of eight prototypes, which were then placed in the homes of volunteers, they used the objects to explore people's experiences of electromagnetic fields in the domestic setting. After the respondents had lived with the artefacts for some time, they were interviewed and their stories recorded. Photographs were also taken of the things in action. The intention was not, then, to see how the things 'worked' or even if they worked, but to understand user experience in a more narrative sense.[17] That is, this was not user testing, it was not meant to create a more efficient tool of any kind, it was to try to understand how people react to such things on an experiential level.

One thing that is noticeable about photographs produced for the *Placebo* project now is how they look like images from a distant past. In the picture that shows the *Compass Table* in use, a person sits writing (Figure 32). Next to her somebody holds a hairdrier, which we are surely meant to understand is turned on and to some degree affecting the numerous compasses embedded in the table top. Behind her is a television set standing on a video recorder, and a compact stereo and speakers. The television is a cathode ray portable, a black cube with a screen that is tiny by today's standards, but the whole thing is bulky and cumbersome all the same. The stereo, being a small CD player would have been quite advanced at the time, though in the front we see a cassette tape deck. The TV is linked to an indoor aerial, which stands on the shelves above. Even if it did not count as state-of-the-art equipment, when the photograph was taken all of this would have appeared at least unremarkable, everyday technology. From the perspective of twenty years later, these devices look archaic, which dates the photograph, particularly as this image was being used at the time to locate a prototype that was meant to be interacting with a new way of living. This then demonstrates a problem that Dunne and Raby have had to contend with since

Figure 32 *Compass Table* photograph from the *Placebo Series*, from Dunne and Raby, *Design Noir*, 2001. Photo: Jason Evans. Image courtesy of the designers

they started working in the field of design and change. At the beginning of the new millennium, they were some of the first people to observe that life was going to alter quite radically because of the way electronic equipment was coming to be folded into everyday life. However, if your practice is going to deal with the material politics of the near future, you are always going to have to run pretty fast to stay ahead of what is being critiqued. This would always have been true in modernity, and would have been difficult in any time. In the past thirty years, things have speeded up to such an extent that even the recent past can look like a distant and antediluvian scenario.

The more anthropological approach was not one that Dunne and Raby pursued with any vigour. After *Design Noir*, their practice became even more gallery based, as they eschewed everyday life experiments as overemphasizing context at the expense of their material value fictions. This seems to suit their intentions. In the presentation of carefully staged scenarios, their work appears primarily intended to make statements, even if these were then intended to 'ask questions'. There is little room for interaction from the user, who is essentially rhetorical, in that we are meant to imagine them, or empathize with their subject position. Yet such a figure is in no way neutral. In the manner that Dunne and Raby's work constructs this mythical subject, a certain form of rhetoric is being employed.

In the introduction to the 2009 exhibition 'What If' held at the Science Gallery in Dublin, which showed works mainly created by students under their tutelage at the RCA, Dunne and Raby suggest that discussion about social issues usually casts us as 'citizens'. However, they note, 'It is only when products are bought that they enter everyday life and have an effect. The act of buying determines the future.' In this way Dunne and Raby's user is quite definitely a consumer, and they observe that it is in this role that 'we help reality take shape'.[18] This then is not to cast the user as a rational entity that is responding to 'carefully crafted questions' at all. It is more to see this person as the subject of advertising messages and the consumption of pleasurable products than as a rational actor. As the social critic Don Slater observes, such consumption 'is about feeling, imaginative desiring and longing rather than reason'.[19] Just as the advertising idiom presents tendentious statements meant to persuade as though they were information, so it seems that in design's critical form what began as a genuine effort to confront the status quo through practice is gently subsiding into an alternative form of consumerism, based in just the economy of desire and consumerist prefiguration it was meant to critique.

Fictional functions

In 2009, Julian Bleecker of the San Francisco-based company Near Future Laboratory wrote an essay about what he called 'design fictions'. Curiously, although referenced, he does not really discuss the work of Dunne and Raby. Instead, he argued for an approach to design that would address the near future, but through methodologies more clearly akin to that of film and sequential narrative. He suggests that a design fiction is a hybrid practice that exists somewhere 'between science fact and science fiction', which is capable of exploring ideas by 'telling stories through objects', which are for him 'conversation pieces in a very real sense'.[20] In explaining how this is possible, he talks about an idea drawn from the theorist David Kirby, that of the 'diegetic prototype'. These are things that exist within the reality of a narrative, the 'diegesis', the props that are accepted by the characters as simply being part of the world they inhabit. In explaining this, he talks about a key scene at the beginning of the 2002 film *Minority Report*, where we see Tom Cruise, playing future cop John Anderton, standing in front of a large transparent visual display, on which data moves and flows in volumetric space, apparently manipulated by hand gestures communicated by special gloves. The production designer Alex McDowell reports that the director, Steven Spielberg, had said that he did not want to make a 'science fiction film', but rather one about 'a future reality'. This McDowell suggests meant that they needed to conduct 'a whole other kind of research'.[21] In order to attain some form of verisimilitude, the interface and the overall physical reality of the film was developed by researchers and designers from industry rather than set designers. The intention was to make a best guess at technologies that could happen – drawing from what was already possible and approaches that were actually in development at the time. As part of the team working on the film, the interface designer John Underkoffler brought to the project his research into how humans interact using gestures. The intention was to develop not just the most realistic version of a computer interface, but the most probable one. Consequently, they created a spatial interface based on a vocabulary of gestures, which they called the 'g-speak Spatial Operating Environment'.[22]

Bleecker notes that such diegetic prototypes are treated as if what was being designed were not only physical propositions but also real objects that could become part of 'everyday life' in the diegesis. According to Kirby, such diegetic prototypes have what he calls a 'rhetorical advantage' over actual material prototypes, in that in the fictional world of the film 'these technologies exist as "real" objects that function properly and which people actually use', within that scenario.[23] To such ends, Kirby describes such fictional prototypes as 'performative artefacts' as well as discussing the role of prototypes in helping contextualize technologies within the social sphere.[24] Thus, Bleecker argues that to attain 'cultural legibility takes more than a scientist demonstrating an idea in a laboratory. What is needed is a broader, context – such as one that great storytellers and great filmmakers can put together into a popular film, with an engaging narrative and some cool gear'.[25] This, however, would seem to be the problem. There is an ideological quality to what is being done. This is rhetorical design not only in that it is 'making a point', or being discursive. It also acts to persuade, to make normal what is presented. In this way, they certainly are performative artefacts, meant to alter reality and not just to reflect it, and this is here being achieved through pathos, an appeal to the emotions. Bleecker is unashamedly commercial in his outlook. He suggests that what he proposes can be 'a way of enhancing the corporate imagination', which certainly seems a long way from the criticality that Dunne and Raby were suggesting in 2001, even if it seems closer to the position they appear to be approaching.

In their 2013 book *Speculative Everything*, which is in many ways an oblique repost to Bleecker's essay, Dunne and Raby directly suggest that their methods are to some degree congruent with the ideas of Kirby. They propose a way of understanding what they describe as the speculative approach to design whereby the objects presented can be understood as 'props for nonexistent films',[26] meant to allow the viewer to imagine their own 'version of the world' to which the thing belongs. Yet, as Dunne and Raby observed some years before in *Design Noir*, there is something of a conceptual and aesthetic balancing act required in the creation of such works, since 'if they are too realistic – that is if they look as they really should be used – objects like this can quickly become ridiculous'. So, the suggestion is that the slightly abstracted nature of work that Dunne and Raby advocate, they believe 'signals that they are intended to be used in the imagination'.[27] As they articulate the basis for what they describe as Speculative Design, this distinction is then important in showing the difference between filmic diegesis and what they claim as actual design practice since they suggest that

> The objects used in design speculations can extend beyond a filmic support function and break away from clichéd visual languages that prop designers are often obliged to use. Yes, it makes reading the objects more difficult but this process of mental interaction is important for encouraging the viewer to actively engage with the design rather than passively consuming it.[28]

Bleecker has suggested that such active engagement can then be captured and used in a quite programmatic way. Thus, for him, the point is not that something like the computer interface in *Minority Report* should serve as a 'canonical origin story for gesture interaction', but rather that such a representation can be 'a powerful, gravity-like force providing a reference point through which science fact and science fiction swap properties', so that 'the film is what gives some sense to a curious speculation that says, in the future people will be flapping their arms around to interact with computers'.[29] This would seem to be precisely the issue. Jaron Lanier is a computer scientist and virtual reality pioneer who also attended the *Minority Report* development sessions. It was him who brought along the glove upon which Anderton's was based, which, he points out, would be very difficult to make work in reality[30] (as has proven to be the case). He notes that manipulating anything in volumetric space without haptic push back from the object is difficult to maintain, and the pose that Anderton adopts would be very painful to hold for any length of time. Arguably what viewers, particularly the more tech-minded, were reacting to was the emotional quality of Cruise's performance as a cop using a computer. Perhaps it was the actor's heroic stance (much better than hunching over a keyboard), that appealed to young men who wanted computers to be cool, rather than anything it said about the manipulation of data.

Movies are highly charged emotive narrative devices. It may be that this is not the best place to test out what we should be doing in the design of everyday life. As Dunne and Raby observe, films require us to empathize with the protagonist, and they require little effort to interact with 'because we are immersed in a high-resolution world designed to push our emotional buttons'.[31]

If the protagonist with whom we are entering into an emotional compact is essentially cast as a consumer, then this is the subject position we will be working from. The intention may be to stimulate reasoned reaction, and this can of course happen, but it will take place in an emotional context of a specific type.

That is to say, because we react emotionally to film, it can be a very poor place to imagine new worlds. If we do, it can be that the main effect is to project the values of today into the future in such a way that it suggests the eternal nature of a politics and philosophy that dominate at the present time.[32]

That the interface in the movie would not work in quite the way that Cruise makes it appear is perhaps not the point. It certainly stimulated discussion. Underkoffler presented a TED talk in 2010 demonstrating the technology in reality. It is interesting to compare his physical posture in doing so to that of Anderton in the film. Underkoffler is more rocked back on his hips than the actor, most actions are performed with one hand, controlled and measured. It just doesn't look as cool. Reading the comments beneath the video is illuminating. Some are saying 'This would never work' – others 'This is the future' and 'What about when the automobile came, nobody saw its potential' and so on.[33] The fictional, through conjoining with the imagined real, becomes part of our habitus. To make hard distinctions between fictions and the real is to misrecognize how we conceptualize reality. According to Kirby, Underkoffler does not just want to make believable films. Rather, his goal is to create believable fictional designs that enter into the wider 'technological imaginative vernacular'.[34] This is then different to making designs that spark debate. It is about shaping what we believe to be possible, plausible and potentially real. Where and how this takes place is then very important, since it is a deeply political practice.

Neuromancer, Gibson's sci-fi fantasy mentioned at the beginning of this chapter, is perhaps a telling example here. In the 1980s and 1990s, this became an ur-text of technophiles, as they reacted to its depiction of a world where technology and biology were merging. In his memoir, Lanier describes how they were 'blown away' by Gibson's depiction of the computational revolution.[35] In *Design Fictions*, Bleecker tells how when he was first working with virtual technologies there was an absence of contextualizing literature. In the circumstances, he explains, science fiction came to fill in the gap, so that there could be mutual reference points. He suggests that 'the objects that authors like William Gibson craft through words are kinds of designed objects that help fill out the vision, inciting conversations, providing backdrops, set pieces and props'.[36] They can also begin to make things look normal, natural and inevitable.

For all the adoration that is heaped upon *Neuromancer*, it should be remembered that it is a darkly dystopian story. It is not a future many people would want, unless, perhaps they were a lonely kid who was into computers and wanted them to become less nerdish in the popular imagination. However, through this yearning, it seems that people have been working to make things in such fictions a reality. The emotional pull of narrative has rendered such imaginings more possible. If the realm of the fictional and the practice of design are to be drawn closer (as is perhaps inevitable), it must then require a discussion about how this should happen, in what contexts, and to what ends. *Minority Report* is also a darkly distressing tale, where 'pre-crime' allows people to be arrested before they have actually done anything wrong. Is this a future we crave? In the film the offices of the police are styled to appear to be a corporate headquarters. This then suggests a bleakly neoliberal future that will be more attractive to some than others. Baudrillard described a world where representation was coming adrift from its referents, so that we were coming to float in a sea of simulacra.[37] As has been noted, when he first started discussing this, it was seen as speculation, now it is manifestly the case. Yes, design fictions can make things more possible, but this suggests an ethical question of what we should be imagining into being, by what methods, and to what ends.

If, as we have seen, speculation and criticality always take place in a context that is, if not entirely determined by emotion (since rational reaction does of course take place and clearly has a part to play), but where the setting of such background tone does serve to establish the parameters of possibility, then how this is managed seems to be a crucial question. One way that this is achieved is by the framing of such work, its placing in a context through a specified metanarrative device that marks it as fictional. In this way, the viewer knows what they are looking at and can calibrate their emotional and logical reaction accordingly. However, as has been discussed, in a world of moving objects, this is becoming an increasingly tricky proposition.

A false tooth

In late spring of 2002, the media was briefly abuzz about a new invention. The images showed a tooth cast in clear resin, which contained a microprocessor. This was the 'Tooth Phone', a tiny telephone receiver that could be implanted into a person's mouth. Though widely referred to as a 'protoype', in a 'Gee whizz, whatever next?!' kind of way, the reports presented this as a product that would fairly soon be commercially available. CBS news reported that its designers were working with the Massachusetts Institute of Technology Media Lab to create a viable version.[38] In November 2002, it appeared on the cover of *Time* magazine. *New Scientist* quoted one of the creators as stating that they were 'looking at commercial uses' for those who may wish to listen to traffic data or stock information.[39]

In an article titled 'Excuse Me Is Your Tooth Ringing?', the tech magazine *Wired* reported that an exhibition at the Science Museum was showing a 'design for a tooth implant that receives digital signals from radios and mobile phones'. Rather breathlessly, the piece reported that 'a micro-vibration device and a wireless receiver is implanted into a natural tooth during routine dental surgery. Sounds are transferred from the tooth into the inner ear by bone resonance (digital signals being converted into audio).' It then went on to reassure readers that for those who might be worried about 'a buzzing mouth', 'sound reception is assured to be totally discreet'. The piece then confidently asserted that 'with health issues being minimal, about the same as the issues raised by the use of mobile phones, the tooth is expected to be available in markets in the near future.'[40] Except it wasn't, because it didn't exist. The 'Tooth Phone' – more properly titled, *Audio Tooth Implant* – was a component from an old television set, mounted in a resin tooth (Figure 33). It was developed at the RCA as part of a Critical Design project by students of Dunne and Raby, James Auger and Jimmy Loizeau.

When the people at *Wired* discovered that the 'invention' they had reported on was in fact a prop to 'make people think' rather than a 'real' product, they were a bit upset. In a follow-up article in 2006 titled 'Lying through Their Teeth', simply attributed to 'Wired staff', the piece recounts how they felt they had been hoaxed. Evocatively suggesting that it was 'just before lunch one weekday afternoon in late spring 2002' when the makers of the 'Tooth Phone' decided

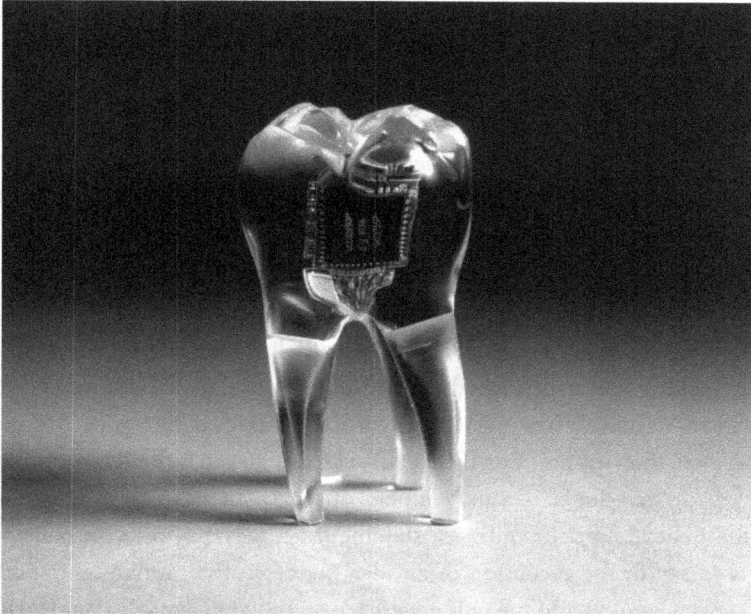

Figure 33 Auger and Loizeau, *Audio Tooth Implant*, 2002. Courtesy of the designers

to start 'lying' about what they had done. According to the piece, Auger and Loizeau had just finished a conversation with a reporter who had rather lost interest when it became clear that the implant was not an 'actual invention' but more of a proposal meant to stimulate discussion. It was at this point, the article suggests, that the designers thought maybe the trick was to 'make it seem a little more real' by allowing people to think that this was actually a viable product that was being shown.[41]

'We never imagined it would become quite as big as it did at the time,' Auger said. 'But if we look back at our original motivation it was a fantastic success.'[42] Yet this is questionable. If the purpose of Critical Design is to make people think about the issues raised, it may be perfectly possible to say that this had been effective. However, in that those seeing the device at this time were initially reacting to what they thought was a real piece of innovation they would have been reacting emotionally in a way very different to if they were seeing this piece in a gallery. As the second *Wired* article makes clear, people can become quite dismayed if they feel they are being deceived.

Sincerity matters in design. One of the reasons that we can accept 'diegetic' objects in film is because we conventionally ascribe a metanarrative frame to the experience. We know that the emotion we are feeling is 'real' in as much as it is experienced in the same way as other everyday emotions in the real world, but, as the sociologist Norbert Wiley notes, in a fictional scenario the emotion does different 'work'.[43] In receiving filmic emotion, we are aware that there is something on the screen and the world around it, this serves to frame the effect. Also, in actual everyday events, the individual is the subject in any emotional reaction, with fiction we register the fact that events are occurring to a character. As Wiley observes, the things depicted are 'only happening to you to the extent that you identify, empathize, sympathize, etc. with that character. Strong as they may be, these emotions are vicarious or "witness emotions"'.[44] Thus, through such knowledge, we can distance and contextualize the reaction we experience. Consequently, what is described as Critical or Speculative Design must do the same in its fictionalizing. As with the Tooth Phone, if this goes wrong or is misdirected, then the emotional effect of such design can be badly compromised.

As the psychologist Daniel Gilbert observes in his essay 'How Mental Systems Believe', understanding a statement actually begins with believing it. That is to say in the reception of an idea or scene, the human tendency is to first assess what it would mean if it were true. Only then can we decide whether to stop believing. This, he notes, is congruent with the way children come to understand the world, in that they react to things in a very credible manner. Thus, when we encounter a scenario, we believe it to be real *first* before thinking it through in any more depth. We do not consider it in detail, mull over its veracity and then believe. We accept it in the first instance, and then according to the context we assess it to be operating in, it is ascribed to a category of relation to the real.[45]

During fictional experience, people necessarily label the emotional content of the stimulus in order to allow it to have an effect, that is to say the content of the experience is categorized to allow for the 'modification of the emotional subjective response'.[46] This means that we are labelling the emotion to make sense of it – we are employing the regulation of emotion to order the world and our reaction to it. These are real feelings, but our reactions have developed to name and comprehend them. One way we do this is through association of the fiction with an author. It is the connection to the perceived origin of the message that guarantees the authenticity of the experience, despite its fictional nature. This is the rhetorical appeal to ethos, the ethics of the author. If the authorship is unclear, or the material becomes loose and untethered from its moorings, as happened with Auger and Loizeau's tooth, then we have trouble framing what we experience, of labelling it so that it is comprehensible and assimilable.

According to Foucault, this is the 'function' of authorship, the attribution of a perceived point of origin. It is something of a riposte to Barthes's observation, discussed in Chapter 2, that many agencies create a work.[47] Yes, says Foucault, but the author persists as a concept because it effectively works as an anchor for discourse, that through such an attribution we know where something is coming from, so to speak, and because of this can make the kind of categorizations discussed above. As Bruce and Stephanie Tharp argue, the effect of Barthes's decentring of the author does not diminish the usefulness in design of at the very least having some knowledge of the author's intentions.[48] As Foucault notes, to make sense of the meaning of texts we encounter, we essentially 'construct the rational entity we call an author', in order to give what we find unity and a sense of authenticity. He suggests that we ascertain this by asking, either explicitly or through how we relate to the work: 'What are the modes of existence of this discourse? Where does it come from; how is it circulated; who controls it? What placements are determined for possible subjects? Who can fulfill these diverse functions of the subject?'[49] In this way, the viewer/user can position the work. The tendency can be reconciled with the technique, or not as the case may be. The answers to these questions will then determine how we can place the encounter and how we feel about it. If we believe ourselves to be interacting on one set of terms, 'this is real product' and it then turns out that we were actually meeting the thing in quite another: 'this is an interesting fiction', there will be emotional fallout in the need to shift categories.

Shock tactics

To encounter a family member in hospital is always disconcerting and not a little disturbing. To find them at home hooked up to a sheep would be a shock. In their desire to provoke a reaction, many works developed under the banner of Critical or Speculative Design are often quite dark. In Revital Cohen's *Life Support* project of 2008, one of the photographs shows a man lying on a bed in a darkened room. From his arm emerges a flexible pipe, which loops down across the room to connect to a strange medical device. On a metal, clinical-looking trolley lies a lamb, which is also rigged up with tubing, so that a pump appears to be transfusing man and beast.

The educator and design critic Stephen Hayward suggests that the reaction to such an image is not '"I must have one of those", but "why do these images disturb, why is there a taboo around the mixing of species and could this aversion be overcome?"[50] Yet, this seems unlikely. Upon being disturbed the first effect cannot be a rational questioning of why this is. To be recognized as disturbing any reaction must first be appraised and brought into the emotional realm. That is to say there is a political process of naming, categorizing and assimilation that precedes any rational questioning: there must be because the subject of reflection, the disturbing nature of the event, can only be discerned once the emotional work of recognizing it has taken place.

Dunne and Raby argue in *Speculative Everything* that 'darkness as an antidote to naïve techno-utopianism can jolt people into action'.[51] This is an idea that Critical Design exponent Matt Malpass stresses: that Speculative Design can act as a form of alienation effect – meant to somehow allow the viewer to be shocked into consciousness.[52] The *verfremdungseffect* developed by Brecht in the 1930s was a technique for stage drama whereby certain incidents in the play were intended to be performed in such a way that they would 'alienate' or distance the viewer. This was then meant to prevent them from experiencing the work as though they were present at a real event. That is, the alienation effect was intended to shatter the illusion that what they were seeing was a part of the real world offered up to them. It was meant to make clear that what they were experiencing was drama, that this was artifice and therefore a constructed reality. By doing away with the fourth wall, directly addressing the audience, using banners and chants, this type of performance was meant to create a rupture in bourgeois culture and cultural reproduction, and allow the dialectical nature of the present to be revealed.[53]

This was a type of theatre then that attempted to show the artificiality of the form to shock the audience into consciousness to allow them to see the realities of their political circumstances. Benjamin was an enthusiastic supporter of Brecht's approach. He believed that the method of 'interruption' allowed for the empathic function of drama to be arrested, that through the shock of stopping the audience cannot help but be extracted from the position in which what is presented looks normal and natural, to then ask why this should be.[54] This does have clear parallels with Critical Design practice, where shocking or troubling elements are presented to cause the viewer to question what they are seeing, yet it is not clear that designed objects can quite be said to operate in the same manner as dramatic performance.

There are clear links here to the work of Shklovsky and the approach of 'making strange' discussed in Chapter 2,[55] yet, in the hands of Brecht, such alienation was primarily to be achieved through the manipulation of form to specific political ends. The effect is created by a formal anti-naturalism in the physicality of the performance that is meant to shock the viewer into consciousness. The person looking is jarred out of complacency by the way in which the thing is presented, not just by what is shown – the content of the work – but how it is offered up to the viewer.[56] As Dunne and Raby have noted, there is a delicate balancing act to be performed in the presentation of critical work. In the photographs of Cohen's speculations, if it is clear that it is a design proposal that is being represented the reaction may be a jolt that leads to questioning. This can be achieved in the gallery, or the lecture room. Yet, if the photographs begin to come loose on the internet, then it seems that quite another reaction is possible. If the author function is in any way destabilized then the position of the work may appear to change as the relationship between tendency and technique is muddled. With Critical Design the alienation effect, in its Brechtian sense, can only really operate if the conditions in which the object is encountered are carefully controlled. Otherwise there is the danger that the images created, or objects presented could be read as real. This then would not be to experience Brecht's alienation, that shock's the viewer into awareness, but perhaps to believe and begin to accept more in Bleecker's sense. As Cameron Tonkinwise asks, 'How does the experience move from an "is" to an "ought," from the affect of uncanniness to the question of whether what is represented is preferable or worrisome?'[57]

Brecht's alienation effect was to be experienced as an interruption, which would allow conscious reflection. This is actually in marked difference to Shklovsky's method that can be discerned in work that takes a more Design Art stance, which was intended to make the thing perceived strange in such a way that it was less normal, acceptable and recognizable, and therefore in further need of consideration through the senses. It is not meant to be a shock that jolts the viewer out of their habituated state, but a strangeness intended to expand, deepen and enliven the perceptual moment in such a way that the 'stoniness of the stone' can be appreciated more fully.[58] This was then not entirely a 'bringing into consciousness', as such, but rather a making more fully available to experience. The 2007 exhibition 'Designing Critical Design' held in Hasselt, Belgium, showed work by Dunne and Raby alongside that of former Droog designer Marti Guixé, and Studio Makkink & Bey. At this time, Bey and his partner were still being generally grouped with the critical tendency, yet it is interesting to see how their method differs from that of the other practitioners discussed here.

In the piece *Vacuum Cleaner Chair* (Figure 34), shown at the exhibition, the bag of a vacuum cleaner has been reformed in the shape of an easy chair. The principle, therefore, seems to be that as one vacuums so the bag will fill,

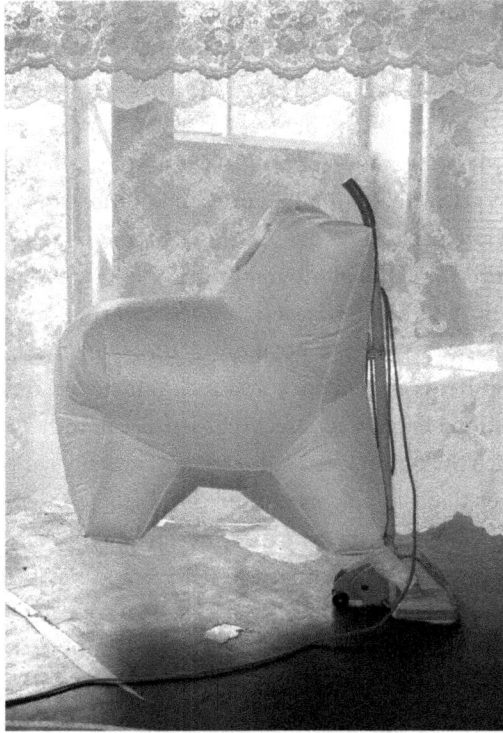

Figure 34 Studio Makkink & Bey, *Vacuum Cleaner Chair*, 2007. Courtesy of Studio Makkink & Bey

gradually stuffing a chair. The piece is preposterous. Yet, if you were to find it in a house, it would still be clear what it was. Here the meaning is embedded in the object, and the emotional reaction to the piece comes from the strangeness intrinsic to it. It does not rely on the context of the gallery to happen. With *Vacuum Cleaner Chair*, the thing can become part of everyday life in a way that does not demand this action, since the contradictions are structured within the object. What Benjamin believed eventually was at the basis of Brecht's interruption was then not the value of shock (though at the time he clearly saw this a viable strategy), but the organizational implications of such a method. He saw that it is in the practices of how we live, which need making strange so that we can see them, that change lies, as he notes that 'events are alterable not at their climaxes', that it is not by dramatic resolution and catharsis that we change how we live, but that such things are only alterable 'in their strictly habitual course'.[59] This is important because it starts to point to another kind of practice altogether.

Design poetics

In CNN news reports during the 2003 invasion of Iraq, the American public started to get to know a particular visual effect. The presenter Miles O'Brien would bring up a satellite image of the country and zoom in to see what was happening on the ground. This seemed like a startling ability, and viewers were excited by this god-like action. In 2004, the company that made this software was acquired by Google, and the package renamed Google Earth. Along with *Streetview*, Google Earth has allowed for a radical shift in how we conceptualize our world. Whereas, before its introduction if we were about to visit somewhere, we might buy a map and pore over it thinking about where we might go. Now we just enter the app and zoom in. Google Earth makes the world so much more available than the abstraction that paper maps provided. It is not just the information, the satellite images, that form the nature of the experience but the ease with which one may glide across the globe. Want to look at Central Park in New York? Here it is. Like to see how Widnes town centre has changed? It is there. Find yourself wishing to linger over the back garden of a house you once shared with that person who promised to be your life partner? Well, here it is (they've built an extension).

At around the same time that Google Earth was being developed, a group of researchers in the UK was creating the *Drift Table* (Figure 35). This was built

Figure 35 Interaction Research Studio, *Drift Table* in use, 2004. Courtesy of the Interaction Research Studio

by an early iteration of the Interaction Research Studio (IRS), a research group established by Bill Gaver and Andy Boucher amongst others, working at this time as part of the Equator Interdisciplinary Research Collaboration between the RCA, University College London, Lancaster University and the Royal Institute of Technology, Sweden. The project brought together interaction designers, computer scientists, and an ethnographer to work together to create a product that would be concerned with play in the home. The device they constructed is a coffee table with a small viewing port set at its centre, which shows a slowly changing aerial view of Britain. It is navigated by exerting pressure upon the surface of the table. This is achieved by pushing down on the table, or applying weights for a more sustained effect.

They did not want to make a device for efficient seeing; they intended to produce something to be played with, a speculative object that would allow new forms of interaction to emerge in its use. This was therefore the development of a poetics of design. This is an idea that designers Ralph Ball and Maxine Naylor have introduced, that design need not be about an instrumental solving of problems, but can be a more expansive practice that is more about an emotional or reflective reaction to manufactured goods than their efficient operation.[60] Although in Ball and Naylor's hands, the approach comes a little nearer to autonomous sculpture, the idea is useful here because it allows for a way of thinking about design that is meant to be more lyrical than functional in a utilitarian manner, or rhetorical in the way of more specifically critical or speculative approaches. In this context, 'lyrical' does not simply mean the personal expression of emotion, as it might in a romantic sense.[61] Drawing from Jonathan Culler, the intention is to see the lyrical quality of things as turning on their relationship to *rituality*, in terms of performance, iterability and discursive indirectness, and *event*, which is not narrative but temporally specific and performative.[62] That is to say, these things are not to be taken as mimetic, as reproducing part of the world for comment, but should rather be understood as being moments that have depth, meaning and resonance in their own right.

Initial research for the interaction project that was to become the *Drift Table* had suggested that people feel a need to escape the here and now, and one way they achieve this is through daydreaming and imagining other places. The designers cited one research subject lying staring at a fish tank, whilst another imagined his room to be a space ship. The idea of looking from a height was influenced by poetic notions of such practices, and the effect that such a vantage point can have on our ability to reflect. It is an abstraction, but also a real representation; it is the world seen from another angle. Another key influence was also the popular book of aerial photographs, published in 2000: *England: The Photographic Atlas.* This was the first time that people had had access to such imagery in a form that could be manipulated at will, and it caused quite a stir. The company behind it also then supplied the data upon which the *Drift Table* depended.[63]

The difficulty was in making a piece such as the *Drift Table* usable enough that it might be a satisfying experience, without overly determining what that would be. To such ends, because the aerial view at this time was essentially quite alien, the makers acknowledged that users would need some help with orientation, so a small text box was added, that would name the place being looked at any given time, whilst a reset button allowed the view to return to the default, which was directly above the user's home. These were then placed on the side of the device, to de-emphasize their role in the functionality of the table (Figure 36).

In this way, the people who made the *Drift Table* had created the potential for experience. The material affordances coded into the piece allowed for certain types of use, and mitigated against others. In order to understand how this could function, how it would be used, the table was then deployed in a real domestic environment. In a paper reporting the experiment, whereby a group of flatmates lived with the *Drift Table* for a six-week period, the researchers describe how the participants related to the piece. One key practice was clearly 'sightseeing',

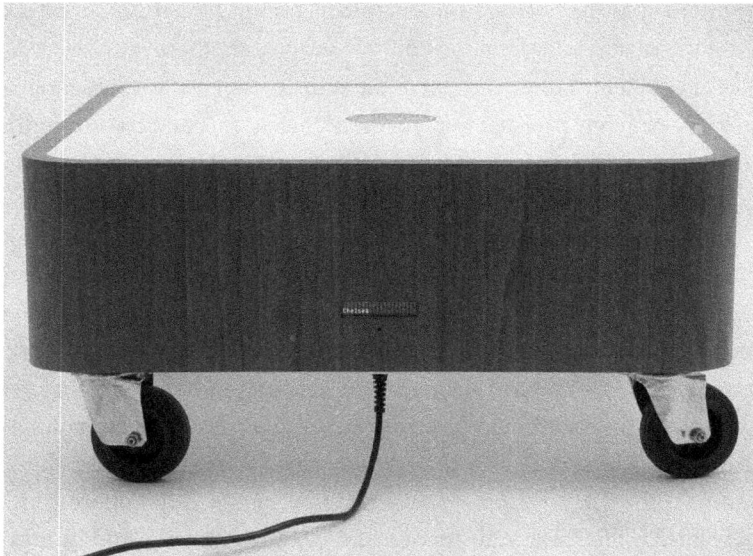

Figure 36 Interaction Research Studio, *Drift Table*, 2004. Courtesy of the Interaction Research Studio

steering the table to well-known locations that would be visible from the air; it was also common for the users to navigate to places that had personal meaning for them.[64] That they would do this again and again shows how such objects allow for the ritualizing of life: apparently 'useless' things, if they are meaningful enough, will begin to find their place in the patterns of life in their performance and iteration.

Thus, as with the playful objects discussed in the last chapter, the intention was to create ludic possibilities. This is to allow for an emotional opening up of subject–object interactions. What then is worth noting is the extent to which such devices have the potential to disrupt the smooth efficiency of much of the design, both tangible and intangible, with which we interact. In terms of utilitarian function, Google Earth does much the same thing as the *Drift Table*, but in a very different way. Because the information that Google Earth delivers to us comes to us through exactly the same route as everything else, through a screen, navigated by a simple intuitive interface, it becomes of the same order. Everything is of the same register of experience. In contrast, through the nature of the affordances and possibilities coded in, the *Drift Table* is materialized poetic possibility. In a very embodied way, it is a medium for play in a way that perhaps makes possible new affective relationships and interactions.

Through experiments such as this, from their base at Goldsmiths, University of London, Gaver and his colleagues in the IRS have been developing technological interventions that they say are intended to 'encourage playfulness, exploration and insight'.[65] Just as with Dunne and Raby's approach, there is no overt attempt to 'solve' a problem, rather the intention is to investigate areas of interest and concern by evolving projects and methodologies. In contrast to Dunne and Raby's later work, which appears finished, complete and only to be used in contemplation, the prototypes created at the IRS are intended to be deployed in everyday situations. This means that whilst the final results may be exhibited or reported through publication, a key part of their process is the requirement that volunteers live with what has been created to 'see how their experiences evolve'. This means that there is a distinctive use phase in the IRS approach, similar to that employed by Dunne and Raby in their early work, but which they seem to have subsequently abandoned in favour of a more museum and gallery-based practice. Thus, whilst the Critical Design approach has emphasized the 'asking of questions', the intervention strategy adopted by the IRS is more concerned with exploring the 'practical encounters' between people and things than creating stand-alone rhetorical work.[66] This allows for a poetics of interaction, the creation of events, which matter in their own functioning.

Figure 37 Interaction Research Studio, *History Tablecloth*, 2004. Courtesy of the Interaction Research Studio

History Tablecloth (Figure 37) is a large, flexible low-resolution display that can lie on a table, just like its title suggests. Protected by a sheet of glass, it has on it a lace-like pattern, reminiscent of doilies and tearooms. When things are left on the table, the pattern beneath the object begins to glow, creating a halo-like effect that slowly expands. When the objects are removed, the glow fades. Here in terms of aesthetics we see echoes of Makkink and Bey's *Linen-Cupboard House*. The archaic quality of the lace is at odds with the technological nature of the sensors and the glow. As the creators note, because it is not 'for' anything, because there is no 'problem' to be solved, the piece becomes emergent, 'the Tablecloth doesn't dictate peoples' reactions, it provides a situation for them to interpret.'[67] In this way, experiments such as this are beginning to deal with the way in which human–object relations are always in a state of becoming, they are concerned with the event nature of such encounters.

Referring to their experience of the tablecloth, a couple who had lived with it for a month talked of how fond of it they had become. 'It's like a cat', they explained. 'It reacts to you, but you can't tell what it will do.' That is, the object is displaying its agency, the experience exists in the in-between, and through the event of the object–person interaction a lyrical space opens up in such a way that new possibilities of action and meaning can come into being.

In this way, the team working at Goldsmiths have been developing an approach that is intended to design in what they refer to as 'ambiguity', which is meant, in their terms, to allow for the engagement of users 'without constraining how they respond.'[68] The concept of ambiguity was outlined in a 2003 paper, written as a collaboration between the IRS and the Mixed Reality Lab at the University of Nottingham, and has been conceptualized as an 'interpretative relationship between people and artefacts.' The suggestion was thus that this condition existed between the intentions of the designers and the state of the user. They argue that what they describe as 'things in themselves' are not to be understood as 'inherently ambiguous', but that this state actually arises in the interplay between the devised script and the interpretation of the user – whether this is semantically in explanation, or behaviourally through practical use. Here, therefore, it seems that ambiguity is to be identified in this disjuncture between intention and effect, which relates the issue back to Foucault's author function. They state that objects 'may give rise to multiple interpretations depending on their precision, consistency, and accuracy on the one hand, and the identity, motivations, and expectations of an interpreter on the other.'[69] Yet, terms like 'precision, consistency, and accuracy' do rather suggest a sense that there is a 'right' way to address the user – to script in such a way that the 'correct' effect can be established. This is perhaps a corollary of the field in which this approach has developed, that of technological systems defined by ideas of usability. The hold of the protocols of Human Computer Interactions approaches, based in ideas of usability, is strong.

This tension is demonstrated in a piece such as *The Light Collector*, developed by the IRS in 2011 as part of the *Indoor Weather Stations* project (Figure 38). This is a small bottle-shaped device with a copper-lined funnel on the top. Inside the base of the top section is a light sensor, which relays information to the interior of the bottle. 'Every five minutes, the device recreates the colour represented by the sensor data as a 1-pixel-wide coloured strip at the top of the display; earlier readings are scrolled down. In this way, the device shows a sedimented view of the last two hours of ambient light with oldest readings at the bottom, and most recent ones at the top.'[70] The purpose of the project was to investigate the possibilities for ludic design in the encouragement of environmental awareness 'while eschewing utilitarian or persuasive agendas'. As can be seen in the design of the object, and this statement, it is not meant to be merely instrumental, but a thing of play and interest in itself. However, the intention that this thing should then encourage ecological sensitivity in the process seems to short-circuit any real openness in the piece.

Figure 38 Interaction Research Studio, *The Light Collector: Indoor Weather Station*, 2011. Courtesy of the Interaction Research Studio

Although they seem to wish to open up a space of ambiguity in design, not least because of the emotional richness this potentially offers, they do not appear to be able to resist what might be described as the teleological collapse of these experiments. The makers suggest that the ambiguity of these pieces will encourage users 'to reflect on the meaning of this aspect of their environment, aesthetically, culturally, and – especially – personally.' But it should be asked whether it is ambiguity in itself that will allow them to do this. In the final analysis, this is the tactic of making strange. It seems to be meant here in quite a Brechtian way, that users will experience the ambiguous and the baffling, and then be shocked into thinking about what has happened. They state that 'ambiguity is not a virtue for its own sake,'[71] which does rather suggest an instrumental attitude, in that if ambiguity has a specific purpose, it is not ambiguity; it is a 'fuzzy' way of achieving a particular teleoscentric goal. It may then be that there is a more Schlovskian way of approaching the designed object as event in the economy of experience.

The radical reciprocity of friendship

The UK-based Italian designer Giovanni Marmont is attempting to devise more a way of acting than a thing. In a piece created in 2018, through what he describes as an 'Enactment', the putting into play of a constructed kinetic machine, his intention has been to create the conditions that allow for what he describes as 'a collective practice of sensing together that could be experimented with in bodily and motional ways' (see Figure 39). In this way, he is attempting to answer Massumi's appeal for those working in the field of affective experimentation to engage with the 'performative, theatrical or aesthetic'[72] forms of action that are capable of meeting '[economizing] affective modulation with [non-economistic] affective modulation'.[73] That is to say, the intention on Marmont's part was to create through a designerly intervention an event space in which the ludic in design could, quite literally, be put into play.

The device consists of two platforms, linked by drive chains to a central hub. When one person sits, nothing happens; when they are joined by another on the other platform, a locking mechanism is freed, and they are released to interact with each other. In this deceptively simple interplay, a whole complexity of human–object, and human–human relationality is revealed. Thus, through human interaction with and through the thing the intention is 'to challenge the inherent experiential boundaries established and rendered desirable through

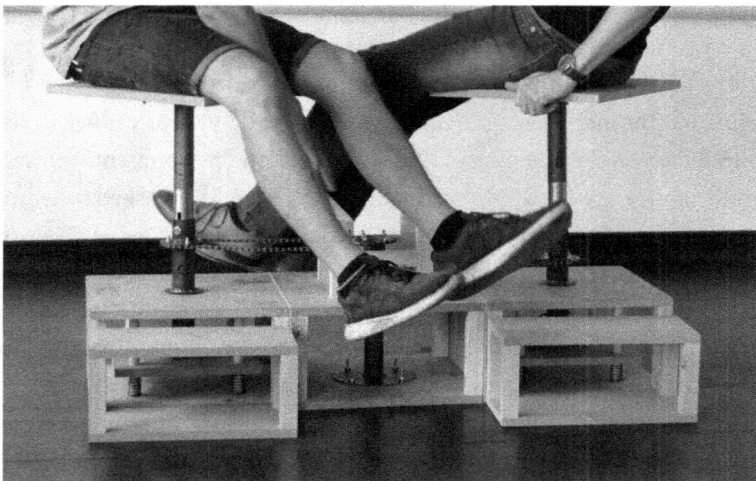

Figure 39 Giovanni Marmont, *kinetic machine enactment*, 2018. Courtesy of the designer

individualized regimes of motion and perception.'[74] That is, the effort is not to create better furniture or products, but to create possibilities of becoming through the creation of circumstances. Rather than being concerned with the teleological end point of what has been made or produced, what is made possible is a certain form of emergence of the self.

Rather radically then the designer is attempting to make artefacts that work not just with play, but the endless reciprocities of friendship. The effort in Marmont's work, then, is to see this behavioural economy as being entirely for itself. It is not concerned with teleological collapse and the application of what is learnt, but rather it is meant to be valuable in and of itself, as action, as play, as human life.

This work is not simply *about* motion, it only exists *in* motion; it acknowledges that to live is to move, and as Massumi notes, motion is indivisible.[75] This is then to reimagine design as the making of possibility, of an endless opening out, an experiment in the creation of new sensibilities, new modes of affect and interaction for changing times, not dictated by the needs of capital or to fit into a market, but as way of living better in what we have. Yet, such a mission is clearly a difficult route to take, not least since it is an effort to do something through an action that refuses to be didactic or instrumental. Necessarily then, there are only presently certain rarified circumstances in which this type of experiment can take place, such as the gallery or in the context of research, and such restrictions will limit what can happen. Thus, the challenge will be whether it is possible to create frames, new contexts of being, where such interventions can extend beyond their present parameters.

Questions answered, questions posed

In order to counter what they saw as the sterility and narrowness of design by optimization, Dunne and Raby agitated for an approach to making things that sought not to answer questions, but to ask them. However, this was not an escape from the rhetorical nature of design, but its employment in a certain way. No matter how much the practitioner suggests that inquiry is the point of the exercise, the making of things to some degree is to make a statement about what should exist in the world. How this is received will depend upon a management of the context to ensure a certain ethical relationship to what has been made or proposed. If this is not very carefully manipulated and controlled, the emotional appeal of the statement can go awry, as it is clear that for all its appeal to logos and the rationality of the argument, that critical and speculative approaches are very much dependent upon pathos and appeals to ethos.

In design, because it is about how we live, it is never enough to make people think. As embodied creatures we also feel the world, and what is created will inevitably be positioned, contextualized and internalized as we interact with it. There will always be an emotive dimension to any design practice, because to be human is to live emotionally, it is just more or less apparent in different forms of practice. As has been demonstrated, work that 'asks questions' may have limited space to operate and minimal opportunity to have any real effect, not least because it claims to be operating on the level of logical inquiry, when it is clearly also functioning very much on an emotional level. In the work of the more lyrical designers, perhaps then a new approach can be seen, one that rejects instrumentality and a need for teleological end points, that attempts to deal not with what could be, but tries to find a new way to access what is. Yet, as Benjamin asked, in such dangerous circumstances, is it acceptable to produce work that does not directly address political issues through direct engagement with the problems we face?[76] Given the ecological collapse of the natural world, and the rise of fascism in human politics, is it not just a little self-indulgent to be making objects that have no discernable purpose, or sitting on platforms feeling things? Well, that does rather depend upon what we consider to be necessary in such circumstances; what, given the crisis we find ourselves a part of, we feel needs to be done, and what potential design has, in such a context. This then is the subject of the next and final chapter of this book.

6

To the ends of the earth

In an article in the *New York Times*, in January 2009, Michael Cannell, the former editor of the 'House and Homes' section of the paper, declared: 'Design Loves a Depression'. In the piece he suggests that the economic collapse of 2007–8 was a good thing for the practice of design. 'The pain of layoffs notwithstanding, the design world could stand to come down a notch or two – and might actually find a new sense of relevance in the process,' he declared, going on to state that the ambition of modernism was the democratization of design, whilst asserting that IKEA and Target 'have shown that the battle for cheap design can be won'. The next challenge, he believed, was to get designers 'to coax us to a more efficient way of living'.[1]

It is telling that Cannell here equates the relevance of design with the extent to which it can provide an 'efficient' mode of life. Indeed, what seemed to exercise Cannell most was how a certain form of decadence appeared to be perceptible in the design that proliferated in the boom years, saying as he did, 'Now, given that all those slick Miami condos are sitting empty in the sky, designers like the Campana Brothers, with their $8,910 Corallo chair, and Hella Jongerius, with her $10,615 Polder sofa, might have a harder time selling their wares.'[2] He goes on to note disapprovingly that in 2007 at the Milan furniture fair (the same year that Sudjic observed that design seemed to have turned 'militantly useless'), Marcel Wanders, whom he describes as 'a Dutch designer known for arty provocations', threw a party at which 'his work was upstaged by his girlfriend, Nanine Linning, who hung upside down half-naked while mixing vodka drinks from bottles affixed to a chandelier'. This appears to have made Cannell very excited. He concluded that 'form followed frivolity' and 'function was left off the guest list'.[3]

Murray Moss, the owner of New York's Moss Gallery, took against this. Calling Cannell's diatribe 'regressive and mean spirited', he responded thus: 'Design loves a depression? I can assure you that design, along with painting, sculpture, photography, music, dance, fashion, the culinary arts, architecture, and theatre, loves a depression no more than it loves a war, a flood, or a plague.' Thus, it is interesting to note how Moss here positioned design as existing within the realm of the liberal arts, alongside painting, sculpture, photography, music, dance and even 'the culinary arts', which he believes are concerned with people's 'emotional, intellectual, cultural, sociological, and political well being.' He then went on to ask: 'When he says "come down a notch or two," does Mr. Cannell mean that Design should retreat from its current expansive, ambitious, fearless, exploratory, guild-breaking, all-encompassing plateau, from its hard-won re-positioning in the Arts?'[4]

Of course, this is exactly what Cannell was saying: that design should be seen as a practical way to achieve a more functional manner of living; that fun and frivolity exist in contradiction to practical problem-solving; that characterizing design as a form of artistic and expressive practice is essentially in opposition to its role of making the world a more rational and efficient place. Moss retorted by saying that design does not thrive in hard times: 'It tends to suffer, like any of the other humanistic disciplines. New ideas do not get championed or realized. Leadership turns to market-driven accommodation.'[5] Though here Moss appeared to be rather ignoring the fact that he too unavowedly operated in a market, it seems that what he was saying was that design, when it is not backed by the economies of art, must operate at the level of being of service to industry and mass production, that the 'efficiency' of design becomes more about its role as a commodity than any more expansive possibilities it may fulfil.

The illustration that accompanied the online version of Cannell's article was apparently meant to exemplify the choice that the author appeared to believe existed in the face of an economic downturn. On the left was an Eames *LCW* plywood chair, standing for the type of efficient modernism for which Cannell was arguing. On the right was an example of the arty decadence that he believed defined the work of those such as the Campana brothers (though it is not actually the chair mentioned in the article). The simple functionality of the Eames chair was meant to contrast with the expressive excess of the more contemporary design. However, Cannell did not actually discuss the nature of the designs he mentioned at all. There was no examination of materials, methods of making or the details of form and function. Rather it was the price of the objects coupled with what he believed to be a wilful disregard for efficiency, as exemplified in the aesthetic of the objects, that appeared to offend him so much. This was then wrapped up into the idea that such work seems to necessarily represent a degenerate form of creativity, which (thankfully, he suggests) would no longer be borne as the world left behind the excesses of the economic bubble of the early

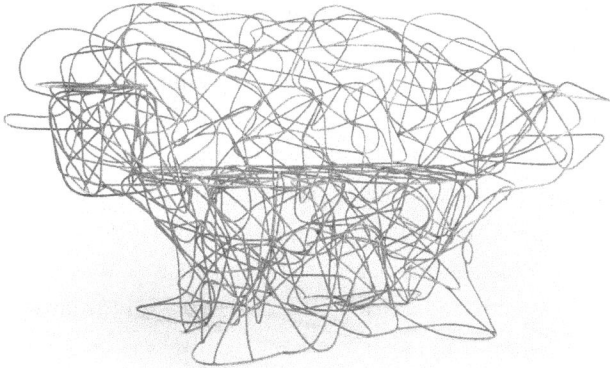

Figure 40 Campana Brothers, *Corallo* chair for Edra, 2004. Courtesy of Edra

twenty-first century. In this sense, anything that is 'art' is in Cannell's definition essentially a decadent luxury. It allows no room for the artistic to have its own value beyond the monetary, it is to regard it as just a frippery when compared to the apparently sensible business of meeting needs.

The Eames chair currently sells for over a thousand pounds, for a relatively simple wooden chair. It is not a good example of austere, democratized design. The *Corallo* chair, made for Edra by the Campana brothers (Figure 40), though expressive and inventive in its form and certainly expensive, is as much an exercise in the use of materials and the possibilities of form as it is any kind of statement. The chair has been made by hand, with the painted steel wire curling and looping into an intricate cloud that holds the sitter. This is the same principle upon which Breuer's *B3* depends for its functioning, that the give and strength of the material should take the weight, not the mass of the piece. The form is convoluted, complex and expressive, but it is still 'solving the problem' of sitting. The dynamic between form and function speaks of new qualities in the relations between user and thing. The spring of the steel will make sitting in it different to conventional chairs, whilst the complexity of the form will provide for a more distributed holding of the body than the rectilinearity of a Bauhaus chair. Yes, there are issues of status and self-image here, but in its form it offers new narratives and novel possibilities for experience on an embodied level.

Yet, Cannell did not appear to be interested in this. For him, such expensive trash simply represented a form of moral regression that Adolf Loos would have recognized. Cannell concluded the article: 'If Ms. Linning's dangling from the ceiling was a cultural moment now passed, we can look forward to others for an age in which beauty and austerity go together.' Here, Cannell seemed to equate expressive and emotive furniture with a person presenting a performance dependent upon her body, seeming quite sure that the reader would disapprove of both. The implication of the article then being that such ridiculousness would be replaced by a more sensible approach to design, more appropriate to straightened times.

Of course, the global financial crisis and the following Great Recession did not serve to make the world a more rational place. Nor did it do much to damage the sales of designers such as the Campanas or Wanders. After a brief hiatus, the market recovered quickly.[6] It seems that with the crash, the forces of international consumer capitalism hit a wall – and kept on going like nothing had changed. But things had altered. The nature of relational politics had shifted in subtle yet profound ways. It was necessary to look quite closely at first, but soon everybody could see that the landscape was different. As people have started to get more scared, as a rising but little-acknowledged panic is setting in, so feeling is beginning to dominate in our interactions. Nostalgia and a yearning for what has gone before are becoming commonplace in the political realm. Anger, fear and resentment seem to be bubbling up to the surface. In such a situation, it might therefore seem reasonable to call for a more rational response to the situation. Surely, if we can simply analyse the problem we can look at all the variables and work out the best solution. Yet, as we have seen, what answer we get, what gets made, will depend upon what questions we ask, and what we consider to be the boundaries of possibility in such a situation.

A case can be made that design has developed to service consumer capitalism.[7] At the beginning of the twenty-first century, Hal Foster argued that the project entered into by idealists like the Russian Productivists and the Bauhausers 'was eventually accomplished, but according to the spectacular dictates of the culture industry, not the liberatory ambitions of the avant-garde. And a primary form of the perverse reconciliation in our time is design'.[8] He argues that 'design is all about desire' and goes on to conclude that 'design seems to advance a new kind of narcissism, one that is all image and no interiority – an apotheosis of the subject that is also its disappearance', whereby he believes we are, quoting Loos's words, 'precluded from all future living and striving, developing and desiring',[9] in a culture that Foster characterizes as 'the neo-Art Nouveau world of total design and Internet plenitude'.[10] This is, therefore, to essentially characterize design as morally bankrupt, seeing it as being entirely in the service of satisfying consumer desire. Yet, as has been demonstrated, there is at least one strand of design that is implicit in an economy of desire, but which may also offer other potential.

In responding to a surge of emotion in public life, the solution cannot be to refute the emotional as a register of discourse. As has been argued, the converse of emotion is not clinical rationalism or an ascetic functionalism. The opposite of sadness is not the absence of feeling, it is happiness; the dialectical obverse of hatred is love. Cannell's position seems to have been that in more straightened times design would be stripped back to what we need, what he sees as functional design, and the unnecessary 'frivolity' of playful and emotive design, would wither away. In this sense, he was adopting a rationalist, problem-solving approach to the practice of design and asserting that such a position is morally superior to other ways of doing things that he regards as decadent and wasteful in such a situation. Yet, it may actually be more reasonable to say that as we come under threat, so we need to react in a way that is different to the orthodoxies that got us here. It may be that a new narrative is needed that sees the emotional qualities of objects not as something that can be harnessed to other ends, but as a quality of life that is essential to our well-being and the state of human flourishing.

Perhaps it is time to try to live in a different way. Nanine Linning, the 'semi-naked' woman whom Cannell so derided in his article, is an internationally recognized choreographer and performance artist. In the piece *Happy Hour Chandelier* to which he refers, she hung from the light-fitting, designed by her partner Wanders, for twenty minutes wearing a rather modest silver bikini, presenting chocolate mousse and champagne to the crowd gathered beneath her. The piece was meant to be exciting and sexy. Was this then morally wrong? It sounds like fun. Yet, for a commentator such as Cannell, the assumption seems to be that to be serious, to be efficient design, it should be amotive, devoid of emotion. Which, as we have seen, is something of an impossibility, and to deny the emotional register of life, to see it as only being of value in that it contributes to other ends, is to impoverish what it means to be alive.

Material messages

Cannell's position depends upon a very narrow ideologically determined understanding of what we need. Throughout the economic crisis (which we are, at this point, still living through of course), the assumption has been that the system makes sense, it just has some problems, that it needs to be reformed; it just needs to work a bit better, to be a bit more efficient. The question that occurs in such a situation, however, is efficient in doing what? As was discussed in earlier chapters, we do not 'need' most furniture or domestic products in any absolute terms. In trying to make sense of what may represent responsible design, the theorist of technology Jesse Tatum observes that the idea that it is possible to rationally work out functionalist needs from a scientific basis is itself an ideology, one that disregards the fact that any such analysis will depend upon what is selected as the evidence from an ultimately underdetermined body of data. As he states, 'we tend to proceed along singular developmental paths as if only one technology were possible. We ask: "What is the most efficient?" or "What is the most cost effective?" and imagine that such a narrow technical analysis can guide us to the best answers.'[11] In such a situation, therefore, the appeal to efficiency or cost-effectiveness actually masks the fact that deciding what is or is not necessary, what counts as 'frivolous' and what is a 'need' is in actuality an ethical question. As the design scholar Alain Findeli notes, 'choosing the technological mediation is a matter of ethics, not technology; in other words, designing an artifact is acting in the field of ethics, not of technology alone.'[12] In this way, all design is a question of ethical practice.

At the basis of such ethical reasoning in design, it is now necessary to break down the subject–object dichotomy, which presupposes that objects can be divorced from their context and considered 'rationally' in abstraction from their actual occurrence, as they appear to us as embodied, necessarily emotional creatures. As emotion becomes more political, it is, therefore, required that we evolve a complex vocabulary of emotionality if our analysis of the situation is to keep pace with its emergence. This need not just be a semantic proposition, however, rather it is perhaps also possible to develop a poetic lexicon of the emotive through the materiality of things.

At first glance, the *Banquette Chair with Pandas* (Figure 41) by the Campana brothers may seem to support Foster's assertion that design is all 'image and no interiority'. This is exactly one of the 'frivolous' designs that Cannell so hated, after all. Here we see a large number of soft toys that have been connected to a steel and canvas armature to create the seat, as with the example that began this book. This is not a functionalist chair. It is however, functional: it is possible to use it to sit down, but it is clearly doing more than simply providing the means to do this.

Just as with the example that sat in Mr West's living room, at the same time as it has the capacity to make those who engage with it smile, it also materially makes manifest a form of overabundance or excess that might be more than a little disturbing if looked at in another way. It seems to be about plenitude, and yes, it is an expensive object. The handmade, the strange, the limited edition,

Figure 41 Campana Brothers, *Banquette Chair with Pandas*, 2006. © DACS 2019

can cost. This is in many ways reprehensible in a world where many want for the most basic things, but the same could be said of many art objects. That it is implicit in such an economy should not preclude it from being considered in other registers, as something that can operate at an emotional level and thus be about a complexity of experience, one which is determined by a set of social relations that takes into account the context of the encounter, the qualities of the piece and the embodied perception of the perceiving entity. What Foster seems to want to deny is that a piece of design can have content, can be about something, and consequently have complexity and depth in a manner akin to art. Yet, what seems clear in pieces such as this is that this is certainly possible, but it will need considering as design, as something that is meant to be used as well as looked at, if such intensities are to be apparent.

If we take this thing seriously as a dialectical object, something that is both in and of a particular moment, then the ways in which is qualities are manifest can to some degree be discerned. In many ways the chair does seem to be celebratory, but we are certainly confronted by the productive capacity of mass-manufacture. Similarly, the very abundance of the piece seems to speak of an uncanny excrescence as the mute and staring bears tumble over each other. Even more than the banquettes of the mixed toys, those such as the panda chair, which use the same toy in multiple, play on the very seriality of the mass-produced. Presented as art in a gallery, this piece would clearly seem to be referencing

Andy Warhol via Jeff Koons. However, if we take it seriously as design, as a use-object, its affordances of possibility reveal another dimension, one that relies upon physicality, movement, experience, affect. Design is concerned with the creation of things that allow others to do things. If art is essentially concerned with *poiesis*, the bringing into being of something that did not previously exist, then design is inevitably involved with *praxis*, whereby theory is enacted.

Studio Makkink & Bey's piece, *Cleaning Beauty Cabinet: Cleanliness Is Next to Godliness* of 2007 (Figure 42), was, like Baas's chair discussed in Chapter 3, created as part of a residency at the Contrasts Gallery in Shanghai. Here the mundane task of cleaning has been reimagined by taking a simple cupboard for the storage of cleaning materials and using Chinese silks and other luxurious materials to make the cabinet a sumptuous thing. This then is a material suggestion that even the simplest quotidian task should be elevated to something deserving of beauty. Contained within it is an irredeemable paradox in present conditions. Since it is made of such high-status materials and because it has been created by Bey

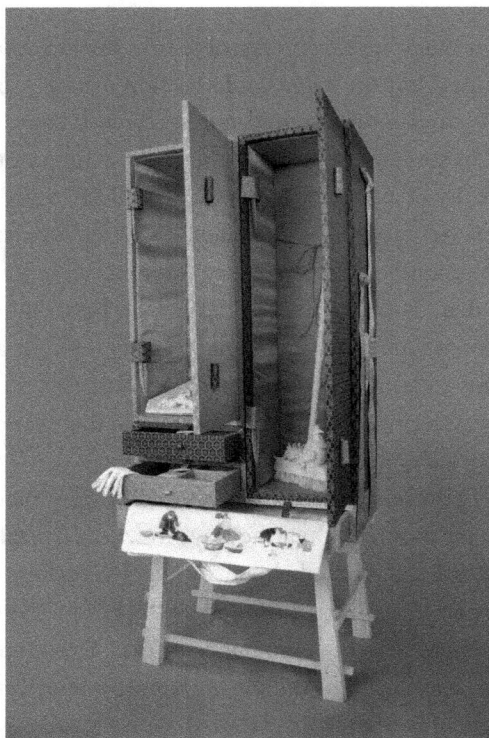

Figure 42 Studio Makkink & Bey, *Cleaning Beauty Cabinet: Cleanliness Is Next to Godliness*, 2007. Courtesy of Studio Makkink & Bey

and his partner's prestigious design firm, it is clearly a valuable object. Yet we do not value cleaning, and we certainly do not celebrate the worth of those who perform this task in our culture.

So who would buy such a thing? The easy answer would be to say that this was never made to be used, that it is again really a designed object that is just an excuse to make a sculpture. Yet, it is too completely worked out, too resolved as a functional object, too full of connection to the actual everyday task of cleaning (in a way that Newson's *Lockheed Lounge* chaise is not in relation to sitting), for this to be an autonomous work of art. Even if it is art when it's in the gallery, they really have made a cupboard full of cleaning equipment, which cries out to be used. If you found it in a car park, it would still operate the same way as it does in the gallery. In the grain of the empirical there can also be wonders. It does not make any claim to be outside of the discourse of the creation of use-objects, it is not sitting at a distance and critiquing something. It is not 'questioning', 'investigating', or otherwise 'depicting'[13] the act of cleaning. Rather it is a physical suggestion as to how such an act might be alternatively carried out. This then is a relational approach to design, one where the context in which objects play out their functionalities is a key determinant in what work they do.

Relational design?

Andrew Blauvelt's 2008 article proposing that design has moved into a phase centrally concerned with context and the performative nature of made objects clearly refers to the rise of Relational Aesthetics in art. The French critic Nicholas Bourriaud, who has done the most to write the term into art history, defined this approach as '[a] set of artistic practices which take as their theoretical and practical point of departure the whole of human relations and their social context, rather than an independent or private space'.[14] This is, therefore, a repudiation of the autonomy of the artwork, whereby relational art is conceptualized as dependent upon the contingencies of its context, its relation to the audience and the social connections formed within this entity; whence this audience is envisaged as a form of community, no matter how transient this may be.

In art, this relational turn can be criticized as misrepresenting the relationship between audience and work. The art historian and critic Claire Bishop suggests that the relational approach in art developed because of the rise of a particular type of work in the 1990s whereby the artist was 'conceived less as an individual producer of discrete objects than as a collaborator and producer of *situations*.[15] The art created in such circumstances was then promoted as 'open' or 'incomplete', to be finally actualized through the participation of a public now conceived of as participants. Yet, she notes that such work actually seems to derive from a misreading of poststructuralist theory, such as Barthes's 'Death of the Author', whereby rather than the '*interpretations* of a work of art being open to continual reassessment the work of art *itself* is argued to be in perpetual flux' (her emphasis).[16] In this regard, Bourriaud has argued, 'Artistic practice appears these days to be a rich loam for social experiments, like a space partly protected from the uniformity of behavioural patterns.'[17] Yet, in adopting such a position, he appears to want it both ways: he suggests that their status as art protects these 'experiments', at the same time that they are somehow radically open to the 'real' world. Indeed, Bourriaud is keen to stress that in his analysis, relational aesthetics is not simply an approach to art which is essentially interactive or that involves participation. Rather he believes it to be a means for positioning such practices within a broader cultural context. In this way, the relational turn in art is characterized as being a response to the increasing virtualization of the life and economics brought about by the development of networked culture.

Yet, it is not clear that the actors of the art world are actually as autonomous as the proselytizers of the open system argue, for as Rancière argues, 'aesthetics has its own politics, or rather its own tension between two opposed politics: between the logic of art that becomes life at the price of abolishing itself as art, and the logic of art that does politics on the explicit condition of not doing it at all'.[18] That is, by being presented *as* art, relational practices can 'do' the politics of interaction only at the expense of being at a remove from its everyday manifestations; the act is absorbed into the protocological structure of the institutions of art.

Of course, if there is a creative practice that actually is open to the real, at the same time as being concerned with social connection, it is design. The relational shift in art has helped to open up a space in which design practice can begin to move beyond the constrictions of a narrow concentration on function. As Blauvelt has more recently noted, 'Relational design is preoccupied not just with design's form or meaning, but with its effects; not with isolated objects, but rather with situations embedded in everyday life.'[19] It is thus in this interface with the everyday that the relational in design can be explored.

There is some degree of redundancy in a term such as 'relational design'. Clearly, all design is to some extent concerned with use, which is a human activity performed in relation to things and other people. However, as Blauvelt has been careful to point out, it is because of changed conditions of existence that the relational qualities of design are coming to the fore, whereby we are experiencing 'the loss of designs that are highly controlled and prescribed and the ascendency of enabling or generative systems; the end of discrete objects, hermetic meanings, and the beginning of connected ecologies.'[20] Through this shift, then, as context within a networked culture becomes ever more important in understanding not just what things mean but what they do, then it seems that an understanding of the material nature of social relations is at the root of understanding design in such times.

Valencies of the relational

The relational in design can be experimented with and explored in very material ways. In the project *100 Chairs in 100 Days* (Figure 43), the furniture designer Martino Gamper spent two years collecting abandoned and unwanted chairs from around London. He then reconfigured the components into new

Figure 43 Martino Gamper, *100 Chairs in 100 Days*, RMIT, Melbourne, Australia, 2007. Photograph by Tobias Titz. Courtesy of the designer

forms, one a day over one hundred days. This was on one level an exercise in construction, an experiment in the manipulation of material affordances, in that in each chair the components have been carefully montaged together. We can see physical rhyme, juxtaposition, tension and compression in any one example. Yet each piece then relates to the others as a part of a series. Each chair makes sense in itself (though there are sly jokes throughout whereby the ad-hoc solutions refer to classic examples and iconic pieces), but it is only in apprehending the relational nature of what has been done that its full complexity can be appreciated.

The components were gathered in a certain geographical location (London) at a specific point in history. The pieces were made in a set time (one day) for a certain duration (one hundred days). Though the assemblages are handmade, the components are fragments of a system of mass production. The fact that they are made from found objects then relates to where the raw material was located, the network that is the sociological context of the city. The construction of the pieces within a given time frame has the effect of emphasizing the particular temporality of the work. The methodology employed, that of assemblage from found elements in an essentially algorithmic frame, in that there were rules applied to the gathering and the making, actually establishes each element as part of a broader temporal economy by demonstrating how artefacts are held within relational dynamics.

Given the entirely contingent quality of the assembled nature of these objects, for all their presence as part of a series or network, each one is then asserted as being entirely and fundamentally unique in space and time. This is not least because the chairs are presented as functionally usable things in their own right, not simply as reflections upon use. As functional objects, they make it possible for those who use them to perform actions, to act and be acted upon.

As has been noted throughout the discussion, the fact that these things get shown in galleries is not unproblematic. Yet it should not make us discount what has been done. Like art, design can exist as a realm of possibilities and ways of thinking about and through the material world. One of the exciting things about Gamper's project is its very realizability. Anybody could do this. In line with Bourriaud's conception of relational aesthetics in art, this newfound emphasis on connection and interrelation in design would seem to point to an increased salience of participatory practice in this field. For the designer and researcher Carl DiSalvo, this would then involve 'opening the design process beyond the experts and including those who might be affected by the designed thing in the activities of imagining, conceptualizing, and creating products and services.'[21]

It is thus the possibility of agency that is one exciting feature about such work. There are hundreds of abandoned chairs in our towns and cities. Smashed and abject furniture is everywhere. We ignore it because, in consumerist terms, it has ended. It is finished. But what if it isn't? What if we see it as the start? A piece such as *One Hundred Chairs in One Hundred Days* illustrates how, as Blauvelt notes, if modernism represented 'a logic of form (aesthetics) or function' then 'today's radical design practices are guided primarily by a social logic'.[22] In this way, such an exercise illustrates how DiSalvo's participatory 'opening up' of the design process could take place.

However, as with the cautionary example of art, how this can then play out will be determined by the practice's relationship to the discourse in which it operates. Celia Lury suggests that the individual subject's relation to any given object is always to some degree dependent upon their relation to the 'object world' of which the thing in question is believed to be a part. This relation can then, in Lury's schema, be understood as a 'network, a series, an ensemble, a closed or open system'.[23] Therefore, any object can be conceptualized as being determined by the protocols of the system in which it is implicit. This is why it is important to think about this kind of emotive work as being design. It is not art. It is not framed by that set of interrelations and it has not been made to work in that world.

One reason why the relational turn is valuable in the understanding of design is because it operates as a counterbalance to a reductivist rationality that claims to know what is necessary in some absolute sense. The really useful point that can be drawn from relational aesthetics is that although the author can create the conditions in which action takes place, they cannot fully control the outcomes of that action. The broader protocols and ideological categorical imperatives will structure what is possible, yet the scenario is predicated upon the involvement of the subject in its object. So it becomes clear that in understanding design as relational it is necessary to conceptualize each new condition to which design is applied as being entangled in a wider system of systems that, in being dynamic and emergent, will always have a unique structure of interrelation and consequence that includes the experiencing subject.

In this way, to take a relational approach to emotive design is to accept that each and every situation is dynamic and therefore unique. It denies the interchangeability of moments, it refutes the action of the commodity form and declares this situation to be generated by its relational, emotional qualities, that are established socially, between us, which must then be weighed by the designer in the act of bringing objects into play.

Futuring

In Gary Hustwit's 2009 documentary *Objectified*, Fiona Raby states, 'We love show rooms, because what is a showroom? You go in there, around IKEA, and you imagine this in your home ... you project yourself into this other space. You could have it at home.' However, Anthony Dunne then adds the observation that 'when you walk into a gallery you don't imagine the sculpture at home and how it's going to impact on your life. But you walk into a shop whether its electronics or furniture or a car showroom, and you do imagine yourself experiencing this thing and enjoying it.' He then continues by arguing that when they create what they call 'conceptual products', they are 'hoping that people will imagine how that will impact on the way they live their lives'.[24] However, as Dunne himself is noting here, it is clear that the context of the shop or showroom is demonstrably not the same as that of the gallery. Different protocols of behaviour and projection are imposed in these types of location.

By coding something as design, whether by naming it as such or creating something that is obviously a functional and functioning use-object, a user is always to one degree or another implied, as is the act of use. Yet, to place design in a gallery is necessarily to bring it into the protocols of a certain type of art. What is useful, then, about the relational turn in art is the extent to which it demonstrates how, even though such actions can never be liminoid and entirely outside of protocol and ideological definition, the unfinishedness of things, their contingent liminality and the need for a user to bring the object into play, suggest the possibility of praxis and therefore change.

Recent discussion of relational aesthetics has created a new sensibility, one that is attentive to questions of situational politics. This has meant that designers have been able to increasingly smuggle the tactics of art into their work. Sometimes this means that such authors can move in their practice from design to art and back again at will. With teams such as Studio Job or Studio Swine, it can be difficult to see what discourse they are working in, and they clearly wish to be able to shift fluidly between registers and roles (though, as we have seen, the effects of this can leave some practices confusing and unclear). With a group such as rAndom International, it is simply impossible to classify in traditional terms what they are doing a lot of the time. With a piece such as *Rain Room* (Figure 44), they presented 'a carefully choreographed downpour', a room in which it rained, everywhere except where the person experiencing it was standing. The press release for the work states that the piece 'invites us to explore what role science, technology and human ingenuity might play in stabilising our environment by rehearsing the possibilities of human adaptation,[25] thus reminding us of the groups' origins on Dunne and Raby's course at the RCA, and showing how such practices flow in and out of the discourse of art. Yet, it may be that we actually need a new terminology to discuss such work, that, as is so often the case, practice is ahead of conceptualization.

By presenting things as use-objects, even if only nominally, functional, the viewer is interpellated into the action of the piece simply through the assertion that this is such a type of thing. If, as the art critic and curator Stephen Wright asserts, art has become 'redundant in every sense of the term,'[26] then design can be seen to be drawing energy from the appropriation of techniques from this field. As Wright suggests, things that borrow from the tactics and competencies of art but are not presented as such have a certain salience because they are less visible *as* art, and this 'impaired visibility' may well be inversely proportional to the work's political potential, 'since it is not partitioned off as "art," that is, as "just art," it remains free to deploy all its symbolic force in lending enhanced visibility and legibility to social processes of all kinds'. In this way, such things can then become 'a form of stealth art' which can infiltrate 'spheres of world-making beyond the scope of work operating unambiguously under the banner of art'.[27] This, therefore, becomes a site of political action, whereby design can operate to change not just how we read the world, but how we feel it.

Figure 44 rAndom International, *Rain Room*, 2012. Courtesy of Carpenters Workshop Gallery

Just as new feelings demand new forms, so as we develop new ways of making things new ways of interpreting our sensual nature will arise. For Danish designer Mathias Bengtsson, the use of technology is an important part of the process, yet his stated intention is to engage those encounter his work on the level of feelings, claiming, 'My work is about challenging the senses: that is its function.' To do this, he begins not by attempting to solve a problem, but by investigating the sensual qualities of what he is making. His design work is always begun with traditional tools, pen and paper or a brush, since he argues that drawing can be said to provide 'the shortest distance between an idea in your imagination and a form'. The problem, he suggests, is then how to translate this into something that can be realized digitally. With his breakthrough piece of 1999, the *Slice Chair* (Figure 45), he first created a wax model, which was then actually physically cut into pieces with a saw. These sections were then scanned and redrawn. Only quite late in the process was CNC technology employed, and even then the elements were put together by hand in the final construction.[28] Therefore, the intention was not to explore the internal protocols of the technology used,

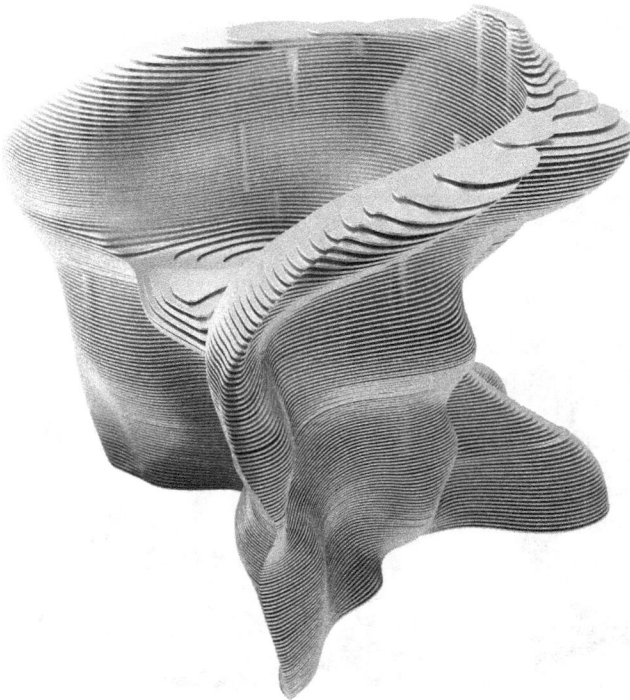

Figure 45 Mathias Bengtsson, *Slice Chair*, 1999. Courtesy of the designer

the ethics of such technological production, so to speak, but to find a means to express feelings that needed working out in such a way.

Increasingly, however, we are coming to live with things where their form is essentially inhuman in its development. This is not to say it is inorganic, often quite the opposite, but rather that what is shaping the work is not the logic of human ethical or aesthetic judgement, but the nature of the machine algorithm at work, where design is increasingly becoming the material realization of data. Though Joris Laarman's *Bone Chair* (Figure 46) looks willfully organic, as though it were a modern Art Nouveau comment on functional form, it is actually the result of the application of high technology to materials. The software that built it was originally developed by a subsidiary of General Motors in Germany, Adam Opel GmbH, to create a more efficient engine mount. The technique works just as the growth of bones does in the body, whereby in the process of modelling the part stresses are applied and what is not needed for structural integrity is removed. Created for the 'Smart Deco' exhibition initiated by Droog and Barry Friedman at Design Miami in 2006, it was made by casting the metal in 3D-printed ceramic moulds specially created by Phil Verdult Castings. Here then the human relation to technology is laid out as materially visible. The organicism of the piece is the result of algorithmic growth, just as our apparently human systems can be seen to be developing not along entirely bio-logics, but

Figure 46 Joris Laarman, *Bone Chair*, 2006. Aluminum. 29 ¾ × 29 ⅞ × 17 ½" (75.6 × 75.9 × 44.5 cm). The Museum of Modern Art, New York © Photo SCALA, Florence

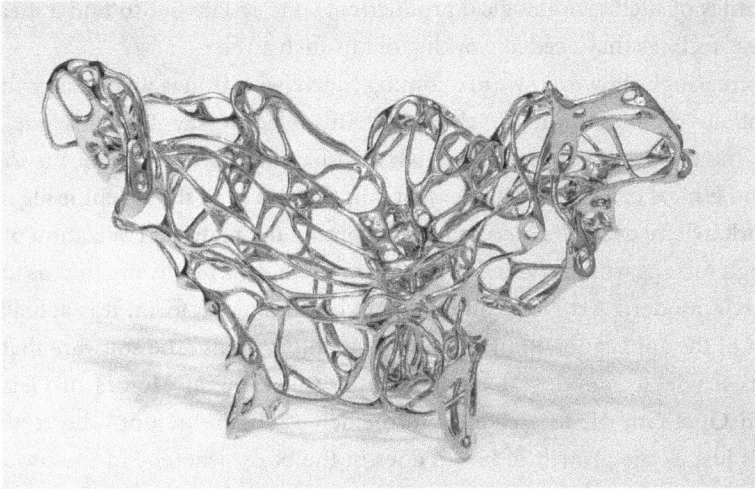

Figure 47 Mathias Bengtsson, *Growth Chair*, 2010. Courtesy of the designer

rather as hybrids created through the nature of anthropogenic approaches to technological production. Bengtsson works with this idea directly in his *Growth* series (from 2010 onwards) (Figure 47), whereby he utilizes this capacity for algorithms to operate as 'seeds', which can then germinate and form structures within the computer. Then using 3D printing, he is able to create beautiful, elegant shapes and interrelations, which push the boundary between art and design to its limits. And yet, these are still chairs and tables. What then is really exciting is to consider the fact that because this is something made to do things with, it will continue to grow through use. Because of the relational nature of design, it will develop and flourish further through engagement with human affectivity, the capacity to affect and be affected. This is then to be attentive to the state of emergence of the thing and the human subjectivities that come into being with it, to be sensitive to their mutual *becoming* as things in motion.

These are examples of design whereby the method of manufacture has created an aesthetic that is at once organic, but which bear the imprint of a wholly new affective relation to materiality. If the *Corallo* chair allows a certain materially determined subjective experience that reflects its careful hand-crafted quality, which is different from the standard weight-bearing methods usually employed in chair design, then these chairs represent what happens when human beings harness and work with things that have begun to grow inside computers. The revolution in digital technologies is manifestly altering our psychology and changing our affective relationship to the world; creating new possibilities of being, strange modes and modulations of feeling that we are only beginning to imagine. New technologies and ways of doing things are creating novel forms, that will allow for emergent ways of feeling and experiencing the material world to come into being, and be expressed. If Gamper's improvised chairs represent a low-tech materialist approach to relational design, the high-tech approach of designers such as Bengtsson and Laarman suggest a method that is just as physical, but looks in a different direction to work with what happens when design becomes data-driven, when the relational includes actors that are not human, but which may be developing intentionality, even if it is not quite conscious (yet).

With new technology, the tendency is to initially use the novel methods to create different versions of the norms and archetypes already existent. Yet new ways of doing things bring with them new sensibilities. A team from UCL and the Bartlett School of Architecture led by Manuel Jiménez Garcia and Gilles Retsin have been trying to examine what it might mean for the whole of life in a house to be digital. This then is not just to imagine how we would live with the everyday things we have now, as might be exemplified by discussions around production processes such as 3D printing, or deployment methods such as the Internet of Things. Instead they are seeking a formal ethics of the digital domestic. That is to say, what are the internal logics of digital production, and how might this manifest in the home? To really consider this might then necessitate the conceptualization of new kinds of feelings, ones that may not be quite human.

With pieces such as the *Voxel 1.0* chair (Figure 48), the development team are trying to imagine ways of making that derive from the affordances of the robots that will be doing the manufacturing. Consequently, the *Voxel 1.0* is not 3D printed in the conventional manner, whereby layers are built up to create parts that are very much like those that have traditionally made up such furniture. Instead, the piece is created in a way that suits the robot more, in one continuous extrusion, a line worked and walked through space by a nozzle to create a form.

'This may look like a Panton chair, but it's actually completely different,' Jiménez Garcia and Retsin point out. 'The Panton chair was a pure surface, optimised to mould. This chair is the opposite: a cloud-like volume, optimised for robotic extrusion.'[29] In the 'cloud-like volume' of the Voxel, it becomes apparent that the conventional boundaries between objects may not matter so much to artificial minds, just as the way that subjectivities are coming to be embedded into their context is rendered visible. Where once there were sharp boundaries between body and chair, now there is only gradations of interplay. This is then a form of design by optimization, but the metrics being worked against are not of

Figure 48 UCL Design Computation Lab, Manuel Jimenez Garcia and Gilles Retsin, *Voxel 1.0*, 2017. Courtesy of UCL Design Computation Lab

our species. What we are left with in formal terms looks strange, inhuman (at the moment), and this is challenging. We will need new narratives to make sense of this, just as we will find ways of relating to the affordances of affect that it makes possible. The *CurVoxel* from the same team pushes this further (Figure 49). It is alien in its aspect. The form is almost disgusting in its complexity, in the way that it has been manufactured to a logic that is not that of the narratives of either functionalism or romanticism, but seems to speak of a future where things will be very different.

The *Mickey Matter* suite of table and chairs (Figure 50) and is perhaps more cheerful. Here the blobby curves of the extrusion suggest we might be having a fun time with our robots, creating marvellous new organic forms on which to sit and be. Yet what is clear is that as we enter a new world of things made in ways that we are just beginning to imagine, so our emotiverse, the cosmology of affect and the possibilities of feeling, will need to alter and take on new forms if we are to have any chance of being comfortable, of being at home in such a world.

Figure 49 UCL Design Computation Lab, Manuel Jimenez Garcia and Gilles Retsin with Hyunchul Kwon, Amreen Kaleel and Xiaolin Li, *CurVoxel*, 2019. Courtesy of UCL Design Computation Lab

Moving objects

The emotive tendency in design has developed because the processes of conventional product design could not deal with the complexity of use, or the depth and strangeness of users. What is termed 'User-Centred Design', or even 'Human-Centred Design', employs in the name of research a process of simplification and reduction that establishes a minimized silhouette that still bears enough of a resemblance to an actual person to persuade that the method is working, but which actually serves to obscure the uncanny strangeness of people, their behaviours and motivations.

User-Centred Design cannot account for the complexity of use. It perforce creates users that are mere sock puppets, humans that are barely recognizable as such. The methodologies employed are so rooted in the commodity structure that the image of the user that emerges is perforce that of an individual consumer

Figure 50 UCL Design Computation Lab, Manuel Jimenez Garcia and Gilles Retsin with Panagiota Spyropoulou, Hyein Lee, Pooja Gosavi and Pratiksha Renake, *Mickey Matter Table*, 2019. Courtesy of UCL Design Computation Lab

of commodities – one who deploys already finished and comprehensible products to achieve defined and quantifiable ends. People are not like this. Our conception of what constitutes design, that which creates to allow action, has been so impoverished by its parentage in consumer capitalism that we have been left with no way to see an alternative, no ability to read and name our own feelings in relation to the use of things. We have become completely schooled in the idea that things are to be used efficiently, even our own selves and our emotions, in the service of achievement.

Emotive design is that which strives to meet the complexity of the world with a concomitant response. Because design is always concerned with things in motion, literally moving objects, it must deal with action. As technology is changing how we can inhabit the world, so our perceptual mechanism changes. As we find new ways of becoming, so we need new forms through which to do so. As we create new forms, so our experience of using things will precipitate novel complexities of affect, which will be brought into the world and named.

To attempt to solve a problem is to look for a solution. To treat such work as a conundrum to be worked out is also to look for this mythical outcome. Even as this is design that is not meant to simply serve a need, neither is this work that you 'get'. Like art, its ambiguity, its play of internal tensions creates an endless unfolding. Yet, unlike art, this does not have to happen elsewhere, in the autonomous zone, it can be here in the now of the everyday. Of course, in contemporary design, there are many objects that are simply conventional everyday things marked-up by being created in fancy ways or made in precious materials. There are also essentially traditional highly crafted objects that occupy a position that would have been recognizable in the eighteenth century, whereby the rich patronized craft ateliers. However, there are other categories of thing that appear to have only really developed in the recent conditions of modernity. Domestic use-objects created from masses of standardized repetitions of the same thing, to the point that the gibbering incontinence of mass production seems to be coalescing into its own self-generated forms; the waste and detritus of a world of ultimate availability becoming new and re-entering consumption as it refuses to go away and die as we were promised it would; the old and the outmoded, that should lie derided in an elderly relative's attic, requiring to be used as it metamorphosizes into life; the things that we were convinced were our mute and attentive servants shuddering into action as they demand their place in the home; memories of ways of being, echoes of other forms of civilization and material knowledge returning from their repression; new methods, materials, techniques and technologies yawning and stretching as they prepare for their time. Some are playful and full of delight. Others are disconcerting. All of this is there and it has come to be when it has because it could, because the conditions for its being have been created in this time.

When the surrealists in the early twentieth century conceived of the uncanny, they did so from a position where the domestic interior had solidified into a carapace within which the bourgeoisie and those who aspired to their condition could retreat from the world. This has now been penetrated by the channels of techno-capitalism as it flows through such spaces with ease, gurgling in and out through screens and handheld devices, welcomed by the bewildered and believing inhabitants as they search for meaning in the infinity in which they are implicit.

In consumerism, the age of the brand, objects with attitude, the reified commodity has been given new life. In this materialist age, we have more physical things than at any other point in history and we have never been so convinced as to their meaning, their import and their capacity to alter our lives to make us happy. But do they? Really? One thing that can be learnt from design that plays with emotion is that the canvas is much bigger than present conditions seem to allow, so perhaps we should start to take back some territory.

As has been demonstrated throughout this analysis, the dichotomy inherent in the commodity is the proposition that it is powerful, that it can satisfy our desires through its consumption, yet at the same time it is characterized as inert, that it is only the will of human beings that animates it into action. This is the mythology of the complete and completed product that magically appears in the marketplace. Concomitant to this is the perverse effect of apparently living in a reified material culture, whereby the possibility of action is conferred on objects whilst subjects appear locked into the inertia of a static now of consumption, unable to act in any way beyond the non-choices offered by consumerism as a mode of life.

The field of the emotive in contemporary design, though it has been contained by being absorbed into a pseudo-art world, has the potential to be a site of domestic creativity and affective inventiveness that can genuinely alter the conditions of everyday life. Though often its relationship to craft production, as is noted above, is that of the conventional position of craftspeople making things for the rich, a significant proportion of the objects that can be described in this way actually speak of the possibilities of a very human production – of the use of what is to hand, and the skills that are available, to make a life. This can now include high technology. Apart from that with which we physically adorn ourselves, such as clothes and jewellery, furniture and our domestic objects are the most intimate things we live with. It is, therefore, at this point that an intervention can be made if we are to construct a new everyday life – a *novi byt* – and these strange and marvellous things, these happy, sad, anxious and excited domestic creatures, suggest this through their form and their function.

At present, many of the designs discussed in this book have a darkness to them, an uncanny quality. Yet, this is not something that is unique to design, it is something that is *visible* in it. The nice shiny commodities we are encouraged to interact with have this quality hidden. In emotive design this can be seen. All things that we interact with are performative. They hail us and demand that we become a new subjectivity in the process. Unfortunately, this is usually the pre-packaged, death-denying onanist that is the consumer. At least the design discussed in this book, which ramps up emotion and plays on our fears and desires, is honest. In demanding we become its co-product, we can see what the deal is based on. We may become clowns or ragpickers, but at least this is a transparent part of the transaction.

At present the boundaries of function, what it means to be functional – for ways of living and being as much as for chairs and tables – are policed by those who believe that life exists to service capital. That all we can do is sell our labour and hope to be able to consume the tawdry devices offered to us. Maybe there is more than this. Maybe we can imagine new ways of living. Not just in the abstract or in the non-space of the gallery, but materially and affectively in what we actually use, in everyday life as it is lived.

At the moment, this practice of design is all too often the making of luxuries for the rich, who can be too stupid or too jaded to really see them. Though, as with Kanye West's living room, it is comforting to think of the way that the dark and the uncanny has been sneaked into the home lives of the wealthy. On this level, all such things really represent is the final act of the commodity. Emotive design can be seen as a last flaring up of the consumerist object just as a new mode of life ascends. The high-water mark has been reached, and the flood has begun to recede. This then has been the generation which has seen the material object burn at its brightest as the remnants of its fuel is consumed. In these dialectical things the mechanisms of our world can be intuited, even if only for a moment as a flickering intersection, and the full horror, and potential, of what we have created, of what we are materially implicated in, can be grasped.

This then does not lead to a moment of realization; it is not a point at which we can see clearly and think our way out of the situation as Brecht may have hoped. Rather, as with all historical experience in the moment of its occurrence, before it is identified, codified and brought into the narrative, it is *felt*. It moves us, as we once believed art could. So, in a humanist approach to the material that sees all creation as an ethical question, in the making of things that demand our engagement and cause us to act, and therefore show that there is the possibility that we can feel differently, *be* differently, there is hope.

By refusing to accept that the borders of what we do are fixed by the sterility of what serves the market and an approach to the material that sees endless consumption as efficient whilst denying the power and importance of our emotional lives, it may then be that we find new purpose. In these moving objects, these things that wear their performativity on their surface, that shout and play, that scream that there are other ways of doing things, it may be that we find not just a way to survive but a new way to live.

Notes

Introduction

1 Humberto Campana in Hannah Martin, 'The Story behind the Campana Brothers' Iconic Stuffed-Animal Chair Design', *Architectural Digest*, https://www. architecturaldigest.com/story/the-story-behind-the-campana-brothers-iconic-stuffed-animal-chair-design (accessed 12 December 2019).

2 For a discussion of the influence of *Casabella* see Penny Sparke, 'Ettore Sottsass and Critical Design in Italy, 1965–1985', in *Made in Italy: Rethinking a Century of Italian Design*, ed. Grace Lees Maffei (London: Bloomsbury Academic, 2013), 63.

3 In conversation with the author.

4 Donald Norman, *The Design of Everyday Things* (New York: Basic Books, 2002); Donald Norman, *Emotional Design; Why We Love (or Hate) Everyday Things* (New York: Basic Books, 2004).

5 Sherry Turkle, *Evocative Objects: Things We Think With* (Cambridge, MA: MIT Press, 2007).

6 Jonathan Chapman, *Emotionally Durable Design: Objects, Experiences and Empathy* (London: Routledge, 2005); Stuart Walker, *Sustainable by Design: Explorations in Theory and Practice* (London: Routledge, 2006).

7 Ibid., 21.

8 Julia Lohmann, Response to Mendini, http://www.julialohmann.co.uk/news/wp-content/uploads/2007/10/julia_lohmann_response.pdf (accessed 21 May 2016).

9 See, for example, Gareth Williams, *Telling Tales: Fear and Fantasy in Contemporary Design* (London: V&A, 2009); and Oliver Bennett, 'Just Don't Sit on the Furniture', *Sunday Times*, suppl. *Style* (27 July 2008): 40–3.

10 Christopher Reed, *Not at Home: Suppression of Domesticity in Art and Architecture* (London: Thames & Hudson, 1996).

11 See Judith Attfield and Pat Kirkham (eds), *Women and Design: A View from the Interior* (London: Women's Press, 1989).

12 See Edward Lucie-Smith, *Furniture: A Concise History* (London: Thames & Hudson, 1979), 149–53.

13 Andrew Blauvelt, 'Towards Relational Design', *Design Observer* (2008), https://designobserver.com/feature/towards-relational-design/7557 (accessed 12March 2017).

14 Glenn Adamson, *Thinking through Craft* (Oxford: Berg, 2007), 35.

15 Peter Dormer, *The Meanings of Modern Design* (London: Thames & Hudson, 1990), 124.

1 Droog: The dry and the moist

1   Peter Frank, 'Cosmopolitan: Las Vegas's Newest Hotel', *Travel+Leisure* (2010)
    http://www.travelandleisure.com/articles/cosmopolitan-las-vegas-newest-hotel#
    (accessed 26 January 2011).

2   Glenn Adamson, *Thinking through Craft* (Oxford: Berg, 2007), 33.

3   Renny Ramakers (ed.), *Simply Droog 10+1* (Rotterdam: 010, 2004), 4.

4   Liberation quoted in Renny Ramakers and Gijs Bakker (eds), *Droog Design: Spirit
    of the Nineties* (Rotterdam: 010, 1998), 92.

5   Gareth Williams, *Telling Tales: Fear and Fantasy in Contemporary Design*
    (London: V&A, 2009), 25.

6   Renny Ramakers, 'Spirit of the Nineties', in *Spirit of the Nineties*, ed. Ramakers and
    Bakker, 30.

7   Paola Antonelli, 'Nothing Cooler Than Dry', in *Spirit of the Nineties*, ed. Ramakers
    and Bakker, 14.

8   Renny Ramakers, 'Q&A with Renny Ramakers about Droog Las Vegas' (2010),
    http://www.droog.com/news/2010/12/qa-renny-ramakers-droog-las-vegas/
    (accessed 15 December 2011).

9   Williams, *Telling Tales*, 16.

10 Jessica Cargill Thompson, 'Design Art Fever', *Blueprint*, no. 261 (2007); Alice
    Rawsthorn, 'The Uses and Misuses of Design Art', *International Herald Tribune*,
    http://www.nytimes.com/2007/10/05/style/05iht-design8.html (accessed 12
    September 2008); Oliver Bennet, 'Just Don't Sit on the Furniture', *Sunday Times*,
    suppl. *Style* (27 July 2008); Sophie Lovell, *Limited Edition: Prototypes, One-Offs and
    Design Art Furniture* (Basel: Birkhauser, 2009).

11 Ramakers, 'Spirit of the Nineties', 34.

12 Ibid., 37.

13 Timo de Rijk, 'So-Called Craft: The Formative Years of Droog Design 1992–1998,'
    Journal of Modern Craft 3, no. 2 (2010): 166.

14 Charles Baudelaire in Walter Benjamin, *Charles Baudelaire: A Lyric Poet of the Era
    of High Capitalism* (London: Verso Classic, 1997), 79.

15 John Heskett, *Toothpicks and Logos: Design and Everyday Life* (Oxford: Oxford
    University Press, 2002), 39.

16 Matt Malpass, *Critical Design in Context* (London: Bloomsbury, 2017), 78.

17 Barry Katz, *Technology and Culture* (Pennsylvania: Pennsylvania State University
    Press, 2005), 388.

18 Mihaly Csikszentmihalyi and Eugene Rochberg-Halton, *The Meaning of
    Things: Domestic Symbols and the Self* (Cambridge: Cambridge University Press,
    1999), 20.

19 Hal Foster, *Design and Crime (and Other Diatribes)* (London: Verso, 2002), 13.

20 Adolf Loos in Foster, *Design and Crime*, 14.

21 Walter Benjamin, *The Arcades Project* (Cambridge MA: Harvard University Press, 2002), 557.

22 Gareth Williams, *The Furniture Machine* (London: V7A, 2006).

23 de Rijk, 'So-Called Craft: The Formative Years of Droog Design 1992–1998,' 162.

24 Ramakers, 'Spirit of the Nineties', 30.

25 Barbara Radice, *Memphis: Research, Experiences, Results, Failures and Successes of New Design* (London: Thames & Hudson, 1985).

26 Penny Sparke, 'Ettore Sottsass and Critical Design in Italy, 1965–1985', in *Made in Italy: Rethinking a Century of Italian Design*, ed. Grace Lees Maffei (London: Bloomsbury Academic, 2013), 59.

27 Mendini in Radice, 25.

28 Sottsass in Ramakers, 'Spirit of the Nineties', 31.

29 Ibid.

30 Ramakers, 'Spirit of the Nineties', 34.

31 Michele De Lucchi in Radice, *Memphis*, 67.

32 Catharine Rossi, 'Memphis as Craft Practice', in *Design and Craft: A History of Convergences and Divergences*, ed. J. Gimeno-Martinez and F. Flore (Weteren: Universa Press, 2010), 322.

33 Hein van Haaren in Ramakers, 'Spirit of the Nineties', 41.

34 Ramakers, 'Spirit of the Nineties', 41.

35 Ibid., 55.

36 Williams, *The Furniture Machine*, 20.

37 Ibid.

38 See Damon Taylor, 'After a Broken Leg; The Performative Function of Jurgen Bey's Do Add Chair', *Design and Culture* 5, no. 3 (2013): 357–74.

39 Achille Castiglioni in Michael Czerwinski, *Fifty Chairs That Changed the World* (London: Design Museum, 2009), 58.

40 John Roberts, *The Intangibilities of Form: Skill and Deskilling in Art after the Readymade* (London: Verso, 2008), 41.

41 Molly Nesbit, 'Ready-Made Originals: The Duchamp Model', *October* 37 (1986).

42 Roberts, *The Intangibilities of Form*, 37.

43 Helen Molesworth, 'Work Avoidance: The Everyday Life of Marcel Duchamp's Readymades', *Art Journal* 57, no. 4 (1998): 50–61.

44 Madeleine Akrich, 'The De-scription of Technological Objects', in *Shaping Technology? Building Society, Studies in Sociotechnological Change*, ed. Wiebe E. Bijker and John Law, 205–24 (Cambridge, MA: MIT Press, 1992).

45 See, for example, Kin Wai Michael Siu, 'Users' Creative Responses and Designers' Roles', *Design Issues* 19, no. 2 (2003): 64–73.

46 Ramakers, 'Spirit of the Nineties', 55.

47   Creative Salvage in Williams, *The Furniture Machine*, 20.

48   Williams, *The Furniture Machine*, 20.

49   Raoul Hausmann in Roberts, *The Intangibilities of Form*, 9.

50   Jurgen Bey in conversation with the author.

51   Antonelli, 'Nothing Cooler than Dry', 12.

52   de Rijk, 'So-Called Craft', 166.

53   Linda Hutcheon, *Irony's Edge: The Theory and Politics of Irony* (London: Routledge, 1994), 33.

54   Nancy Walker, *Feminist Alternatives: Irony and Fantasy in the Contemporary Novel by Women* (Jackson: Uninversity Press of Mississippi, 1990), 24.

55   Hutcheon, *Irony's Edge*, 15.

56   Ibid., 13.

57   Claire Colebrook, *Irony* (London: Routledge, 2004), 18.

58   Aaron Betsky, 'Re: Droog', in Ramakers, *Simply Droog: 10+1*, 20.

59   Hutcheon, *Irony's Edge*; Colebrook, *Irony*.

60   Hutcheon, *Irony's Edge*, 178.

61   de Rijk, 'So-Called Craft', 170.

62   Jacques Ranciere, 'Problems and Transformations in Critical Art', in *Participation*, ed. Claire Bishop (London: Whitechapel, 2006), 84.

63   Dick Van Hoff in Ramakers and Bakker, *Spirit of the Nineties*, 64.

64   Ramakers, 'Spirit of the Nineties', 124.

65   Roger Caillois in Jane Alison, 'The Surreal House', in *The Surreal House: The Architecture of Desire* (London: Yale University Press, 2010), 20.

66   Julia Lohmann in conversation with the author, 2010.

67   Hal Foster, *Compulsive Beauty* (Cambridge, MA: MIT Press, 1995).

68   Alison, 'The Surrealist House', 22.

69   Foster, *Compulsive Beauty*, 19.

70   Benjamin, *The Arcades Project*.

71   Foster, *Design and Crime*.

72   Ramakers, 'Spirit of the Nineties', 52.

73   Danny Miller, *Material Culture and Mass Consumption* (London: Blackwell, 1987); Danny Miller, *Home Possessions: Material Culture behind Closed Doors* (Oxford: Berg, 2001).

74   Pierre Bourdieu, *Distinctions: A Social Critique of the Judgement of Taste* (Boston: Harvard University Press, 1987).

75   Michel Foucault, *Power Knowledge: Selected Interviews and Other Writings, 1972–1977* (London: Pantheon Books, 1980), 57.

76   Anthony Giddens, *Modernity and Self Identity* (London: Polity Press, 1991).

77   Ramakers, *Simply Droog 10+1*.

78   Jeroen Junte, 'Droog Makes Surprise Move to Las Vegas', Design.nl (2010), http://www.design.nl/item/droog_makes_surprising_move_to_las_vegas (accessed 22 February 2011).

79 Hutcheon, *Irony's Edge*, 123.

80 Ramakers, 'Spirit of the Nineties', 123.

2 Framing design art

1   Gareth Williams, *Telling Tales: Fear and Fantasy in Contemporary Design* (London: V&A, 2009).

2   See Damon Taylor, 'Contingent Autonomy and Gallery Envy', in *Design Objects and the Museum*, ed. Liz Farrelly, 91–6 (London: Bloomsbury, 2016).

3   Ibid.

4   For an interesting discussion of this elision, see Lionel Shriver, 'Semantic Drift', *Harper's Magazine*, August 2019 https://harpers.org/archive/2019/08/semantic-drift/ (accessed 14 September 2019).

5   See, for example, Rebecca Houze, 'Postmodernisms: Introduction 1967–2006', in *The Design History Reader*, ed. Grace Lees-Maffei and Rebecca Houze, 175–9 (London: Berg, 2010).

6   Williams, *Telling Tales*, 24.

7   See, for example, John Thackara (ed.), *Design after Modernism: Beyond the Object* (London: Thames & Hudson, 1988); John Heskett, *Toothpicks and Logos: Design and Everyday Life* (Oxford: Oxford University Press, 2002); Deyan Sudjic, *The Language of Things* (London: Allen Lane, 2008).

8   Ida Engholm and Karen Lisa Salamon, 'Design Thinking between Rationalism and Romanticism – A Historical Overview of Competing Visions', *Journal of Design Practice* 4, no. 1 (2017): E1.1–E1.18.

9   Max Weber, 'Science as a Vocation', in *Max Weber: Essays in Sociology*, trans. and ed. Hans Gerth and C. Wright Mills (New York: Oxford University Press, 1946), 129–56.

10 Aren Kurtgözü, 'From Function to Emotion: A Critical Essay on the History of Design Arguments', *Design Journal* 6, no. 2 (2003): 51.

11 Anne Massey, *Chair* (London: Reaktion Books, 2011).

12 A. Adolf Loos, 'Ornament and Crime', 1908, www.sjsu.edu/people/thomas.leddy/courses/c2/s1/Loos.doc (accessed 17 June 2015).

13 Massey, *Chair*.

14 Richard Buchanan, 'Declaration by Design: Rhetoric, Argument, and Demonstration in Design Practice', *Design Issues* 2, no. 1 (1985): 4–22.

15 George Marcus, *Functionalist Design* (Munich: Prestel Verlag, 1995), 9–16.

16 Buchanan, 'Declaration by Design', 8–9.

17 Jean Baudrillard, *The System of Objects* (London: Verso, 2005), 60.

18 Victor Shklovsky, 'Art as Technique' (1925), http://www.culturalagents.org/int/biblio/pdf/shklovsky.pdf (accessed 22 February 2016).

19 Rianne Makkink and Jurgen Bey, '3038 Linenchesthouse', http://www.studiomakkinkbey.nl/list/projects/3038_linenchesthouse (accessed 12 July 2015).

20 Michael Rock, 'The Designer as Author', *Eye Magazine*, 1996 http://www.eyemagazine.com/feature/article/the-designer-as-author (accessed 12 August 2017).

21 Roland Barthes, 'The Death of the Author', in *Image Music Text* (London: Fontana Press, 1977).

22 Marshall McLuhan, *Understanding Media* (London: Routledge Classics, 2001).

23 Roland Barthes, 'The Death of the Author', in *Image, Music, Text* (London: Fontana, Press 1977), 148.

24 Louis Althusser, *Essays on Ideology* (London: Verso, [1970] 1993), 40.

25 J. L. Austin, *How to Do Things with Words* (Oxford: Oxford University Press, 1976).

26 Jacques Derrida, 'Signature Event Context', in *Limited Inc* (New York: Northwestern University Press, 1988).

27 Judith Butler, *Gender Trouble: Feminism and the Subversion of Identity* (London: Routledge, 1990); Judith Butler, *Excitable Speech: A Politics of the Performative* (London: Routledge, 1997).

28 For a discussion of the concept of 'the emotive' in this context, see William Reddy, 'Against Constructionism: The Historical Ethnography of Emotions', *Current Anthropology* 38, no. 3 (1997): 327–51.

29 James J. Gibson, *The Ecological Approach to Visual Perception* (New York: Psychology Press, 1986).

30 Donald Norman, *Emotional Design: Why we Love (or Hate) Everyday Things* (New York: Basic Books, 2004), 67.

31 See, for example, Donald Norman and Eli Spencer, 'Community-Based Human Centered Design', 1 January 2019, https://jnd.org/community-based-human-centered-design/ (accessed 12 September 2019).

32 Bruno Latour, *Reassembling the Social* (Oxford: Oxford University Press, 2007), 72.

33 Madeleine Akrich, 'The De-scription of Technological Objects', in *Shaping Technology? Building Society, Studies in Sociotechnological Change*, ed. W. E. Bijker and J. Law, 205–24 (Cambridge, MA: MIT Press, 1992).

34 Kjetil Fallan, 'De-scribing Design: Appropriating Script Analysis to Design History', *Design Issues* 24, no. 4 (2008): 64–5.

35 Ben Matthews, Marcella Steinstra and Tom Djajadiningrat, 'Emergent Interaction: Creating Spaces for Play', *Design Issues* 24, no. 3 (2008): 58–71.

36 Makkink and Bey, '3038 Linenchesthouse'.

37 Charles Darwin, *The Expression of Emotion in Man and Animals* (New York: Appleton, 1897).

38 Paul Ekman and Wallace Friesen, 'Constants across Cultures in Face and Emotion', *Journal of Personality and Social Psychology* 17, no. 2 (1971); Paul Ekman, Robert Levenson and Wallace Friesen, 'Autonomic Nervous System Distinguishes among Emotions', *Science* 221, no. 4616 (1983).

39 Lisa Feldman Barrett, *How Emotions Are Made: The Secret Life of the Brain* (London: Macmillan, 2017), 17–21.

40 Barrett, *How Emotions Are Made*, 72.

41 James Russell, 'Core Affect and the Psychological Construction of Emotion', *Psychological Review* 110, no. 1 (2003): 145–72.

42 Magda Arnold, *Emotion and Personality* (New York: Columbia University Press, 1960).

43 Klaus Scherer, Angela Shorr and Tom Johnstone (eds), *Appraisal Processes in Emotion: Theory, Methods, Research* (Canary, NC: Oxford University Press, 2001).

44 See, for example, Richard Lazarus, 'Progress on a Cognitive-Motivational-Relational Theory of Emotion', *American Psychologist* 46, no. 8 (1991): 819–34.

45 Antonio Damasio, *Descartes' Error: Emotion, Reason and the Human Brain* (New York: Avon, 1994).

46 Ibid.

47 Bill Gaver, 'Designing for Emotion (among Other Things)', *Philosophical Transactions of The Royal Society, Biological Sciences* (December 2009): 3597.

48 Sarah Ahmed, *The Cultural Politics of Emotion* (London: Routledge, 2007), 8.

49 Erin Manning, *Relationscapes: Movement, Art, Philosophy* (Cambridge, MA: MIT Press, 2009), 95.

50 Brian Massumi, *Parables for the Virtual; Movement, Affect, Sensation* (Durham, NC: Duke University Press, 2002).

51 Massumi, *Parables for the Virtual*, 28.

52 Bertolt Brecht, Marc Silberman, Steve Giles and Tom Kuhn (eds), *Brecht on Theatre* (London: Bloomsbury, 2015), 190.

53 Peter Desmet, 'Product Emotion', in Product Experience, ed. Paul Hekkert and Heinrich Schifferstein (San Diego: Elsevier, 2008), 388.

54 Norman, *Emotional Design*, 63.

55 Desmet, 'Product Emotion'.

56 Norman, *Emotional Design*, 7.

57 Catherine A. Lutz, 'Gender, Power and the Rhetoric of Emotional Control in American Discourse', in *The Emotions: Social, Cultural and Biological Dimensions*, ed. Rom Harré and Gerrod Parrott (London: Sage, 1996), 289.

58 Ibid., 289–90.

59 Ibid., 291.

60 Keith Oatley, *A Brief History of Emotions* (Oxford: Blackwell, 2004), 43.

61 Jonathan Chapman, *Emotionally Durable Design: Objects, Experiences and Empathy* (London: Routledge, 2005), 108.

62 Ben Highmore, *Everyday Life and Cultural Theory* (London: Routledge, 2001), 1.

63 Pierre Bourdieu, *Outline of a Theory of Practice* (Cambridge: Cambridge University Press, 1977).

64 Matthews et al., 'Emergent Interaction: Creating Spaces for Play'.

65 Highmore, *Everyday Life and Cultural Theory*, 12.

66 Ibid.

67 Guy Debord, *The Society of the Spectacle* (London: Soul Bay Press, [1967] 2009), 28.

68 Ibid., 29.

69 Karl Marx, *Capital Volume 1* (London: Penguin, [1867] 1979), 162.

70 Ibid.

71 Ibid., 187.

72 Don Slater, *Consumer Culture and Modernity* (Cambridge: Polity Press, 1997).

73 Roberts, *The Intangibilities of Form*, 20.

74 Georg Lukács, *History and Class Consciousness* (London: Merlin Press, 1974), 83.

75 Susan Buck Morrs, *The Dialectics of Seeing: Walter Benjamin and the Arcades Project* (Cambridge, MA: MIT Press, 1979), 2.

76 Lukács, *History and Class Consciousness*, 84.

77 Stuart Sim, *George Lukács* (London: Prentice Hall, 1994), 29.

78 BorisArvatov, 'Everyday Life and the Culture of the Thing (Towards a Formulation of the Question), *October* 81 (1997), 121.

79 Theodore Adorno and Max Horkheimer, *Dialectic of Enlightenment* (London: Verso, [1947] 1979).

80 Slater, *Consumer Culture and Modernity*, 102–3.

3 Viscerealities

1 For a discussion of Adorno's theories of autonomy and how they relate to design see Damon Taylor, 'Contingent Autonomy and Gallery Envy', in *Design Objects and the Museum*, ed. Liz Farrelly (London: Bloomsbury, 2017), 91–6.

2 Suzanne Ngai, *Ugly Feelings* (Cambridge, MA: Harvard University Press, 2007), 5.

3 Judy Attfield, *Wild Things: The Material Culture of Everyday Life* (Oxford: Berg, 2000), 245.

4 Maurice Mearleau-Ponty, *The Primacy of Perception: And Other Essays on Phenomenological Psychology, the Philosophy of Art, History and Politics* (Evanston: Northwestern University Press, 1963).

5 Richard G. Erskine, *Relational Patterns, Therapeutic Presence: Concepts and Practice of Integrative Psychotherapy* (London: Routledge, 2015).

6 Tim Dant, *Materiality and Society* (Maidenhead: Open University Press, 2005), 64.

7 Tiffany Watt Smith, *The Book of Human Emotions: An Encyclopedia of Feeling from Anger to Wanderlust* (London: Wellcome Collection, 2015), 80.

8 Priyatna, correspondence with the author.

9 Donald Winnicott, *Playing and Reality* (London: Routledge, 2008).

10 Ibid., 2–8.

11 Julia Kristeva, *Powers of Horror: An Essay on Abjection* (New York: Columbia University Press, 1982).

12 Sarah Ahmed, *The Cultural Politics of Emotion* (London: Routledge, 2007), 90.

13 Stuart Jeffries, *Grand Hotel Abyss: The Lives of the Frankfurt School* (London: Verso, 2017), 82.

14 Georg Lukács, 'Reification and the Consciousness of the Proletariat', in *History and Class Consciousness* (London: Merlin Press, 1967).

15 See, for example, Theodor Adorno and Max Horkheimer, *Dialectic of Enlightenment* (London: Verso, 1997).

16 Le Corbusier, *Precisions: On the Present State of Architecture and City Planning* (Cambridge, MA: MIT Press, 1991), 79.

17 It was also impregnated with pheromones, though since the science for this is not proven, it is not discussed here.

18 Karl F. MacDorman and Hiroshi Ishiguro, 'The Uncanny Advantage of Using Androids in Social and Cognitive Science Research', *Interaction Studies* 7, no. 3 (2006).

19 See Brian Massumi, *Parables for the Virtual: Movement, Affect, Sensation* (Durham, NC: Duke University Press, 2002); Linda C. Lin and Eva H. Telzer, 'An Introduction to Cultural Neuroscience', in *The Handbook of Culture and Biology*, ed. Jośe M. Causadias, Eva H. Telzerand and Nancy A. Gonzales (London: Wiley, 2018).

20 See, for example, Lisa Feldman Barrett, *How Emotions Are Made: The Secret Life of the Brain* (London: Macmillan, 2017); Heejung S. Kim and Joni Y. Sasaki, 'Cultural Neuroscience: Biology of the Mind in Cultural Contexts', *Annual Review of Psychology* 65 (2014): 487–514.

21 William Davis, *Nervous State: How Feeling Took Over the World* (London: Jonathan Cape), 38.

22 Watt Smith, *The Book of Human Emotions*, 3.

23 Walter Benjamin, *Illuminations* (London: Jonathan Cape, 1979), 224.

24 Michel Foucault, *The Archaeology of Knowledge* (London: Tavistock, 1986).

25 Ibid.

26 Michel Foucault, 'The Confession of the Flesh', in *Power/ Knowledge: Selected Interviews and Other Writings, 1972-1977*, ed. C. Gordon (New York: Pantheon 1980).

27 Walter Benjamin, *The Arcades Project* (Cambridge, MA: Harvard University Press, 2002), 9.

28 Scott Lash, *Intensive Culture* (London: Sage, 2010).

29 Hal Foster, *Compulsive Beauty* (Cambridge, MA: MIT Press 1995), 190.

30 See https://www.techopedia.com/definition/24967/ieee-80211 (accessed 12 December 2016).

31   Galen Cranz, *The Chair; Rethinking Culture, Body and Design* (New York: Norton, 1998), 112.

32   Ibid.

33   Elizabeth Shove, Matthew Watson, Martin Hand and Jack Ingram, *The Design of Everyday Life* (Oxford: Berg 2003), 24.

34   Witold Rybczynski, *Home: A Short History of an Idea* (London: Penguin, 1986), 97.

35   Bonnie Alter, 'Is This the World's Most Famous Chair?', *Treehugger*, https://www.treehugger.com/sustainable-product-design/is-this-the-worlds-most-famous-chair.html (accessed 14 May 2012).

36   Quite who 'designed' the monobloc is contested and unclear, and different sources attribute its origination to different points in history and several designers. See, for example: Design Boom, 'Monobloc Plastic Chair' https://www.designboom.com/design/db-history-monobloc-plastic-chair/ (accessed 9 February 2010); Ricardo Biannchi, 'The History of Plastic Monobloc Chairs', https://www.inexhibit.com/marker/the-history-of-monobloc-plastic-chairs-on-view-at-vitra-shaudepot/ (accessed 12 June 2019).

37   Stuart Walker, 'Sambo's Stones; Sustainability and Meaningful Objects', *Design and Culture* 2, no. 1 (2010): 52.

38   Fonds Mercator, *Flemish Art* (London: Arch Cape, 1988).

39   Bethan Ryder, 'In Conversation with Studio Job', *The Telegraph*, 20 April 2016 https://www.telegraph.co.uk/luxury/design/studio-job-interview/ (accessed 17 December 2017).

40   Job Smeets, Studio Job, *Perished Furniture*, https://www.studio-job.com/work/art/perished-furniture (accessed 23 October 2018).

41   See, for example, Charlotte Fiel and Peter Fiel, *Modern Chairs* (Cologne: Taschen, 1993); Patricia Bueno, *Just Chairs* (New York: Harper Design, 2003); Michael Czerwinski, *Fifty Chairs That Changed the World* (London: Design Museum, 2009).

42   Cranz, *The Chair*; Mel Byars, *New Chairs, Design Technology Materials* (London: Lawrence King, 2006); Peter Opsvik, *Rethinking Sitting* (New York: Norton, 2008).

43   Tom Fisher, 'What We Touch, Touches Us: Materials, Affects, and Affordances', *Design Issues* 20, no. 4 (2004): 30.

44   Robert Stadler CV reproduced at Traversee.com, http://www.traversee.com/Kuenstler/Robert_Stadler/T_RS/RS_CV_web.pdf (accessed 14 April 2020).

45   Scott Lash and Celia Lury, *Global Culture Industry* (Cambridge: Polity, 2007), 133.

46   Walter Benjamin in Susan Buck-Morss, *The Dialectics of Seeing: Walter Benjamin and the Arcades Project* (Cambridge, MA: MIT Press, 1979), 97.

47   Donald Norman, *Emotional Design: Why We Love (or Hate) Everyday Things* (New York: Basic Books, 2004); Jonathan Chapman, *Emotionally Durable*

Design: Objects, Experiences and Empathy (London: Routledge, 2005); Walker, 'Sambo's Stones'.

48 Andrew Benjamin, 'The Decline of Art: Benjamin's Aura', *Oxford Art Journal* 9, no. 2 (1986): 32.

49 Henri Bergson, 'Time and Free Will', *Internet Archive* (1910), 105, http://www. archive.org/details/timeandfreewilla00berguoft (accessed 9 May 2016).

50 Ibid., 226.

51 Ibid., 237.

52 Paul Rozin, Jonathan Haidt and Clark R. McCauley, 'Disgust: The Body and Soul Emotion', in *Handbook of Cognition and Emotion*, ed. Tim Dalgleish and Mick Power, 429–45 (London: Wiley, 1999).

53 Watt Smith, *The Book of Human Emotions*, 81.

54 Julia Lohmann, CV and Portfolio, julialohmann.co.uk (accessed 19 January 2016).

55 Alessandro Mendini, http://www.julialohmann.co.uk/news/wp-content/uploads/ 2007/10/alessandro_mendini_letter.pdf (accessed 21 May 2016).

56 Julia Lohmann, Response to Mendini, http://www.julialohmann.co.uk/news/wp-content/uploads/2007/10/julia_lohmann_response.pdf (accessed 21 May 2016).

57 Arthur Danto, *The Transfiguration of the Commonplace: A Philosophy of Art* (Cambridge, MA: Harvard University Press, 1981), 25.

58 Alexander Groves in Kristin Hohenadel, 'Jewelry Boxes, Combs and Mirror Frames Made of Human Hair', *Slate* (2014), http://www.slate.com/blogs/the_eye/2014/07/ 21/studio_swine_hair_highway_uses_human_hair_from_china_to_create_high_ design.html?via=gdpr-consent (accessed 12 August 2017).

59 Other examples of projects using human hair include Sanne Visser's 'The New Age of Trichology' and 'The Colour of Hair' by Fabio Hendry and Martijn Rigters. See Kate Franklin and Caroline Till, *Radical Matter: Rethinking Materials for a Sustainable Future* (London: Thames & Hudson, 2018).

60 Siri Hustvedt, 'Notes towards a Theory of Hair', *The New Republic* (2015), https://newrepublic.com/article/122893/notes-toward-theory-hair (accessed 10 September 2016).

61 Emma Tarlo, *Entanglement: The Secret Lives of Hair* (London: Oneworld, 2017), 43.

62 J. G. Ballard, *Miracles of Life Shanghai to Shepperton: An Autobiography* (London: Fourth Estate, 2008), 4–5.

63 Jonathan Swift, 'A Modest Proposal and Other Short Pieces', https://www. globalgreyebooks.com/modest-proposal-ebook.html (accessed 14 May 2019).

64 Tomás Moldonado, *Design, Nature and Revolution* (London: Harper & Row, 1972), 18.

65 There is insufficient space in this work to discuss the idea of embodiment in design any real detail. For a discussion of the concept of embodied cognition, see Francisco J. Varela, Eleanor Rosch and Evan Thompson, *The Embodied*

Mind: Cognitive Science and Human Experience (Cambridge, MA: MIT Press, 1993).

4 Valuing emotive design

1   See, for example, Deyan Sudjic, *The Language of Things* (London: Allen Lane, 2008); Sophie Lovell, *Limited Edition: Prototypes, One-Offs and Design Art Furniture* (Basel: Birkhauser, 2009).

2   Sotheby's, 'By the Numbers: Marc Newson Lockheed Lounge', https://www.sothebysinstitute.com/news-and-events/news/marc-newson-lockheed-lounge-chair/ (accessed 12 January 2019).

3   Peter Dormer, *The Meanings of Modern Design* (London: Thames & Hudson, 1990), 124.

4   Lovell, *Limited Edition*, 111.

5   Sudjic, *The Language of Things*, 100.

6   Pierre Bourdieu, *Distinctions: A Social Critique of the Judgement of Taste* (Cambridge, MA: Harvard University Press, 1987), 56.

7   Sudjic, *The Language of Things*, 177.

8   Rolf Fehlbaum in Lovell, *Limited Edition*, 171.

9   Ibid., 111.

10 Gareth Williams, *Telling Tales: Fear and Fantasy in Contemporary Design* (London: V&A, 2009).

11 Loic Le Galliard, 'Curating in Design Art', *Telling Tales Symposium* (London: Victoria & Albert Museum, 16 October 2009).

12 Murray Moss, moss-gallery.com/about (accessed 12 October 2010).

13 Lovell, *Limited Edition*, 167.

14 Richard Wright in Lovell, *Limited Edition*, 225.

15 Lovell, *Limited Edition*, 226.

16 Anthony Giddens, *Modernity and Self Identity* (London: Polity Press, 1991).

17 Igor Kopytoff, 'The Cultural Biography of Things: Commoditization as Process', in *The Social Life of Things: Commodities in Cultural Perspective*, ed. Arun Appadurai (Cambridge: Cambridge University Press, 1986), 64.

18 See George Simmel, *The Philosophy of Money* (London: Routledge Classics, 2011).

19 Ibid., 69.

20 Ibid., 70.

21 Thorstein Veblen, *The Theory of the Leisure Class* (London: Dover, 1994).

22 Donna Bergenstock and James M. Maskulka, 'The De Beers Story: Are Diamonds Forever?', *Business Horizons* 44, no. 3 (2001): 37–44.

23 Sudjic, *The Language of Things*, 177.

24 Bourdieu, *Distinctions*, 230.

25 See, for example, Hal Foster, *The Return of the Real* (London: MIT Press, 1996).

26 Lovell, *Limited Edition*, 167.

27 Jean Baudrillard, 'The Hyper-realism of Simulation', in *Art in Theory; 1900–1990*, ed. C. Harrison and P. Wood, 1018–20 (Oxford: Blackwell, 1996).

28 Javier Serrano-Puche, 'Emotions and Digital Technologies: Mapping the Field of Research in Media Studies', Media@LSE Working Paper series, http://www.lse. ac.uk/media@lse/research/mediaWorkingPapers/pdf/WP33-FINAL.pdf (accessed 12 January 2017).

29 Scott Lash and Celia Lury, *The Global Culture Industry* (Cambridge: Polity, 2007), 37.

30 Ibid.

31 Kevin Roberts, *Lovemarks: The Future Beyond Brands* (New York: Powerhouse Books, 2006).

32 Renny Ramakers, *Less + More: Droog Design in Context* (Rotterdam: 010, 2002), 21.

33 Walter Benjamin, *Illuminations* (London: Jonathan Cape, 1979), 222.

34 Ibid., 223.

35 See Damon Taylor, 'After a Broken Leg; The Performative Function of Jurgen Bey's Do Add Chair', *Design and Culture* 5, no. 3 (2013): 357–74.

36 Matt Malpass, *Critical Design in Context* (London: Bloomsbury, 2017), 47.

37 Boris Arvatov, 'Everyday Life and the Culture of the Thing (Towards a Formulation of the Question)', *October* 81 (1997).

38 Madeleine Akrich, 'The De-scription of Technological Objects', in *Shaping Technology? Building Society*, ed. Wiebe E. Bijker and John Law (Cambridge, MA: MIT Press, 1992).

39 Louise Schouwenburg, 'Inevitable Ornament', in *Simply Droog: 10+3* (Rotterdam: Droog Design, 2006), 42.

40 Kristina Neidderrer, 'Designing Mindful Interaction: The Category of the Performative Object', *Design Issues* 23, no. 1 (2007).

41 Judith Butler, *Gender Trouble: Feminism and the Subversion of Identity* (London: Routledge, 1997), 25.

42 Jan Konings in conversation with the author, 2009.

43 Ben Matthews, Marcella Steinstra and Tom Djajadiningrat, 'Emergent Interaction: Creating Spaces for Play', *Design Issues* 24, no. 3 (2008): 62.

44 Warren Motte, 'Playing in Earnest', *New Literary History* 40, no. 1 (2009): 25.

45 Johan Huizinga, *Homo Ludens: A Study of the Play Element in Culture* (London: Routledge Kagan Paul, 1970).

46 Jacques Ehermann, '*Homo Ludens* Revisited', in *Game, Play, Literature*, ed. Jacques Ehrmann (Boston: Beacon, 1971), 33.

47 Alvin Toffler, *The Third Wave* (London: Bantam, 1984).

48 Julka Almquist and Julia Lupton, 'Affording Meaning: Design-Oriented Research from the Humanities and Social Sciences', *Design Issues* 26, no. 1 (2010).

5 Rhetorical devices and lyrical things

1   See, for example, Matt Malpass, *Critical Design in Context* (London: Bloomsbury); Cameron Tonkinwise, 'How We Intend to Future: Review of Anthony Dunne and Fiona Raby, *Speculative Everything: Design, Fiction, and Social Dreaming*', *Design Philosophy Papers* 12, no. 2 (2014): 187; Bruce Tharp and Stephanie Tharp, *Discursive Design: Critical, Speculative and Alternative Things* (Cambridge, MA: MIT Press, 2019).

2   Roland Barthes, 'Death of the Author', in *Image Music Text* (London: Fontana Press, 1977), 142–7.

3   Walter Benjamin, 'The Author as Producer', in *Walter Benjamin: Selected Writings, Volume 2, Part 2, 1931–34*, ed. Michael W. Jennings, Howard Eiland and Gary Smith, 507–30 (Cambridge, MA: Harvard University Press, 1999).

4   See, for example, Malpass, *Critical Design in Context*, 47; Tharp and Tharp, *Discursive Design*, 189.

5   Jennifer Richards, *Rhetoric* (Abingdon: Routledge, 2008).

6   Anthony Dunne, *Hertzian Tales: Electronic Products, Aesthetic Experience and Critical Design* (London: MIT Press, [1999] 2008), xvii.

7   Ibid., xvii.

8   Ibid., 22.

9   Dunne, *Hertzian Tales*, 36.

10 Anthony Dunne and Fiona Raby, *Design Noir: The Secret Life of Electronic Objects* (London: August/Birkhauser), 58.

11 Ibid., 64.

12 Ibid., 8.

13 Ibid., 46.

14 Ibid., 12.

15 Anthony Dunne and William Gaver, *The Pillow: Artist Designers in the Digital Age*, in CHI '97 Extended Abstracts on Human Factors in Computing Systems (New York: ACM, 1997), 361.

16 Ibid.

17 Dunne and Raby, *Design Noir*, 75.

18 Anthony Dunne and Fiona Raby, 'What If' Introduction, http://dunneandraby. co.uk/content/bydandr/496/0 (accessed 14 September 2019).

19 Don Slater, *Consumer Culture and Modernity* (Cambridge: Polity Press, 1997), 95.

20 Julian Bleecker, 'Design Fiction: A Short Essay on Design, Science, Fact and Fiction', 8 http://blog.nearfuturelaboratory.com/2009/03/17/

design-fiction-a-short-essay-on-design-science-fact-and-fiction/ (accessed 17 March 2017).

21 Alex McDowell, 'Designing Minority Report', https://www.denofgeek.com/ movies/15773/alex-mcdowell-interview-designing-minority-report (accessed 12 February 17).

22 Jonathan Gorczyca, 'Minority Report Fifteen Years Later', *Helm Experience and Design* https://medium.com/helm-experience-design/minority-report-15-years-later-328b15a7845a (accessed 12 July 2017).

23 David Kirby, 'The Future Is Now: Diegetic Prototypes and the Role of Popular Films in Generating Real-World Technological Development', *Social Studies of Science* 40, no. 1 (2010), 43.

24 Ibid.

25 Bleecker, 'Design Fiction', 41.

26 Anthony Dunne and Fiona Raby, *Speculative Everything: Design, Fiction and Social Dreaming* (London: MIT Press, 2014).

27 Dunne and Raby, *Design Noir*, 64.

28 Dunne and Raby, *Speculative Everything*, 90.

29 Bleecker, 'Design Fiction', 41.

30 Jaron Lanier, *Dawn of the New Everything: A Journey Through Virtual Reality* (London: Bodley Head, 2017).

31 Dunne and Raby, *Speculative Everything*, 91.

32 Rodrigo Gonzatto, Fredrick van Amstel, Luis Ernesto Merkle and Timo Hartmann, 'The Ideology of the Future in Design Fictions', *Digital Creativity* 24, no. 1 (2013): 36.

33 John Underkoffler, 'Pointing to the Future of UI', TED, https://www.ted.com/talks/ john_underkoffler_drive_3d_data_with_a_gesture?language=en (accessed 19 June 2017).

34 Kirby, 'The Future Is Now', 50.

35 Lanier, *Dawn of New Everything*, 245–6.

36 Bleecker, 'Design Fiction', 29.

37 Jean Baudrillard, 'Simulacra and Simulations', in *Jean Baudrillard: Selected Writings*, ed. Mark Poster, 166–84 (Stanford: Stanford University Press, 1988).

38 Brian Dakks, 'Talk of the Tooth', CBS News (2002), https://www.cbsnews.com/ news/talk-of-the-tooth/ (accessed 24 May 2016).

39 Will Knight, 'Tooth-Phone Provides Covert Chat', *New Scientist* (2002), https:// www.newscientist.com/article/dn2436-tooth-phone-provides-covert-chat/ (accessed 24 May 2016).

40 Lakshmi Sandhana, 'Excuse Me, Is Your Tooth Ringing?' *Wired* (2002), https:// www.wired.com/2002/06/excuse-me-is-your-tooth-ringing/ (accessed 12 May 2016).

41 Wired Staff, 'Lying through Their Teeth', *Wired* (2006), https://www.wired.com/2006/04/lying-through-their-teeth/) (accessed 12 May 2016).

42 Ibid.

43 Norbert Wiley, 'Emotion and Film Theory', *Studies in Symbolic Interaction* 26 (2003): 171.

44 Ibid., 174.

45 Daniel Gilbert, 'How Mental Systems Believe', *American Psychologist* 46, no. 2 (1991): 107–19.

46 Marco Sperduti, Margherita Arcangeli, Dominique Makowski and Prany Wantzen, 'The Paradox of Fiction: Emotional Response toward Fiction and the Modulatory Role of Self-Relevance', *Acta Psychologica* 165 (2016): 53–9.

47 Barthes, 'Death of the Author'.

48 Tharp and Tharp, *Discursive Design*, 66.

49 Michel Foucault, 'What Is an Author', Open University, 314, https://www.open.edu/openlearn/ocw/pluginfile.php/624849/mod_resource/content/1/a840_1_michel_foucault.pdf (accessed 12 January 2017).

50 Stephen Hayward, 'Design for Debate May Be Very Interesting; but How Do We Know If It's Any Good?' *Central St. Martins Catalogue*, 2012.

51 Dunne and Raby, *Speculative Everything*, 38.

52 Malpass, *Critical Design*.

53 Bertolt Brecht, Marc Silberman, Steve Giles and Tom Kuhn (eds), *Brecht on Theatre* (London: Bloomsbury, 2015).

54 Walter Benjamin, *Understanding Brecht*, trans. Anna Bostock (London: Verso, 2003).

55 There is evidence that Brecht had learnt about Shklovsky's work and ideas during a visit to Russia in 1935, see Douglas Robinson, *Estrangement and the Somatics of Literature: Tolstoy, Shklovsky, Brecht* (Baltimore: Johns Hopkins University Press, 2008).

56 Brecht et al., *Brecht on Theatre*.

57 Tonkinwise, 'How We Intend to Future', 187.

58 Victor Shklovsky, 'Art as Technique' (1925), http://www.culturalagents.org/int/biblio/pdf/shklovsky.pdf (accessed 22 February 2016).

59 Benjamin, 'The Author as Producer', 779.

60 Ralph Ball and Maxine Naylor, *Form Follows Idea: An Introduction to Design Poetics* (London: Black Dog, 2005).

61 Stephen Bygrave, *Romantic Writings* (London: Routledge, 1996).

62 Jonathan Culler, *Theory of the Lyric* (Cambridge, MA: Harvard University Press, 2017).

63 William Gaver, John Bowers, Andy Boucher, Hans Gellersen, Sarah Pennington, Albrecht Schmidt, Anthony Steed, Nicholas Villar and Brendan Walker, 'The Drift Table: Designing for Ludic Engagement', Extended abstracts of the 2004 Conference on Human Factors in Computing Systems, CHI, Vienna, Austria (2004), https://

www.researchgate.net/publication/221516001_The_drift_table_designing_for_
ludic_engagement (accessed 12 July 2015).

64 Ibid.

65 Gaver et al., https://www.gold.ac.uk/interaction/ (accessed 17 March 2017).

66 Gaver et al., 'The Drift Table: Designing for Ludic Engagement'.

67 Gaver et al., https://research.gold.ac.uk/5527/1/History_Table_Cloth.pdf (accessed
    22 October 2016).

68 William Gaver, Jacob Beaver and Steve Benford, 'Ambiguity as a Resource for
    Design', Conference on Human Factors in Computing Systems – Proceedings
    (2003), https://www.researchgate.net/publication/221516884_Ambiguity_as_a_
    resource_for_design/citation/download (accessed 23 November 2017).

69 Ibid.

70 Indoor weather stations, https://www.academia.edu/17970268/Indoor_weather_
    stations (accessed 7 January 2018).

71 Gaver, Beaver and Benford, 'Ambiguity as a Resource for Design'.

72 Brian Massumi, *Politics of Affect* (Cambridge: Polity Press, 2015), 34.

73 Massumi in Giovanni Marmont, 'Nanopoetics of Use: Kinetic Prefiguration and
    Dispossessed Sociality in the Undercommons', unpublished PhD thesis (2019).

74 Marmont, 'Nanopoetics of Use', 58.

75 Brian Massumi, *Parables for the Virtual: Movement, Affect, Sensation* (Durham,
    NC: Duke University Press, 2002), 6.

76 Benjamin, 'Author as Producer', 507.

6 To the ends of the earth

1 Michael Cannell, 'Design Loves a Depression', *New York Times online* (2009)
   http://www.nytimes.com/2009/01/04/weekinreview/04cannell.html (accessed 22
   April 2016).

2 Ibid.

3 Ibid.

4 Murray Moss, 'Design Hates a Depression', *Design Observer* (2009), http://
   observatory.designobserver.com/entry.html?entry=7757 (accessed 22 April 2011).

5 Ibid.

6 Daniella Ohad, 'On Collectible Contemporary Design', COBO, https://www.
   cobosocial.com/dossiers/on-collectible-contemporary-design-i/ (accessed 19
   March 2019).

7 See Damon Taylor, 'A Brief History of (Un)Sustainable Product Design', in *The
   Routledge Handbook of Sustainable Product Design*, ed. Jonathan Chapman, 11–24
   (London: Routledge, 2017).

8 Hal Foster, *Design and Crime (and Other Diatribes)* (London: Verso, 2002), 69.

9   Adolf Loos in Ibid., 72.

10 Ibid., 72.

11 Ibid., 69.

12 Ibid., 59.

13 Steven Wright, 'The Future of the Reciprocal Readymade (The use-value of art)',
    Apexart (2004), http://www.apexart.org/exhibitions/wright.php (accessed 21
    April 2011).

14 Nicolas Bourriaud, *Relational Aesthetics* (Paris: Les Presses du Reel, 2002), 113.

15 Claire Bishop, *Artificial Hells* (London: Verso, 2012), 2.

16 Claire Bishop, 'Antagonism and Relational Aesthetics', *October* 110 (2004), 52.

17 Bourriaud, *Relational Aesthetics*, 9.

18 Jacques Rancière, 'Problems and Transformations in Critical Art', in *Participation*,
    ed. C. Bishop (London: Whitechapel, 2006) 83.

19 Andrew Blauvelt, 'The Rise of the Relational: Five Themes in relational Design',
    Journal of Design Strategies (2019), http://sds.parsons.edu/designdialogues/?post_
    type=article&p=68 (accessed 12 June 2019).

20 Andrew Blauvelt, 'Towards Relational Design', *Design Observer* (2008), https://
    designobserver.com/feature/towards-relational-design/7557 (accessed 12
    March 2017).

21 Carl DiSalvo, *Adverserial Design* (Cambridge, MA: MIT Press, 2012), 124.

22 Blauvelt, 'Towards Relational Design'.

23 Celia Lury in Guy Julier, 'Value, Relationality and Unfinished Objects: Guy Julier
    Interview with Scott Lash and Celia Lury', *Design and Culture* 1, no. 1 (2009): 97.

24 Dunne and Raby in Gary Hustwit (dir.), *Objectified* [Film] (2009).

25 rAndom International, *Rain Room*, https://www.barbican.org.uk/rain-room-
    random-international (accessed 12 September 17).

26 Stephen Wright, *Toward a Lexicon of Usership*, 54, https://museumarteutil.net/
    wp-content/uploads/2013/12/Toward-a-lexicon-of-usership.pdf (accessed 22
    June 2019).

27 Wright, 'The Future of the Reciprocal Readymade'.

28 http://www.mathiasbengtsson.com/ (accessed 2 December 2019).

29 Jiménez Garcia and Gilles Retsin in Rima Sabina Aouf, 'Robot-Made Voxel Chair
    Designed Using New Software by Bartlett Researchers', *Dezeen* (17 May 2017),
    https://www.dezeen.com/2017/05/17/robot-made-voxel-chair-new-software-
    bartlett-researchers-design-furniture-technology-chairs-robots/ (accessed 10
    January 2018).

Select Bibliography

Adamson, Glenn. *Thinking through Craft*. Oxford: Berg, 2007.

Adorno, Theodor, and Max Horkheimer. *Dialectic of Enlightenment*. London: Verso, 1997.

Ahmed, Sarah. *The Cultural Politics of Emotion*. London: Routledge, 2007.

Akrich, Madeleine. 'The De-scription of Technological Objects'. In *Shaping Technology? Building Society, Studies in Sociotechnological Change*, edited by Wiebe E. Bijke and John Law. Cambridge, MA: MIT Press, 1992: 205–24.

Albena, Yaneva. 'Making the Social Hold; Towards an Actor Network Theory of Design'. *Design and Culture* 1, no. 3 (2009): 273–88.

Alison, Jane. 'The Surreal House'. In *The Surreal House: The Architecture of Desire*. London: Yale University Press, 2010.

Almquist, Julka, and Julia Lupton. 'Affording Meaning: Design-Oriented Research from the Humanities and Social Sciences'. *Design Issues* 26, no. 1 (2010): 3–14.

Althusser, Louis. *Essays on Ideology*. London: Verso, [1970] 1993.

Antonelli, Paola. 'Nothing Cooler than Dry'. In *Spirit of the Nineties*, edited by Renny Ramakers, 12–29. Rotterdam: 010, 1998.

Arvatov, Boris. 'Everyday Life and the Culture of the Thing (towards a Formulation of the Question)'. *October* 81, (1997): 119–28.

Austin, J. L. *How to Do Things with Words*. Oxford: Oxford University Press, 1976.

Ballard, J. G. *Miracles of Life Shanghai to Shepperton: An Autobiography*. London: Fourth Estate, 2008.

Bardzell, Shaowen, Jeffrey Bardzell, Jodi Forlizzi, John Zimmerman and John Antanitis. 'Critical Design and Critical Theory: The Challenge of Designing for Provocation'. DIS 2012 • In the Wild https://www.researchgate.net/publication/232251471, (accessed 17 May 2017).

Barrett, Lisa Feldman. *How Emotions Are Made: The Secret Life of the Brain*. London: Macmillan, 2017.

Barthes, Roland. 'The Death of the Author'. In *Image Music Text*, 142–7. London: Fontana Press, 1977.

Baudrillard, Jean. 'Simulacra and Simulations'. In *Jean Baudrillard: Selected Writings*, edited by Mark Poster, 166–84. Stanford: Stanford University Press, 1988.

Baudrillard, Jean. 'The Hyper-Realism of Simulation'. In *Art in Theory; 1900–1990*, edited by C. Harrison and P. Wood, 1018–20. Oxford: Blackwell, 1996.

Baudrillard, Jean. *The System of Objects*. London: Verso, 2005.

Benjamin, Andrew. 'The Decline of Art: Benjamin's Aura'. *Oxford Art Journal* 9, no. 2 (1986): 30–5.

Benjamin, Walter. *Illuminations*. London: Jonathan Cape, 1979.

Benjamin, Walter. *Charles Baudelaire: A Lyric Poet of the Era of High Capitalism*. London: Verso Classic, 1997.

Benjamin, Walter. 'The Author as Producer'. In *Walter Benjamin: Selected Writings, Volume 2, Part 2, 1931–34*, edited by Michael W. Jennings, Howard Eiland and Gary Smith, 507–30. Cambridge, MA: Harvard University Press, 1999.

Benjamin, Walter. *The Arcades Project*. Cambridge, MA: Harvard University Press, 2002.

Bergson, Henri. 'Time and Free Will'. *Internet Archive 105* (1910), http://www.archive. org/details/timeandfreewilla00berguoft (accessed 9 May 2016).

Betsky, Aaron. 'Re: Droog'. In *Simply Droog: 10+1*, edited by Renny Ramakers, 14–22. Rotterdam: Droog Design, 2004.

Bishop, Claire. 'Antagonism and Relational Aesthetics'. *October* 110 (2004): 51–79.

Bishop, Claire. *Artificial Hells*. London: Verso, 2012.

Blauvelt, Andrew. 'Towards Relational Design'. *Design Observer* (2008). https:// designobserver.com/feature/towards-relational-design/7557 (accessed 12 March 2017).

Bleecker, Julian. 'Design Fiction: A Short Essay on Design, Science, Fact and Fiction' (2009). http://drbfw5wfjlxon.cloudfront.net/writing/DesignFiction_WebEdition.pdf (accessed 22 April 2020).

Bourdieu, Pierre. *Distinctions: A Social Critique of the Judgement of Taste*. Boston: Harvard University Press, 1987.

Bourriaud, Nicolas. *Relational Aesthetics*. Paris: Les Presses du Reel, 2002.

Bratu Hansen, Miriam. 'Benjamin's Aura'. *Critical Inquiry* 34, no. 2 (2008): 336–75.

Brecht, Bertolt, Marc Silberman, Steve Giles and Tom Kuhn (eds). *Brecht on Theatre*. London: Bloomsbury, 2015.

Buchanan, Richard. 'Declaration by Design: Rhetoric, Argument, and Demonstration in Design Practice'. *Design Issues* 2, no. 1 (1985): 4–22.

Buck-Morss, Susan. *The Dialectics of Seeing: Walter Benjamin and the Arcades Project*. Cambridge, MA: MIT Press, 1979.

Bueno, Patricia. *Just Chairs*. New York: Harper Design, 2003.

Butler, Judith. *Gender Trouble: Feminism and the Subversion of Identity*. London: Routledge, 1990.

Butler, Judith. *Excitable Speech: A Politics of the Performative*. London: Routledge, 1997.

Bygrave, Stephen. *Romantic Writings*. London: Routledge, 1996.

Cannell, Michael. 'Design Loves a Depression'. *New York Times online* (2009), http:// www.nytimes.com/2009/01/04/weekinreview/04cannell.html (accessed 22 April 2016).

Causadias, Jose M., Eva H. Telzerand and Nancy A. Gonzales (eds). *The Handbook of Culture and Biology*. London: Wiley, 2018.

Chapman, Jonathan. *Emotionally Durable Design: Objects, Experiences and Empathy.* London: Routledge, 2005.

Colebrook, Claire. *Irony.* London: Routledge, 2004.

Cranz, Galen. *The Chair; Rethinking Culture, Body and Design.* New York: Norton, 1998.

Csikszentmihalyi, Mihaly, and Eugene Rochberg-Halton. *The Meaning of Things: Domestic Symbols and the Self.* Cambridge: Cambridge University Press, 1999.

Culler, Jonathan. *Theory of the Lyric.* Cambridge, MA: Harvard University Press, 2017.

Czerwinski, Michael. *Fifty Chairs That Changed the World.* London: Design Museum, 2009.

Damasio, Antonio. *Descartes' Error: Emotion, Reason and the Human Brain.* New York: Avon, 1994.

Dant, Tim. *Materiality and Society.* Maidenhead: Open University Press, 2005.

Danto, Arthur. *The Transfiguration of the Commonplace: A Philosophy of Art.* Cambridge, MA: Harvard University Press, 1981.

Darwin, Charles. *The Expression of Emotion in Man and Animals.* New York: Appleton, 1897.

Davis, William. *Nervous States: How Feeling Took Over the World.* London: Jonathan Cape, 2018.

de Rijk, Timo. 'So-Called Craft: The Formative Years of Droog Design 1992–1998'. *Journal of Modern Craft* 3, no. 2 (2010): 161–78.

Debord, Guy. *The Society of the Spectacle.* London: Soul Bay Press, [1967] 2009.

Derrida, Jacques. 'Signature Event Context'. In *Limited Inc.* New York: Northwestern University Press, 1988.

Desmet, Peter. 'Product Emotion'. In *Product Experience*, edited by Paul Hekkert and Heinrich Schifferstein, 379–94. San Diego: Elsevier, 2008.

Dormer, Peter. *The Meanings of Modern Design.* London: Thames & Hudson, 1990.

Dunne, Anthony. *Hertzian Tales: Electronic Products, Aesthetic Experience and Critical Design.* London: MIT Press, [1999] 2008.

Dunne, Anthony, and William Gaver. *The Pillow: Artist Designers in the Digital Age.* In CHI '97 Extended Abstracts on Human Factors in Computing Systems, 361–2. New York: ACM, 1997.

Dunne, Anthony, and Fiona Raby. *Design Noir: The Secret Life of Electronic Objects.* London: August/Birkhauser, 2001.

Dunne, Anthony, and Fiona Raby. *Speculative Everything: Design, Fiction and Social Dreaming.* London: MIT Press, 2014.

Eagleton, Terry. *Walter Benjamin.* London: Verso, 1981.

Ehermann, Jacques. '*Homo Ludens* Revisited'. In *Game, Play, Literature*, edited by Jacques Ehrmann, 31–57. Boston: Beacon, 1971.

Ekman, Paul, and Wallace Friesen. 'Constants across Cultures in Face and Emotion'. *Journal of Personality and Social Psychology* 17, no. 2 (1971): 124–29.

Ekman, Paul, Robert Levenson and Wallace Friesen. 'Autonomic Nervous System Distinguishes Among Emotions'. *Science* 221, no. 4616 (1983): 1208–10.

Engholm, Ida, and Karen Lisa Salamon. 'Design Thinking between Rationalism and Romanticism – A Historical Overview of Competing Visions'. *Journal of Design Practice* 4, no. 1 (2017): E1.1–E1.18.

Erskine, Richard G. *Relational Patterns, Therapeutic Presence: Concepts and Practice of Integrative Psychotherapy*. London: Routledge, 2015.

Fiel, Charlotte, and Peter Fiel. *Modern Chairs*. Cologne: Taschen, 1993.

Findeli, Alain. 'Ethics, Aesthetics and Design'. *Design Issues* 10, no. 2 (1994): 49–68.

Fisher, Tom. 'What We Touch, Touches Us: Materials, Affects, and Affordances'. *Design Issues* 20, no. 4 (2004): 20–31.

Foster, Hal. *Compulsive Beauty*. Cambridge, MA: MIT Press, 1995.

Foster, Hal. *The Return of the Real: The Avant Garde at the End of the Century*. London: MIT Press, 1996.

Foster, Hal. *Design and Crime (and Other Diatribes)*. London: Verso, 2002.

Foucault, Michel. *Power Knowledge: Selected Interviews and Other Writings, 1972–1977*. London: Pantheon Books, 1980.

Foucault, Michel. 'The Confession of the Flesh'. In *Power/Knowledge: Selected Interviews and Other Writings, 1972–1977*, edited by C. Gordon, 194–228. New York: Pantheon 1980.

Foucault, Michel. *The Archaeology of Knowledge*. London: Tavistock, 1986.

Foucault, Michel. 'Subjectivity and Truth'. In *The Essential Works of Michel Foucault, 1954–1984, Vol. 1: Ethics: Subjectivity and Truth*, edited by P. Rabinow, 87–92. London: Allen Lane, 1987.

Foucault, Michel. 'Preface to the History of Sexuality, Volume II'. In *The Foucault Reader*, edited by P. Rabinow, 333–9. London: Penguin, 1991.

Foucault, Michel. 'What Is an Author'. Open University, 314. https://www.open.edu/ openlearn/ocw/pluginfile.php/624849/mod_res ource/content/1/a840_1_michel_ foucault.pdf (accessed 12 January 2017).

Garcia, Manuel Jiménez, and Gilles Retsin, in Rima Sabina Aouf. 'Robot-Made Voxel Chair Designed Using New Software by Bartlett Researchers'. *Dezeen* (17 May 2017). https://www.dezeen.com/2017/05/17/robot-made-voxel-chair- new-software- bartlett-researchers-design-furniture-technology-chairs- robots/ (accessed 10 January 2018).

Gaver, William, Jacob Beaver and Steve Benford. 'Ambiguity as a Resource for Design'. *Conference on Human Factors in Computing Systems – Proceedings* (2003). https:// www.researchgate.net/publication/221516884_Ambiguity_as_a_ resource_for_ design/citation/download (accessed 23 November 2017).

Gaver, William, John Bowers, Andy Boucher, Hans Gellersen, Sarah Pennington, Albrecht Schmidt, Anthony Steed, Nicholas Villar and Brendan Walker. 'The Drift Table: Designing for Ludic Engagement'. Extended abstracts of the 2004 Conference on Human Factors in Computing Systems, CHI. Vienna, Austria (2004). https://

www.researchgate.net/publication/221516001_The_drift_table_ designing_for_ ludic_engagement (accessed 12 July 2015).

Gibson, James J. *The Ecological Approach to Visual Perception*. New York: Psychology Press, 1986.

Giddens, Anthony. *Modernity and Self Identity*. London: Polity Press, 1991.

Gilbert, Daniel. 'How Mental Systems Believe'. *American Psychologist* 46, no. 2 (1991): 107–19.

Gonzatto, Rodrigo Fredrick, van Amstel, Luis Ernesto Merkle and Timo Hartmann. 'The Ideology of the Future in Design Fictions'. *Digital Creativity* 24, no. 1 (2013): 36–45.

Gross, Danile M. *The Secret History of Emotion: From Aristotle's Rhetoric to Modern Brain Science*. Chicago: University of Chicago Press, 2006.

Hayward, Stephen. 'Design for Debate May Be Very Interesting; but How Do We Know If It's Any Good?' *Central St. Martins Catalogue*, 2012.

Heidegger, Martin. 'The Thing'. In *The Object Reader*, edited by Fiona Candlin and Guins, 113–24. London: Routledge, [1927] 2009.

Heskett, John. *Toothpicks and Logos: Design and Everyday Life*. Oxford: Oxford University Press, 2002.

Highmore, Ben. *Everyday Life and Cultural Theory*. London: Routledge, 2001.

Houze, Rebecca. 'Postmodernisms: Introduction 1967–2006'. In *The Design History Reader*, edited by Grace Lees-Maffei and Rebecca Houze, 175–9. London: Berg, 2010.

Huizinga, Johan. *Homo Ludens: A Study of the Play Element in Culture*. London: Routledge Kagan Paul, 1970.

Hutcheon, Linda. *Irony's Edge: The Theory and Politics of Irony*. London: Routledge, 1994.

Jeffries, Stuart. *Grand Hotel Abyss: The Lives of the Frankfurt School*. London: Verso, 2017.

Katz, Barry. *Technology and Culture*. Pennsylvania: Pennsylvania State University Press, 2005.

Kim, Heejung S., and Joni Y Sasaki. 'Cultural Neuroscience: Biology of the Mind in Cultural Contexts'. *Annual Review of Psychology* 65 (2014): 487–518.

Kirby, David. 'The Future Is Now: Diegetic Prototypes and the Role of Popular Films in Generating Real-World Technological Development'. *Social Studies of Science* 40, no. 1 (2010): 41–70.

Kjetil, Fallan. 'De-scribing Design: Appropriating Script Analysis to Design History'. *Design Issues* 24, no. 4 (2008): 61–75.

Kjetil, Fallan. *Design History: Understanding Theory and Method*. Oxford: Berg, 2010.

Kopytoff, Igor. 'The Cultural Biography of Things: Commoditization as Process'. In *The Social Life of Things: Commodities in Cultural Perspective*, edited by Arun Appadurai, 64–91. Cambridge: Cambridge University Press, 1986.

Kurtgözü, Aren. 'From Function to Emotion: A Critical Essay on the History of Design Arguments'. *Design Journal* 6, no. 2 (2003): 49–59.

Lanier, Jaron. *Dawn of the New Everything: A Journey Through Virtual Reality*. London: Bodley Head, 2017.

Lash, Scott. *Intensive Culture*. London: Sage, 2010.

Lash, Scott, and Celia Lury. *Global Culture Industry*. Cambridge: Polity, 2007.

Latour, Bruno. *Reassembling the Social*. Oxford: Oxford University Press, 2007.

Lazarus, Richard. 'Progress on a Cognitive-Motivational-Relational Theory of Emotion'. *American Psychologist* 46, no. 8 (1991): 819–34.

Le Corbusier. *Precisions: On the Present State of Architecture and City Planning*. Cambridge, MA: MIT Press, 1991.

Loos, Adolf. 'Ornament and Crime' (1908). www.sjsu.edu/people/thomas.leddy/courses/c2/s1/Loos.doc (accessed 17 June 2015).

Lukács, Georg. 'Reification and the Consciousness of the Proletariat'. In *History and Class Consciousness*. London: Merlin Press, 1974.

Lury, Celia, in Guy Julier, 'Value, Relationality and Unfinished Objects: Guy Julier Interview with Scott Lash and Celia Lury'. *Design and Culture* 1, no. 1 (2009): 93–104.

Lutz, Catherine. 'Gender, Power and the Rhetoric of Emotional Control in American Discourse'. In *The Emotions: Social, Cultural and Biological Dimensions*, edited by Rom Harré and Gerrod Parrott, 89–116. London: Sage, 1996.

MacDorman, Karl F., and Hiroshi Ishiguro. 'The Uncanny Advantage of Using Androids in Social and Cognitive Science Research'. *Interaction Studies* 7, no. 3 (2006): 297–337.

Malpass, Matt. *Critical Design in Context*. London: Bloomsbury, 2017.

Manning, Erin. *Relationscapes: Movement, Art, Philosophy*. Cambridge, MA: MIT Press, 2009.

Marcus, George. *Functionalist Design*. Munich: Prestel Verlag, 1995.

Margolin, Victor. 'Design Research: Towards a History'. *Proceedings of the Design Research Society International Conference 'Design & Complexity'*. Montreal, Canada, Université de Montréal, 7–9 July 2010.

Marmont, Giovanni. 'Nanopoetics of Use: Kinetic Prefiguration and Dispossessed Sociality in the Undercommons' (unpublished PhD thesis, University of Brighton, 2019).

Marx, Karl. *Capital Volume 1*. London: Penguin, [1867] 1979.

Massey, Anne. *Chair*. London: Reaktion Books, 2011.

Massumi, Brian. *Parables for the Virtual: Movement, Affect, Sensation*. Durham, NC: Duke University Press, 2002.

Matthews, Ben, Marcella Stienstra and Tom Djajadiningrat. 'Emergent Interaction: Creating Spaces for Play'. *Design Issues* 24, no. 3 (2008): 58–71.

McLuhan, Marshall. *Understanding Media*. London: Routledge Classics, 2001.

Merleau-Ponty, Maurice. *The Primacy of Perception: And Other Essays on Phenomenological Psychology, the Philosophy of Art, History and Politics*. Evanston: Northwestern University Press, 1963.

Miller, Danny. *Material Culture and Mass Consumption*. London: Blackwell, 1987.

Miller, Danny. *Home Possessions: Material Culture Behind Closed Doors*. Oxford: Berg, 2001.

Moldonado, Tomás. *Design, Nature and Revolution*. London: Harper and Row, 1972.

Molesworth, Helen. 'Work Avoidance: The Everyday Life of Marcel Duchamp's Readymades'. *Art Journal* 57, no. 4 (1998): 50–61.

Moss, Murray. 'Design Hates a Depression'. *Design Observer* (2009). http://observatory.designobserver.com/entry.html?e ntry=7757 (accessed 22 April 2011).

Motte, Warren. 'Playing in Earnest'. *New Literary History* 40, no. 1 (2009): 25–42.

Neidderer, Kristina. 'Designing Mindful Interaction: The Category of the Performative Object'. *Design Issues* 23, no. 1 (2007): 3–17.

Nesbit, Molly. 'Ready-Made Originals'. *October* 37 (1986): 53–64.

Ngai, Suzanne. *Ugly Feelings*. Cambridge, MA: Harvard University Press, 2007.

Nietzsche, Friedrich. 'On the Genealogy of Morals; A Polemical Tract' (1887). http://records.viu.ca/~johnstoi/Nietzsche/genealogytofc.htm (accessed 23 March 2015).

Nietzsche, Friedrich. *Twilight of the Idols*. London: Penguin, [1889] 1979.

Norman, Donald. *User-Centered System Design: New Perspectives on Human-Computer Interaction*. New York: CRC Press, 1986.

Norman, Donald. *The Design of Everyday Things*. New York: Basic Books, 2002.

Norman, Donald. *Emotional Design: Why We Love (or Hate) Everyday Things*. New York: Basic Books, 2004.

Oatley, Keith. *A Brief History of Emotions*. Oxford: Blackwell, 2004.

Opsvik, Peter. *Rethinking Sitting*. New York: Norton, 2008.

Radice, Barbara. *Memphis: Research, Experiences, Results, Failures and Successes of New Design*. London: Thames & Hudson, 1985.

Ramakers, Renny. *Spirit of the Nineties*. Rotterdam: 010, 1998.

Ramakers, Renny (ed.). *Simply Droog 10+1*. Rotterdam: 010, 2004.

Ranciere, Jacques. 'Problems and Transformations in Critical Art'. In *Participation*, edited by Claire Bishop, 83–95. London: Whitechapel, 2006.

Redström, Johan. 'Towards User Design? On the Shift from Object to User as the Subject of Design'. *Design Studies* 27, no. 2 (2006): 123–29.

Reed, Christopher. *Not at Home: Suppression of Domesticity in Art and Architecture*. London: Thames & Hudson, 1996.

Richards, Jennifer. *Rhetoric*. Abingdon: Routledge, 2008.

Roberts, John. *The Intangibilities of Form: Skill and Deskilling in Art After the Readymade*. London: Verso, 2008.

Robinson, Douglas. *Estrangement and the Somatics of Literature: Tolstoy, Shklovsky, Brecht*. Baltimore: Johns Hopkins University Press, 2008.

Rock, Michael. 'The Designer as Author'. *Eye Magazine* (1996). http://www.
eyemagazine.com/feature/article/the-designer-as-author (accessed 12 August 2017).

Rossi, Catharine. 'Memphis as Craft Practice'. In *Design and Craft: A History of
Convergences and Divergences*, edited by J. Gimeno-Martinez and F. Flore, 322–5.
Weteren: Universa Press, 2010.

Rozin, Paul, Jonathan Haidt and Clark R. McCauley. 'Disgust: The Body and Soul
Emotion'. In *Handbook of Cognition and Emotion*, edited by Tim Dalgleish and Mick
Power, 429–45. London: Wiley, 1999.

Russell, James. 'Core Affect and the Psychological Construction of Emotion'.
Psychological Review 110, no. 1 (2003): 145–72.

Rybczynski, Witold. *Home: A Short History of an Idea*. London: Penguin, 1986.

Scherer, Klaus, Angela Schorr and Tom Johnstone (eds). *Appraisal Processes in
Emotion: Theory, Methods, Research*. Canary, NC: Oxford University Press, 2001.

Schouwenburg, Louise. 'Inevitable Ornament'. In *Simply Droog: 10+3*, 72–81.
Rotterdam: Droog Design, 2006.

Serrano-Puche, Javier. 'Emotions and Digital Technologies: Mapping the Field of
Research in Media Studies'. Media@LSE Working Paper series, http://www.lse.ac.uk/
media@lse/research/mediaWorkingPapers/pdf/ WP33-FINAL.pdf (accessed 12
January 2017).

Shklovsky, Viktor. 'Art as Technique' (1925). http://www.culturalagents.org/int/biblio/
pdf/shklovsky.pdf (accessed 22 February 2016).

Shove, Elizabeth, Matthew Watson, Martin Hand and Jack Ingram. *The Design of
Everyday Life*. Oxford: Berg, 2003.

Sim, Stuart. *George Lukács*. London: Prentice Hall, 1994.

Slater, Don. *Consumer Culture and Modernity*. Cambridge: Polity Press, 1997.

Sparke, Penny. 'Ettore Sottsass and Critical Design in Italy, 1965–1985'. In *Made in
Italy: Rethinking a Century of Italian Design*, edited by Grace Lees Maffei, 59–72.
London: Bloomsbury Academic, 2013.

Sperduti, Marco, Margherita Arcangeli, Dominique Makowski and Prany Wantzen. 'The
Paradox of Fiction: Emotional Response Toward Fiction and the Modulatory Role of
Self-Relevance'. *Acta Psychologica* 165 (2016): 53–9.

Sudjic, Deyan. *The Language of Things*. London: Allen Lane, 2008.

Tarlo, Emma. *Entanglement: The Secret Lives of Hair*. London: Oneworld, 2017.

Taylor, Damon. 'After a Broken Leg: The Performative Function of Jurgen Bey's Do Add
Chair'. *Design and Culture* 5, no. 3 (2013): 357–74.

Taylor, Damon. 'Contingent Autonomy and Gallery Envy'. In *Design Objects and the
Museum*, edited by Liz Farrelly, 91–96. London: Bloomsbury, 2016.

Taylor, Damon. 'A Brief History of (Un)Sustainable Product Design'. In *The Routledge
Handbook of Sustainable Product Design*, edited by Jonathan Chapman, 11–24.
London: Routledge, 2017.

Thackara, John (ed.). *Design After Modernism: Beyond the Object*. London: Thames &
Hudson, 1988.

Tharp, Bruce, and Stephanie Tharp. *Discursive Design: Critical, Speculative and Alternative Things*. Cambridge, MA: MIT Press, 2019.

Thorstein, Veblen. *The Theory of the Leisure Class*. London: Dover, [1899] 1994.

Toffler, Alvin. *The Third Wave*. London: Bantam, 1984.

Tonkinwise, Cameron. 'How We Intend to Future: Review of Anthony Dunne and Fiona Raby'. *Speculative Everything: Design, Fiction, and Social Dreaming' Design Philosophy Papers* 12, no. 2 (2014): 169–87.

Varela, Francisco, Eleanor Rosch and Evan Thompson. *The Embodied Mind: Cognitive Science and Human Experience*. Cambridge, MA: MIT Press, 1993.

Walker, Nancy. *Feminist Alternatives: Irony and Fantasy in the Contemporary Novel by Women*. Jackson: Uninversity Press of Mississippi, 1990.

Walker, Stuart. *Sustainable by Design: Explorations in Theory and Practice*. London: Routledge, 2006.

Walker, Stuart. 'Sambo's Stones; Sustainability and Meaningful Objects'. *Design and Culture* 2, no. 1 (2010): 45–62.

Weber, Max. 'Science as a Vocation'. In *Max Weber: Essays in Sociology*, edited and translated by Hans Gerth and C. Wright Mills, 129–56. New York: Oxford University Press, 1946.

Wiley, Norbert. 'Emotion and Film Theory'. *Studies in Symbolic Interaction* 26 (2003): 169–87.

Williams, Gareth. *The Furniture Machine*. London: V&A, 2006.

Williams, Gareth. *Telling Tales: Fear and Fantasy in Contemporary Design*. London: V&A, 2009.

Williams, Raymond. *Politics and Letters: Interviews with New Left Review*. London: NLB, 1979.

Winnicott, Donald. *Playing and Reality*. London: Routledge, 1971.

Wright, Stephen. 'The Future of the Reciprocal Readymade (The Use-Value of Art)'. *Apexart* (2004). http://www.apexart.org/exhibitions/wright.php (accessed 21 April 2011).

Index